THE CONFESSIONAL IMAGINATION

For somehow I am not praised when my judgment of myself is not praised. . . . Am I then doubtful of myself in this matter?

Augustine, *Confessions*

THE CONFESSIONAL IMAGINATION

A READING OF WORDSWORTH'S *PRELUDE*

FRANK D. MCCONNELL

THE JOHNS HOPKINS UNIVERSITY PRESS
BALTIMORE AND LONDON

This book has been brought to publication with
the generous assistance of the Andrew W. Mellon
Foundation.

The Johns Hopkins University Press, Baltimore, Maryland 21218
The Johns Hopkins University Press Ltd., London

Library of Congress Catalog Card Number 73-19333
ISBN 0-8018-1574-6

Library of Congress Cataloging in Publication data
will be found on the last printed page of this book.

This book is for Carolyn

CONTENTS

Preface   ix

Introduction   1

CHAPTER ONE   The Poem to Coleridge   15

CHAPTER TWO   The Sense of the Human   59

CHAPTER THREE   The Tyrant Eye   99

CHAPTER FOUR   Edenic Words   147

APPENDIX ONE   James Nayler   191

APPENDIX TWO   William Cowper   193

APPENDIX THREE   Silas Told   197

Bibliography   201

Index   209

PREFACE

In its original form, this book was written under the guidance of Harold Bloom. It is a great pleasure here to record my gratitude to Mr. Bloom for that, and other, guidance. It is an equal pleasure to thank my teachers at Yale and Notre Dame: Walter Davis, Seymour Gross, Edward Vasta, William Wimsatt, Louis Martz, John Pope, Talbot Donaldson, and D. G. James. They are responsible for whatever is good in this book.

Any fresh Ph.D. beginning a teaching career knows the curious injunction, Turn it into a book. In my case, the transubstantiation could not have occurred without the aid, advice, and kindness of a number of colleagues and friends: Peter Conn, Richard Schwartz, Philip Marcus, Robert Hume, Thomas Hill, Arthur Mizener, Samuel Hynes, Jean Hagstrum, and Alfred Appel, Jr. Barbara Kraft of the Johns Hopkins University Press has helped greatly in making my argument readable.

For my wife, to whom this book is dedicated, there are not adequate words to record my debt. And the good reader of Wordsworth should learn, at least, when to abandon words altogether.

THE CONFESSIONAL IMAGINATION

INTRODUCTION

"What Mr. Wordsworth will produce, it is not for me to prophecy: but I could pronounce with the liveliest convictions what he is capable of producing. It is the FIRST GENUINE PHILOSOPHICAL POEM." This was Coleridge's judgment in the *Biographia Literaria*. And he wrote better than he knew, though not better than he might have known. For though, by 1817, his great friend was already well into that long last phase of his career so many critics call "the decline," and though Wordsworth was never to complete the philosophical epic he himself projected as his magnum opus, yet *The Prelude* had been and was being written. Coleridge had heard Wordsworth read the first, 1805 version of the poem, and Wordsworth was in process of that forty-year revision, realignment, and tinkering with his masterpiece which is one of the oddest stories in English literary history. Thinking of Lucretius, Dante, or Spenser, we may not wish to call *The Prelude* the *first* genuine philosophical poem. But there can be little doubt that *The Prelude* stands in an almost archetypal relationship to all that has come since.

It is one of the assumptions of this book, at any rate, that *The Prelude* represents not only a magisterial triumph in Wordsworth's own imaginative life but a problematic pattern for the entire imaginative and philosophical tradition of "the modern." To read the poem at all is to invoke, at a rather serious level, the question of Romanticism, its nature, extent, and continuing power over our own best writing. Harold Bloom has recently argued that literary inheritances in our tradition are a matter of the "anxiety of influence": each generation of poets, that is, struggling against and willfully deforming the great accomplishments of their predecessors.[1] In such a reading, *The Prelude* should stand not only as archetype but also as countertype to the achievements of Shelley, Keats, and Whitman or, in our time, to the shattered, despairing confessions of Hart Crane's *The Bridge* and John Berryman's *The Dream Songs*. But my concern here is primarily with the archetypal quality of the poem, the ways in which it develops and defines concepts of language, time, and narrative which inevitably guide and influence—whatever the degree of their anxiety—the writers who succeed Wordsworth.

It is interesting that both Coleridge and Wordsworth should have failed to recognize the "first genuine philosophical poem"—at least of Romanticism—when it was, so to speak, locked in the poet's desk all along. For at the heart of their error is a crucial, epoch-making transformation of the sense of the word *philosophical*: a transformation whose prime movers include Wordsworth and Coleridge themselves. If *philosophy* is what Wittgenstein, Heidegger, Sartre, or the structuralists do, it is a philosophy much closer to the erratic narrative explorations of the *Biographia* or *The Prelude* than to the discursive structures of Hume, Berkeley, or Hartley: closer not simply in form but in the inevitable pressure of form upon thought. What has been heralded as the "death of metaphysics" in the modern era is not, indeed, a death but the distinctively Romantic growth of a metaphysics of the individual personality, a philosophy whose central methods are introspection and self-examination, along with an acute sense of the interchange between abstract speculation and the most idiosyncratic structures of the single self. Under such a dispensation, philosophical writing cannot help but become a much more meditative—in fact, confessional—activity, in which the theoretical content of assertion comes to rely more and more profoundly upon the imaginative, self-conscious *act* of assertion itself. *The Prelude*, to which Wordsworth habitually referred as "the poem on the growth of my own mind," illuminates and is illuminated by the intellectual history which it helped transform.

There is, however, an inherent danger in such a reading of this,

1. Harold Bloom, *The Anxiety of Influence: A Theory of Poetry* (New York, 1973).

or any, poem. We have learned over the last two decades that the tools of psychoanalysis, phenomenology, and structural linguistics immeasurably deepen our understanding of the key works of Romanticism. And this is so, I suggest, precisely because these disciplines are Romanticism's still vital manifestations, its more professorial godchildren, just as so many contemporary fictions are its more cantankerous grandchildren. But whenever we locate the influence, the living continuation of a text or body of texts, we run the risk of losing the original in the mob of its offspring—of losing, indeed, the "tradition" we seek to describe by losing the sense of individual, independent works which realize and incarnate that tradition. In the wealth of new lights currently being focused on Romanticism, it is possible to feel, sometimes, that the lights are perhaps too bright: that the tools of analysis borrowed from contemporary modes of thought, by being overemployed, in fact over-contemporize their object, thereby obscuring the very historical inheritance from Romanticism to modernism which they seek to clarify. It is to our advantage to recognize the family resemblance between *The Prelude* and *The Dream Songs* or the *Philosophical Investigations*; but it is at our peril that we forget the gulfs which separate them.

Yeats observed that we make poetry out of our quarrel with ourselves, rhetoric out of our quarrel with others. Criticism is, or should be, made out of the quarrel between poetry and rhetoric: the creative tension in the reader's mind between the text in its own immitigable inwardness and the text as unit of a larger, public literary continuity. The second, rhetorical aspect of *The Prelude* involves the considerations we have already invoked, the poem's identity as shaping agent and ancestor of the modern tradition. The first aspect—the inwardness of *The Prelude*—involves, in my reading, close attention to the literary and psychological conventions which underlie and—perhaps unconsciously—shape the language structures of the poem itself and which the poem, in its turn, transforms through its own distinctive vision. These inner pressures on the poem I identify specifically as the tradition of Augustinian and English Protestant religious confession.

Like M. H. Abrams in his recent book, *Natural Supernaturalism*, I find in St. Augustine one of the most suggestive analogues for the Wordsworthian quest for lost time and for the redemptive power of memory. Unlike Abrams, however, I am more concerned with similarities between the two writers than with the differences between them: I am more concerned, therefore, with the Augustinian tradition of confession in England during the two centuries immediately preceding Wordsworth. The idea of Romanticism, particularly in its Wordsworthian variety, as a secularization of Protestant piety is no new thing, of course, among critics of the age. But it has not been sufficiently noticed that radical Protestantism itself, particularly the great movements of the Society of Friends and the Methodists, is a first, highly subtle and self-conscious version of exactly this secularizing process. The progressive rejection by the Friends and the Methodists of sacramental and liturgical forms of worship, and their resolute insistence on an inward Kingdom of God in *this* world, is one of the most crucial and least-examined phases in the transformation of the post-Renaissance English mind. And the distinctive art form of these men, the art of confession founded upon the ideal of Augustinian piety, may well prove to be an even more vital force in the genesis of the Romantic imagination than the philosophy of Locke or Berkeley or the poetry of Cowper or Smart.

In religious confession the central narrative impulse is best described in that favorite term of the confessants themselves, *justification*. It is possible for the confessant to own his past only because the plot of his past is a divinely ordained plot manifesting the grace of God: the confessant experiences a sense of being written by the divine Author Himself. Confession, then, is to be distinguished from the less specifically determined art of autobiography, as we find it in Gibbon, Hume, or even—despite the title—the *Confessions* of Jean-Jacques Rousseau. It is, most centrally, a self-ratifying statement of election. "Is it better to call upon you, to know you, or to love you?" Augustine asks his God on the first page of the *Confessions*. What he discovers—and what largely characterizes all Protestant piety since Luther—is that these three acts are indistinguishable from each other. The movement of heart, will, and intellect is, for the true Protestant confessant, a single act of speech; and if it fails to become such, if it fragments itself into "head-knowledge" as opposed to "heart-knowledge," then the confessant knows that something is wrong, that his election is not yet complete. Eschewing the more conservative, sacramentally tinged quest for "evidences of election" in the outer world (as with Donne or Vaughan), the confessant leaves himself nowhere to look for his proof of salvation except within his own heart or—most crucially— within the language of his own heart. Such English confessants as John Newton, William Nelson, and Silas Told were capable, indeed, of extraordinarily bad writing and sometimes extraordinarily off-putting pietism. But they were also capable of a truly astounding narrative self-consciousness and control, a sense of the rightness of language which arises, surely, from the exigencies of their chosen form—one of the most demanding, murderously self-critical forms of religious writing we know.

The fundamental similarity between the general shape of con-fession and the concerns and procedures of *The Prelude* is striking. It becomes even more striking as one realizes that this cannot be a matter of Wordsworth's consciously copying the techniques of the Protestant confessants; rather, the similarity springs from a shared concern, a psychic isomorphism between the radical Protestants and this most radical of poets. Anyone who has taught Wordsworth's poetry to undergraduates has had to face the widespread cliché (or prejudice) about Wordsworth as "nature poet." He is a "nature poet" only in the most difficult, most contradictory way: the same way in which we might choose to call George Fox, founder of the Society of Friends, a "churchman" or a "minister." Wordsworth's attempt to redeem nature—to integrate it with the rhythms of his own consciousness—finally led him to a vision of self-in-nature which all but obscures the conventional imagery and existence of the natural world, turning that world rather into an almost abstract principle of otherness, of alternate resistance and support to the life of the mind, whose sensory qualities are important mainly for their functioning within this eternal give-and-take. It is the same deeply motivated response which the confessants have to sacra-mental "evidences of election," turning them to use only as elements in the inner tension between the mind, the heart, and the memory.

One example will suffice to indicate the kinds of connections I am concerned with. It is the example which was, in fact, the genesis of this book, Wordsworth's short poem "Nutting." There he relates how one morning, as a boy, he left home early on a nutting expedition:

> Tricked out in proud disguise of cast-off weeds
> Which for that service had been husbanded,
> By exhortation of my frugal Dame—
> Motley accoutrement, of power to smile
> At thorns, and brakes, and brambles,—and in truth
> More ragged than need was!
>
> (9–14)

He came to a secluded bower, isolated and luxuriant:

> A little while I stood,
> Breathing with such suppression of the heart
> As joy delights in; and with wise restraint
> Voluptuous, fearless of a rival, eyed
> The banquet;—or beneath the trees I sate
> Among the flowers, and with the flowers I played;
> A temper known to those who, after long
> And weary expectation, have been blest
> With sudden happiness beyond all hope.
>
> (21–29)

This idyllic and incipiently sexual state of enjoyment lasted only for a short while, however, for soon the boy erupted into a wanton, absolutely unmotivated act of destruction:

> Then up I rose,
> And dragged to earth both branch and bough, with crash
> And merciless ravage: and the shady nook
> Of hazels, and the green and mossy bower,
> Deformed and sullied, patiently gave up
> Their quiet being: and unless I now
> Confound my present feelings with the past,
> Ere from the mutilated bower I turned
> Exulting, rich beyond the wealth of kings,
> I felt a sense of pain when I beheld
> The silent trees, and saw the intruding sky.
>
> (43–53)

In the last three lines of the poem, the poet turns to his auditor (obviously Dorothy) in much the same surprising, yet completely natural, way he turns to his sister in the last section of "Tintern Abbey":

> Then, dearest Maiden, move along these shades
> In gentleness of heart; with gentle hand
> Touch—for there is a spirit in the woods.
>
> (54–56)

This remarkable poem "belongs" to *The Prelude* in a number of important ways. It was included in manuscript in a December 1798 letter from the Wordsworths to Coleridge, along with the Stolen Boat and Skating episodes from book 1 of *The Prelude* and two Lucy poems. "Few before him," one critic writes of Wordsworth, "would have been inspired by the event recorded in 'Nutting.' "[2] This is true, of course, of the history of English, and for that matter, of European, poetry. But at least one very remarkable man both could have been and was inspired deeply by an experience quite like that of "Nutting." The man was St. Augustine and the experience was the episode of the pear tree, perhaps the most famous passage in the *Confessions*:

> For I stole that, of which I had enough, and much better. Nor cared I to enjoy what I stole, but joyed in the theft and sin itself. A pear tree there was near our vineyard, laden with fruit, tempting neither for colour nor taste. To shake and rob this, some lewd young fellows of us went, late one night (having according to our pestilent custom prolonged our sports in the streets till then), and took huge loads, not for our eating, but to fling to the very hogs, having only tasted them. And this, but to do what we liked only, because it was misliked. Behold my heart, O God, behold my heart, which Thou hadst pity upon in the bottom of the bottomless pit.
>
> (2. 9)[3]

2. Geoffrey Hartman, *Wordsworth's Poetry, 1797–1814* (New Haven, 1964), p. 73.

3. *The Confessions of Saint Augustine*, trans. Edward B. Pusey (New York, 1958). I use the Pusey translation throughout, for its convenience and close (if plodding) accuracy; references to the conventional paragraph numeration of the Latin text are my own interpolation and follow references to chapter.

There are significant differences of circumstance here, of course, from "Nutting": Wordsworth goes out in the morning, Augustine at night; Wordsworth is alone, Augustine with his "pestilent" boyhood companions; Wordsworth is entranced by the natural object of his appetite, while Augustine takes pains to note the plainness and commonness of the pear tree. But these circumstantial divergences only underscore the nearly identical imaginative form of the episodes. In both instances, a grown man relates how, as a boy, he once approached nature as the object of his appetites; how this appetitive approach transformed itself, apparently without rational motivation, into a violently destructive impulse; and how now, as a man ("unless I now / Confound my present feelings with the past"), he realizes this apparently trivial act to have been a signal of something crucial in his moral life. For both men, the true, life-giving relationship between mind and experience, soul and nature, is caught in the formulation from "Tintern Abbey":

> . . . all the mighty world
> Of eye, and ear,—both what they half create,
> And what perceive . . .
>
> (105–107)

although of course for Augustine the "creation" is a secondary creation, a recognition of the inspiriting power of God. The beautiful and seductive forms of the world become changed, through the confessant's narrative, into the mental forms of the writer's struggle to

> . . . recognize
> In nature and the language of the sense
> The anchor of my purest thoughts, the nurse,
> The guide, the guardian of my heart, and soul
> Of all my moral being.
>
> (107–111)

This struggle, the struggle of the religious confessant or the confessional poet, is linguistic in an especially intense manner. We have observed that, for the confessant, there is *no* guarantee of his salvation except the carefully maintained rectitude of his own confession, his own language. Throughout my reading of *The Prelude*, I concentrate upon the verbal texture of the poem, its own evolving sense of the proper language for poetic celebration, as one of its most intensely confessional aspects and also one of its most creative anticipations of later modes of thought and writing. A number of recent studies of Wordsworth have emphasized a more or less psychoanalytic approach to the poet: tracing the ways in which his emotional and intellectual problems shape the language of his poetry.[4] But my interest here is in the ways language itself shapes consciousness, not the other way around. Whether we are speaking simply of language or of the rather specific linguistic sanctions of confessional rhetoric, we need to realize that the grammar of our experience, the verbal grid through which we receive and shape the world, goes far toward determining the nature of the experience itself. As Wittgenstein observes at several points in *The Brown Book* and *The Philosophical Investigations*, to imagine a language is to imagine a way of life. And, indeed, our own century has grown increasingly aware of the primacy of linguistic controls over our attempts to name the "real" world. Wittgenstein is a particularly dramatic instance of this concern, since his major work, like that of Wordsworth and the confessants, is a lifelong attempt to discover the underlying conditions of speech which will allow him to believe in, to trust, his own self-consciousness: *bene dicere* leading to and constituting *bene esse*.

A reading of "Nutting" first led me to notice the remarkable similarities between that poem and Augustine's practice in the *Confessions*. Then, speculating on *The Prelude* as a whole and, later, on English religious confessions, I was led to reexamine the idea of language in these works, and I turned to Wittgenstein, among other writers, for a better grasp of modern viewpoints on the problem of language. And at this point in my reading, I was struck and excited by a coincidence which is not, I think, simply a *post hoc* justification of my research, for not only Wordsworth but Wittgenstein too is "Augustinian" in a peculiar manner. We know that Wittgenstein was fascinated with Augustine's power of faith—a faith the later thinker could never quite attain—and that the epigraph to the *Philosophical Investigations*, the springboard for that whole immense exploration of language, is a passage from the *Confessions*

4. See especially Richard J. Onerato, *The Character of the Poet: Wordsworth in The Prelude* (Princeton, 1972).

on the validity and meaning of words. But this quest itself leads Wittgenstein at points into an uncannily Wordsworthian—not Augustinian—diction. The final goal of the confessant's speech is what I call in my fourth chapter "Edenic Words": a language, that is, which recreates the lost Eden of Man's innocence within the successful narrative of each man's private life. And Wittgenstein, revising his early positivism, writes at the beginning of the *Philosophische Bemerkungen*: "Phenomenological or 'primary' speech, as I called it, is not now my concern; I no longer think it important. All that is possible or necessary is to distinguish the inmost nature of *our* speech [*das Wesentliche u n s e r e r Sprache*] from its nonessentials."[5] This important passage, and especially the key phrase *das Wesentliche u n s e r e r Sprache*, inevitably and astoundingly reminds the reader of Wordsworth of the poet's own announced hopes for a purified, Edenic language in the Prospectus to *The Excursion*:

> Paradise, and groves
> Elysian, Fortunate Fields—like those of old
> Sought in the Atlantic Main—why should they be
> A history only of departed things,
> Or a mere fiction of what never was?
> For the discerning intellect of Man,
> When wedded to this goodly universe
> In love and holy passion, shall find these
> A simple produce of the common day.
> —I, long before the blissful hour arrives,
> Would chant, in lonely peace, the spousal verse
> Of this great consummation—and, by *words*
> *Which speak of nothing more than what we are,*
> Would I arouse the sensual from their sleep
> Of death. . . .
>
> (47–61, italics mine)

It is similarities such as these—and, of course, their attendant dissimilarities—which the present study attempts to map, always keeping its central focus upon an attempt to understand and read

---

5. Ludwig Wittgenstein, *Philosophische Bemerkungen* (Oxford, 1964), p. 51 (my translation).

efficiently *The Prelude* itself. Each chapter is intended to center upon a basic aspect of Wordsworth's confessional procedure in writing the poem. Thus, he is confessing *to* someone; he is confessing his past life from the viewpoint of the present; he is confessing a life which he regards mainly as a development and refinement of his perception of the outer and inner worlds; and finally, most radically, he is confessing through words, he is *speaking*. Chapter 1 is an examination of the peculiarities involved in the mode of address to *The Prelude*'s definitive auditor, Coleridge, and of the ways this auditor, as felt presence, shapes the overall form of the poem. Chapter 2 is a general discussion of the confessional—and Wordsworthian—view of the human career, contrasting the holistic and organic ideal of man's development with a more ancient and allegorical, or *daemonic*, view against which the confessional vision struggles. Chapter 3 carries the argument to the more fundamental level of the *shape* of the experiences narrated: it is necessarily a discussion of the senses of sight and hearing, since these are the "real" senses for Wordworth's pre-Proustian and, indeed, pre-Keatsian kind of poetry. And chapter 4 deals with language itself, the irreducible counters of Wordsworth's vision, and the highly specialized confessional language of "Edenic words." The general direction of my reading, then, is a narrowing of focus from the most general to the most specific, definitive features of the confessional act.

I have attempted, following the example of my great primary texts, to avoid a specialized, technical diction and to use words which speak of nothing more than what *The Prelude*, in my view at least, is. But there is one term, in frequent use in this study, which deserves some initial clarification: the *daemonic*.

Daemon, in pre-Olympian Greek mythology, refers to a kind of supernatural agent, less than divine and more than human, capable of compelling human beings to act in certain obsessive, excessive ways. The daemon is the linguistic ancestor of our *demon*, of course; but he is not primarily an agent of evil. The compulsion through which the daemon possesses and drives a man may be for either good or evil, but it is fundamentally something which comes to a man from *outside* himself, something which seems to force him to act despite his conscious will. The wrath—the *Ménin*—of Achilles announced as the subject of the *Iliad*, for example, is not simply Achilles' anger but a *daemonic principle* of wrath, a semi-detached agent which possesses the Achaean hero. The *daemonic*, then, describes a state of mind in which one sees his best or worst actions as, in some way, *not part of himself* but thrust upon him from without. The Freudian idea of obsession-compulsion is a good analogue to this sense of the daemonic, although obsessive-compulsive actions are always accompanied, in our culture, with a feeling of guilt. And the very nature of the daemonic is, really, to deny the possibility of guilt. E. R. Dodds, in his magisterial book *The Greeks and the Irrational*, discusses the daemon as the central figure of a primitive Greek "shame-culture": a culture, that is, in which shame or embarrassment, rather than the sense of sin or guilt, is the prime motivating factor of ethics: "This daemon has, apparently, nothing to do with perception or thought, which Empedocles held to be mechanically determined; the function of the daemon is to be the carrier of man's potential divinity and actual guilt. It is nearer in some ways to the indwelling spirit which the shaman inherits from other shamans than it is to the rational 'soul' in which Socrates believed. . . ."[6] Dodds's thesis is that the great accomplishments of fifth-century Athenian culture transformed the Greek moral universe from "shame-culture" to "guilt-culture." Through the morality of Socrates and Aeschylus, among others, the daemon was denuded of his role as guilt-carrier, and the sense of *sin*, of personal responsibility for one's actions and therefore of the need for purification and penance, was introduced into Western culture.

We may remark that the daemonic, as Dodds describes it, is by no means an obsolete notion. Indeed, it seems to be a perennial possibility of moral thought, in constant battle with the more unitary vision of the soul as creator of its own guilts and triumphs. If the daemon finds his most receptive host in the figure of the shaman, the soul in need of purification is ministered to most efficiently by the shaman's historical successor, the priest. But our own century, both in literature and in politics, has seen how easy it is for the shaman and his attendant daemons to reassert their hegemony over the mind.

At any rate, the daemonic, as undying competitor of the unified moral soul, is a particularly important attitude for the confessant—

6. E. R. Dodds, *The Greeks and the Irrational* (Berkeley, 1951), p. 153.

recorder and narrator of the progress of the soul toward unity—to overcome. Augustine's quarrel with the Manichaeans, the quarrels of the English confessants with various forms of sacramental "superstition," and Wordsworth's quarrel with the obsessive, disembodied rationalism of David Hartley, are all versions of the struggle against the daemonic. In fact, the confessant's progress toward a true vision of unity-in-time almost always becomes, in this way, a minihistory of the cultural upheaval Dodds traces. The confessor needs to establish his own guilt as real guilt precisely so that he can overcome it through the saving speech of his confession. And in order to do this, he needs to find a stage in his past where he was under a daemonic dispensation: a dispensation, that is, which would not allow him to recognize the true processes of his soul.

Milton, one of the few great poets who is also a great theologian, was acutely aware of this problem, both in his own life and in the great celebratory work of his life. I preface my discussion, in the second chapter, of Wordsworth's sense of the daemonic with a discussion of *Paradise Regained*. It is perhaps the profoundest myth we have of a battle, in the persons of Satan and the Son of God, between the principles of daemonism and moral unity. It is a "preconfessional" poem, since it works out, with extraordinary clarity and precision, those moral and verbal oppositions which underlie the techniques of confessional writing for invoking and then circumventing daemonism.[7]

The term has, in fact, recently become rather current in literary criticism. Angus Fletcher's *Allegory* and Bloom's *Anxiety of Influence*, among other books, use daemonism in immensely suggestive ways to describe processes and techniques basic to all poetic creation. My own use of the term is intended to suggest both its general relevance to certain eternal problems of moral thought and writing and its particular usefulness in dealing with Wordsworth's narrative of the growth of his own—archetypally modern—mind. The struggle in Yeats between Self and Soul and in Robert

7. An excellent discussion of *Paradise Regained* in relation to the whole tradition of the Romantic epic is Stuart Curran's "The Mental Pinnacle: *Paradise Regained* and the Romantic Four-Book Epic," in *Calm of Mind*, ed. Joseph Anthony Wittreich, Jr. (Cleveland, 1971). Curran's reading of the nature of the Son of God agrees essentially with my own, although he does not discuss *Paradise Regained* in specific relation to *The Prelude*.

Lowell between the will to sanity and the dementia of "Skunk Hour"—indeed, the great warfare in contemporary writing between poetry as cure and poetry as deep disease—are all among the directions in which this Wordsworthian and confessional strife seems to survive and develop.

As a final point, I wish to reemphasize my subtitle: this is *a* reading of *The Prelude*, one which I think makes good sense of the poem but which would not be possible without a great body of Wordsworth criticism, although, indeed, it sometimes contradicts it. Wordsworth has been blessed, among a number of ways, in the critics who have written about him: I think it would be difficult to find another author whose modern commentators include so many readers of such a consistently high level of perception. And in an age not distinguished by the generosity of its literary critics, it is refreshing to note the tone of most discussions of, and even debates over, the nature of his work. Perhaps the poet's personality— at least, his literary personality—has a gentling effect on writers who approach it. Or perhaps his work, and especially *The Prelude*, is simply capacious enough to allow even antithetical interpreters to dwell in fellowship. Whatever the cause, the effect cannot but be to inspire further study in the same spirit of reasoned, generous, and humane criticism. I have attempted, in my reading, to be faithful to the high standard of that exegesis as well as to *The Prelude*.

CHAPTER
ONE

THE
POEM
TO
COLERIDGE

Taking up the subject, then, upon general grounds, I ask what is meant by the word Poet? What is a poet? To whom does he address himself? And what language is to be expected from him? He is a man speaking to men. . . .

Wordsworth, *Preface* to *Lyrical Ballads*

Nothing is more familiar or characteristic among Christians than assertion. Take away assertions, and you take away Christianity. Why, the Holy Spirit is given to Christians from heaven in order that He may glorify Christ and in them confess Him even unto death. . . .

Luther, *The Bondage of the Will*

Perhaps the greatest irony we encounter in *The Prelude* is the poem's title. Wordsworth, of course, originally did think of it as a prelude to his proposed philosophical epic. But that later epic he never found the strength to complete, and the title so suggestive of promise and beginnings was given the poem by his wife on its posthumous publication in 1850. It was actually called, in William and Dorothy's letters, "the Poem on his own Life" or "the poem on the growth of my own mind."[1] But it has a different, much more interesting, name on the title page of the 1805–6 manuscripts:

POEM
Title not yet fixed upon
by
WILLIAM WORDSWORTH
Addressed to
S. T. COLERIDGE

This "title," which corresponds closely to Wordsworth's habitual reference within his own household to "the poem to Coleridge,"[2] is reproduced in de Selincourt's editions of the 1805 and the combined 1805 and 1850 texts. And in its refusal to settle on a conventional title, it may be the most meaningful name we have for the poem. For as the "Poem Addressed to S. T. Coleridge," *The Prelude* reveals the first of its distinctively confessional aspects: its sense of an *audience* as necessary not only for the rhetorical decorum of the poem but for the poem's very existence. The phrase, "Title not yet fixed upon," is in fact an admission of uncertainty which finally belies its own diffidence. For Coleridge, in all he represented for Wordsworth, is in a profound way the only *fact* in the poem which can be "fixed upon" in the way we normally fix upon the title of a major work of imagination.

To understand the novelty of this, we must understand the importance of titles in Western epic tradition—the tradition in which, rightly or wrongly, Wordsworth thought he was working. Kenneth Burke and Francis Fergusson have both pointed out the importance of title in conventional epic as the identification of a central action, a dynamic paradigm which, repeated in varying modalities (high, middle, or low style) and intensities (successful,

1. William Wordsworth, *The Prelude*, ed. Ernest de Selincourt and Helen Darbishire (Oxford, 1959), pp. xx, xxxvii.
2. Ibid., p. xxxvii.

abortive, or equivocal), defines the moral universe or the theme of the work.[3] Thus, for example, in *The Iliad*, the paradigmatic action of "destruction of a city" ramifies itself throughout the action in various versions of subjection or cruelty. (This process is brilliantly described by Simone Weil, who calls *The Iliad* "The Poem of Force."[4]) *Gerusalemme Liberata* and *Paradise Lost* exemplify titles which are actually paradigms of an action to be replayed, in one way or another, throughout their narratives. And epics titled after heroic central characters, such as *The Odyssey*, *The Aeneid*, and even *Beowulf*, display the same principle of paradigmatic organization, with the added sophistication of epitomizing the central action as a dramatic characteristic of a single man.

The "Romance" epics of the Renaissance, however, present a special problem for this sort of interpretation. And one such epic, which Wordsworth knew intimately—Spenser's *Faerie Queene*—may be allowed to stand for this class and to introduce an interesting perspective on *The Prelude*.

In Spenser's poem, the exuberant projection of ideal types around—and symbolically within—the elusive Gloriana tends to split the poem into a series of more or less independent paradigms of action and to suggest that the unfinished epic may be virtually untitled, or without an analogical, paradigmatic center. Most responsible lines of interpretation of *The Faerie Queene* confront this problem and suggest that the poet's continuing address to Elizabeth provides a clue to its total organization.[5] If this is correct, then the paradigmatic action of *The Faerie Queene* is not an action *described* but an action *performed* in the telling of the tale: the action of courtly praise, whose roots have been traced by such scholars as E. R. Curtius to the centrality of epideictic oratory in medieval Latin literature.[6] The key passage here would perhaps be the chronicles of British and Elvin kings in the House of Alma (book 2, canto 10), itself a series of praises, where we learn that

3. Francis Fergusson, *The Idea of a Theater* (New York, 1953), p. 250.
4. Simone Weil, *The Iliad, or the Poem of Force* (Wallingford, Eng., 1962).
5. See Northrop Frye, *Fables of Identity* (New York, 1963), pp. 69–87, and William Nelson, *The Poetry of Edmund Spenser* (New York, 1963), pp. 111–46.
6. Ernst Robert Curtius, *European Literature in the Latin Middle Ages* (New York, 1963), pp. 115 ff.

the quest of Arthur for Gloriana is, in its full meaning, the quest of historical process for the purity of moral ideas, of mutability for permanence. So that the deification of Elizabeth, her symbolic conversion into ideality, becomes the prime motive of *The Faerie Queene*, unifying the legends of allegorical knights of virtue, the exercises in political commentary, and the occasional neoplatonic pastorals of Spenser's book. In some sense, then, Spenser's impulse to *address*, as itself an epic action, serves to de-allegorize or de-mythologize even his own supreme exercises in allegory. This itself is significant, since I shall have much to say in this study about the way Wordsworth's poem, an even more radical version of address as action, resolutely opposes itself to the resources and techniques of moral allegory, of verbal daemonism.

The Faerie Queene, then, is an important predecessor of *The Prelude* in epic tradition precisely because it, like *The Prelude*, appears to be an epic whose sense of address is crucial for the whole fabric of the poetry (it will be remembered that Wordsworth's early *Guilt and Sorrow* is a highly Spenserian, though not imitative, poem). Indeed, Janet Spens, in her study of Spenser, devotes some suggestive pages to the mutual illumination of the two poets.[7] Even more useful, however, is the way the comparison emphasizes the real newness of Wordsworth's practice. His poem is not "dedicated" but "addressed" to S. T. Coleridge, and in that choice of word and attitude lies one source of a new mode in English poetry.

As subtle as is Spenser's modulation of epic action from the matter to the manner of praise, that praise remains an essentially public act, dignified and constituted by the importance of Queen Elizabeth. Praise, both as a classical *topos* and as a human activity, necessitates the fixation and isolation of the person praised:

> And with them [the gods and Muses] eke, O Goddesse
> heauenly bright,
> Mirrour of grace and Maiestie diuine,
> Great Lady of the greatest Isle, whose light
> Like *Phoebus* lampe throughout the world doth shine,
> Shed thy faire beames into my feeble eyne,
> And raise my thoughts too humble and too vile,

7. Janet Spens, *Spenser's Faerie Queene* (London, 1934), pp. 54 ff.

To thinke of that true glorious type of thine,
The argument of mine afflicted stile:
The which to heare, vouchsafe, O dearest dred a-while.

(1, Induction. 4)[8]

In this passage the epic of praise achieves its barest articulation: the poem, as private encomium of a public exemplar of virtue, is imaginatively determined by the exaltation of its auditor—not necessarily her personality, that is, but the very fact of her great distance from the poet. Thus the poem seeks to transcend its own subjectivity by the public ratification of its auditor. In a great age of patronage, it is among the most subtle and eloquent defenses of preferment for art's sake.

But now compare Wordsworth, at an analogous stage of *The Prelude*, the end of book 1, and his musings on a proper theme for his poem:

Nor will it seem to thee, O Friend! so prompt
In sympathy, that I have lengthened out
With fond and feeble tongue a tedious tale.
Meanwhile, my hope has been, that I might fetch
Invigorating thoughts from former years;
Might fix the wavering balance of my mind,
And haply meet reproaches too, whose power
May spur me on, in manhood now mature,
To honourable toil. Yet should these hopes
Prove vain, and thus should neither I be taught
To understand myself, nor thou to know
With better knowledge how the heart was framed
Of him thou lovest; need I dread from thee
Harsh judgments, if the song be loth to quit
Those recollected hours that have the charm
Of visionary things, those lovely forms
And sweet sensations that throw back our life,
And almost make remotest infancy
A visible scene, on which the sun is shining?

(617–635)

---

8. *The Poems of Edmund Spenser*, ed. J. C. Smith and Ernest de Selincourt (London, 1960).

The opening of the passage is remarkable for its simultaneous dependence upon and easy assumption of the approval of the "Friend so prompt in sympathy," and even more for the use of the word "Meanwhile" at line 620. That word is obviously used to differentiate two temporal sequences: first, the narrating of the "tedious tale" of Wordsworth's youth and, second, his reexamination of his earliest memories for renewed stability and purpose. In actual fact, however, the two sequences have been, throughout book 1, not only parallel but identical. The "Meanwhile," then, is disturbingly difficult to understand, because it takes account of a disjunction in the poetry of book 1 which had not been previously acknowledged: the disjunction between expression and intent, between speech and the purpose of speech.

It is necessary, as we shall see in the following chapter, that Wordsworth make such an admission at this point, but here it is important to note that the admission itself is couched in a curious dubiety. The "tedious tale," the personal recitation of past experience, certainly in one sense belongs to the private sphere, while the purpose of the tale's being told, as a preparation for a fully epic work, surely belongs to the public. But this ostensive organization contradicts the speech itself, since it is the address to the Friend which, in normal rhetoric, would be the public element of speech, while the purpose of that address, as all purposes, is a private intention. The pivotal point for this transvaluation of public and private is simply that the speaker identifies his auditor as a "Friend"—with all the inherent ambiguities of that word, implying an intimacy at once more than courtly and less than passionate. Unlike the rhetoric of Spenser, here the action of address does not limit and define the rhetorical status of the poetry but rather becomes the poetry itself as a necessary transaction between impulse and achievement. The personality of the auditor does not determine the nature of the discourse: the discourse, with its typical Wordsworthian drive toward "images of interaction" between the self and the other,[9] interacts so strongly with the "other" person to whom it is addressed that, in an inevitable manner, *it* determines *him*.

The last eleven lines of the passage cited are a more striking

9. The phrase is from Herbert Lindenberger, *On Wordsworth's Prelude* (Princeton, 1963), the title of chapter 2.

instance of this technique. For there the poet begins with the admission of possible failure in his public task and moves, through the medium of address, to an intimation of what is to be the triumphant myth of renewal and salvation of *The Prelude*. Certainly, to make

> . . . remotest infancy
> A visible scene, on which the sun is shining

is Wordsworth's central accomplishment and the first tentative intimation of the idea of "spots of time," described by Hartman as temporalized liberations of spatial experiences.[10] It is also one of the most arresting single images of the whole poem. What makes it so is the extraordinary fashion in which it is contained and, in the full sense of the word, articulated by the activity of address to a friend. Grammatically, the image of the "visible scene" is the weakest member of an already too subordinated sentence: it is the end phrase of a question too long to be read as a question. And this is precisely its strength, since poetically it is the most assertive phrase of the whole self-effacing and apologetic passage. The question asked by Wordsworth of Coleridge, "Need I dread from thee / Harsh judgments," is not what we would term a rhetorical question, since its demand for an appropriate answer is stronger than that of the normal rhetorical question.

The rhetorical question, in fact, is a homely paradigm of Spenserian epic, since its answer, while implied, depends upon the personality of the auditor as somehow outside the world of discourse for its effectiveness. In the classical example, Cicero asks Catiline, "Do not the night watches on the Palatine, do not the vigils of the city, does not the fear of the people . . . move you?" and the implied force of the questions is in the silence following their utterance—a silence filled in, as it were, by the presence of the auditor. But Wordsworth writes differently: he continues to talk after finishing his question, and each addition to the question tends to answer it more definitely. In an inversion of periodic style, he moves into ever looser subordinate clauses and into more and more confident assertions of the value of his art: from "song" to "recol-

10. Geoffrey Hartman, *Wordsworth's Poetry, 1797–1814* (New Haven, 1964), pp. 212 ff.

lected hours" to "visionary things" to "lovely forms" and finally to the powerful last couplet. That couplet does end in a question, however, and the mark of interrogation serves to reenclose, with rather a jolt, the progressive expansion of the sentence in the movement of conversation and of public-private address.

Indeed, the presentation of the "visible scene" tends to annihilate the third dimension, for the phrase which gives us that scene, in terms of the grammar of the sentence, is the most heavily subordinated and therefore, in a "normal" reading, the most dispensable piece of information. And yet, poetically, it is the most arresting image of the passage: it is both subordinate to and subordinates the rest of its sentence, depending upon whether we read it grammatically or imagistically. The double existence of the "visible scene," as detail in the poet's narrative and as visually striking "spot of time," is beautifully articulated through Wordsworth's syntax here: the phrase itself vibrates between existences as an element of process (the unfolding of grammar) and a fixed, stable image. This use of the speaking voice to overcome or integrate the fixedness of the visual is one which we shall see to have profound implications for Wordsworth's procedure in *The Prelude*. And it is suggestive that here, in one of its first occurrences, it should be manifested through the form of a question to the "Friend," Coleridge.

The importance of Coleridge as auditor of *The Prelude* has been noted by a number of critics. Herbert Lindenberger, whose valuable study *On Wordsworth's Prelude* reads the poem more or less within the canons of traditional epic, describes the poet's "use" of Coleridge as a technique approximating Horatian epistle:

> What goes on in the poem is a constant flight from the subjectivity of private experience to the assertion of publicly communicable and valid truths. The epistolary convention becomes a means of achieving the sense of an audience—if only an audience of one—and thus of giving a public definition to a state of mind which might otherwise have remained meaningful to the poet alone.[11]

Another critic, however, Francis Christensen, sees Coleridge as the vehicle of an intellectual love which converts Wordsworth *away*

11. Lindenberger, *On Wordsworth's Prelude*, p. 7.

from public address to a "gentle and tender" quietism and conservative humility.[12] Christensen's concern is with the themes of
The Prelude, as opposed to Lindenberger's interest in its rhetoric,
and he bases his argument upon the passage toward the end of
the poem:

> Imagination having been our theme
> So also hath that intellectual Love,
> For they are each in each, and cannot stand
> Dividually.
>
> (14. 206–209)

But we have already seen how theme and rhetoric—private
purpose and public articulation—tend to change roles in Wordsworth's poem. Lindenberger's Horatian poet and Christensen's
quietist one are, in this way, both combined and transcended in
the speaker of *The Prelude*. And the passage Christensen cites
should probably be read as another instance of what we have
already seen occurring at the end of book 1: a momentary division
of elements which have been imaginatively identical in the poetry
itself, whose retrospective separation only serves to underscore the
binding energy of the poetry. The lines immediately preceding this
passage, in fact, make explicit the identity of "imagination" and
"intellectual love." And the fact that they are "addressed to S. T.
Coleridge" abrogates the distinction between public and private
inspiration:

> This spiritual Love acts not nor can exist
> Without Imagination, which, in truth,
> Is but another name for absolute power
> And clearest insight, amplitude of mind,
> And Reason in her most exalted mood.
> This faculty hath been the feeding source
> Of our long labour: we have traced the stream
> From the blind cavern whence is faintly heard
> Its natal murmur; followed it to light
> And open day; accompanied its course

12. Francis Christensen, "Intellectual Love: The Second Theme of *The
Prelude*," *PMLA* 80 (1965–66):69.

Among the ways of Nature, for a time
Lost sight of it bewildered and engulphed:
Then given it greeting as it rose once more
In strength, reflecting from its placid breast
The works of man and face of human life. . . .

(14. 188–202)

When Wordsworth describes the creation of *The Prelude* as "our labour," he is employing more than an editorial plural, for Coleridge is surely here being absorbed into the Wordsworthian personality. But it is an absorption which includes a graceful compliment, for the course of "imagination" in the passage is a reprise of Coleridge's description, in *Kubla Khan*, of the course of the sacred river Alph. Characteristically, too, Wordsworth revises Coleridge's image of the river as an emblem of the fitful and potentially violent power of poetry. Its emergence from concealment is not in a disruptive fountain but in a smooth flow, reflecting not the dark caverns and lifeless ocean of imaginative occlusion but the one face of human community—"The works of man and face of human life." *Kubla Khan* ends with a vision of society as necessarily inimical to, since threatened by, the power of the poet: "All should cry, Beware! Beware! / His flashing eyes, His floating hair!" But Wordsworth tries to reconcile the energies of independent imagination and social morality, not only through, but largely because of, his sense of the poem as an intimate dialogue with a "Friend."

There is, quite simply, no real analogue in previous English poetry for the speaker-audience relationship in *The Prelude*. Critics like Lindenberger and Christensen, who attempt to describe that relationship by reference to conventions of seventeenth- or eighteenth-century lyric or epic, inevitably distort it, for in the major traditions of English verse, as with Spenser, the existence of an audience is a definitive but external context for the rhetorical motives of the poem: the audience determines the role of the poet. But it is a central aspect of the speech of *The Prelude* that *the speaker in the act of speaking constitutes his audience*. As we shall see, Wordsworth's effort to recreate his own past is inseparable from his effort to remake the personality of his friend Coleridge, and a prime implication of this motive is that the standard of success which *The Prelude* poses for itself is a kind of edification previously unattempted by serious—that is, professional—English poets.

David Ferry, in *The Limits of Mortality*, comes close to describing this "rhetoric of edification" when he says that Wordsworth's view of human nature required a complete revision of what we normally understand as human, in order for the poet to regard it as at all worthy of love.[13] But the closest approximation to the view I am maintaining is made by a critic who is, on the whole, unsympathetic to its literary and ethical implications. F. W. Bateson writes in *Wordsworth: A Reinterpretation*,

> [Wordsworth's relationship with his public] was a poet-audience relationship different in kind from that of a Spenser, a Milton, a Dryden or a Pope, partly because of its oral basis and partly because of its emotional overtones. To a typical Wordsworthian Wordsworth was so much more than just another good poet. The process of discovering his poetry was more like a religious conversion, an experience from which the convert emerged with the whole of his way of looking at the world permanently and profoundly changed.[14]

"Religious conversion" is precisely the term. And throughout the nineteenth century, the recorded instances of "Wordsworthian" experiences—by Hazlitt, De Quincey, Mill, Arnold, and even Oscar Wilde[15]—testify to the power and resiliency of Wordsworth's imagination along this line. But in *The Prelude* itself, the intended and crucial convert is Coleridge. And Coleridge, in a moving document, records his reaction to the poem addressed to him in terms which illuminate our own reading of it.

"To William Wordsworth" is Coleridge's description of hearing the 1805 "Poem on the Growth of an Individual Mind." He recapitulates briefly the story of *The Prelude*, from Wordsworth's youth to his disappointment with the French Revolution to his return to "the dread watchtower of man's absolute self," and he then

---

13. David Ferry, *The Limits of Mortality: An Essay on Wordsworth's Major Poems* (Middletown, 1959), p. 50.

14. F. W. Bateson, *Wordsworth: A Reinterpretation* (London, 1963), p. 195.

15. See Robert Langbaum, *The Poetry of Experience* (New York, 1963), p. 35.

turns to a reflection upon his own imaginative life. This reflection
is described as occurring while Wordsworth reads his own retrospect aloud, but its outcome is painfully contrary to Wordsworth's
own eventual triumph:

> Sense of past Youth, and Manhood come in vain,
> And Genius given, and Knowledge won in vain;
> And all which I had culled in wood-walks wild,
> And all which patient toil had reared, and all,
> Commune with thee had opened out—but flowers
> Strewed on my corse, and borne upon my bier
> In the same coffin, for the self-same grave!
>
> That way no more! and ill beseems it me,
> Who came a welcomer in herald's guise,
> Singing of Glory, and Futurity,
> To wander back on such unhealthful road,
> Plucking the poisons of self-harm! And ill
> Such intertwine beseems triumphal wreaths
> Strew'd before thy advancing!
>
> (69–82)

This vision, culminating in the image of Coleridge literally
being plowed under by Wordsworth's greater genius, is an eloquent
testimonial to *The Prelude* as the record of a conversion. For the
aim of conversion-narrative is not so much to spur others to greater
effort as to reshape their imaginative and spiritual world and lead
them, too, into the difficult experiences of retrospect and the
memory of guilt. Confession addresses itself not so much to the
pragmatic will of its audience as to their affective intellect. In fact,
confession, regarded as the distinctively radical Protestant narrative
technique, is fundamentally inimical to the idea of pragmatic will,
since such will is thought to interfere with the affective reconstitution of its audience. As the nonconformist divine John Newton
writes at the beginning of his own confession:

> We may collect indisputable proof, from the narrow circle of our
> own concerns, that the wise and good providence of God watches
> over his people from the earliest moment of their life, overrules
> and guards them through all their wanderings in a state of ignorance,

leads them in a way they know not, till at length his providence and grace concur in those events and impressions, which bring them to a knowledge of him and themselves.[16]

This is precisely the effect we can see in Coleridge's poem on *The Prelude*: he has literally remade himself, for the moment, into the image of the "Friend" which Wordsworth has projected through the long personal confession which is his poem. But at this point it is necessary to examine more closely the characteristics of confession itself.

The literature of Protestant confession is immense—it is probably one of the few bodies of writing not, in our time, overbalanced by the volume of latter-day commentary. In the case of the Quakers, for example, who account for by far the greater bulk of religious confessions before the rise of Methodism in the mid-eighteenth century, Luella M. Wright, in *The Literary Life of the Early Friends*, estimates that between 1653 and 1725 from two and a half to four million tracts were printed and issued by the Friends.[17] Even allowing for high percentages of polemical essays and sermons among these works, the number of books which either in whole or in part may be termed "confessions" is considerable. And as the creative energy of dissenting Protestantism passed from the Quakers to the Methodists in the middle of the century, so the impulse to confession and "accounts of convincement" flourished within the younger movement: besides the individually published narratives, Wesley's *Arminian Magazine* (first issued in 1778) contained in every issue the serialized journal of a prominent Wesleyan preacher. These were collected in 1837 by Thomas Jackson in *The Lives of the Early Methodist Preachers* in six volumes.

That these books are important for the history of English

16. "An Authentic Narrative, &c.," in *The Works of the Reverend John Newton* (Philadelphia, 1834) 1:79.

17. Luella M. Wright, *The Literary Life of the Early Friends* (New York, 1932), p. 8.

autobiography, few scholars have questioned. But small account has been taken of the fact that they also form an original and highly consistent subgenre of narrative art and that, indeed, they are in the best sense of the word an important version of fictive technique. This, rather than their frequent implication of egalitarian sentiments, their predilection for humble style, or their general aura of enthusiasm, is the focal point of their significance for English Romantic poetry, particularly for Wordsworth. Demonstration of a continuity of thought between the confessing Protestants and the Romantics—the approach loosely called "history of ideas"—has been attempted frequently and with interesting but equivocal results. But while it is alarming (though intriguing) to claim that "an atmosphere of Quakerism was felt among the literary celebrities of the Lake School of Poets and Writers,"[18] what *is* demonstrable is the extent to which the distinctive narrative form of a religion contributes to the distinctive poetic form of a revolution in secular imagination. And though styles of expression, if they are meaningful, necessarily arise from modes of thought, we can usefully discuss such styles while keeping speculation about ideological forms to a minimum.

We are concerned with the relationships between the distinctive sense of audience exhibited by *The Prelude* and similar forms of public-private address in the religious confessions of the seventeenth and eighteenth centuries. How does the Wordsworthian technique resemble the sensibility which informed these confessions, and how does it differ from it? The key concept, for both *The Prelude* and Protestant confession, is that of edification: confession seeks a mode of conviction beyond rhetoric, since it attempts to confront human form with human form, consciousness with consciousness at the most introspective level. Thereby the will is moved to action and the perception, memory, and sense of self to literal re-formation. Newton, whose confession is notable both because of its intrinsic power and because of the influence Newton had as a preacher during the late eighteenth century, distinguishes two sorts of

18. Quoted in Henry J. Cadbury, "The Influence of *The Journal of George Fox*," in *The Journal of George Fox*, ed. Rufus M. Jones (New York, 1963), p. 13.

Christian conversion: the gradual, an imperceptible turning to God of which the converted "can give little account," and the exemplary, done "in thunder and tempest" after the pattern of Paul, Augustine, and Luther.[19] It is the latter form—the form, of course, of Newton's own experience—which is, he asserts, the more valuable to tell of, precisely because of its potential influence for edification, an influence he specifically relates to the creative power of the divine Word:

> They [the exemplary] are, beyond expectation, convinced, pardoned, and changed. A case of this sort indicates a divine power no less than the creation of a world: and it is evidently the Lord's doing, and it is marvellous in the eyes of all those, who are not blinded by prejudice and unbelief.[20]

Edification, then, implies in the confessions a closer and more aggressive relationship of speaker to auditor or auditors than is implied in other, more meditative styles of devotional writing. Ideally, the confession does not issue in an impulse toward conversion but actually *is* a conversion for the auditor. In the journal of John Nelson, one of Wesley's most energetic and effective disciples, we have an important account of the process whereby the confession of another becomes the content and motive of one's own conversion experience. Nelson's narrative deserves discussion in some detail.

Nelson begins life in a state highly receptive to radical Protestant ideas of the efficacious and overpowering Word: he relates how, at nine years, as his father was reading aloud from the twentieth chapter of Revelation (the Last Judgment), "the word came with such light and power to my soul, that it made me tremble. . . ."[21] The years of his early manhood were spent, as is typical among the confessants, in a search for convictions of justification and what Thomas Traherne and John Wesley both call "the riches of the full assurance." As is also typical, he does not seem to have found in his marriage a great deal of spiritual companionship, and he constantly bemoans his lack of a sympathetic auditor and counselor for his difficulties:

19. Newton, "An Authentic Narrative, &c.," p. 80.
20. Ibid.
21. *Extract from the Journal of John Nelson* (New York, 1831), p. 5.

In all these troubles I had none to open my mind to, so I wandered up and down in the fields when I had done my work, meditating what course to take to save my soul.[22]

Nelson examines carefully all possible forms of religious belief and finds none of them satisfying, although the Quakers seem to offer him more solace than anyone else. Then Whitefield comes to preach in his vicinity, and Nelson feels the first stirrings of his attraction to Methodism; a short while later Wesley himself arrives, and the stirrings grow stronger, more personal. For some time afterward, Nelson wrestles manfully with his conviction of guilt, trying to accept faith in his redemption by Christ, but he cannot. Then one day, "a little after Michaelmas," leaving the Park at Westminster, he is attracted to a crowd gathered about a soldier who is confessing the history of his own conversion to Methodism by Charles Wesley. Nelson takes pains to record in his own narrative this soldier's oral confession, as nearly as possible verbatim. It is evidently a crystallizing experience for him, and within two weeks, after some final struggles with despair, he pronounces himself converted.

What is important here is that Nelson, in relating his experience, structures it around three distinct versions of the Word—those of Whitefield, Wesley, and the anonymous soldier—and gives us what almost amounts to a thumbnail *ars rhetorica* of radical Protestant speech. Of the three speakers who shape Nelson's convictions, Whitefield, the most poised rhetorician and "public" reformer, comes off the poorest:

He was to me as a man that could play well on an instrument, for his preaching was pleasant to me, and I loved the man. . . . But I did not understand him, though I might hear him twenty times for aught I know. . . .[23]

Wesley, the great journal-writer and advocate of plain, forthright style, moves Nelson in a manner beyond public persuasion and closer, in Nelson's mind at least, to direct personal confrontation:

22. Ibid., pp. 13–14.
23. Ibid., p. 16.

O that was a blessed morning to my soul! As soon as he got upon the stand, he stroked back his hair, and turned his face toward where I stood, and I thought fixed his eyes on me: his countenance struck such an awful dread upon me, before I heard him speak, that it made my heart beat like the pendulum of a clock; and when he had done, I said, this man can tell the secrets of my heart. . . .[24]

But the soldier whose tale Nelson repeats is presented with a minimum of description, in spite of his catalytic influence on Nelson's conversion. His story is repeated at length, and Nelson says:

These sayings of the soldier were a blessing to me, for they sunk deep into my mind, and made me cry more earnestly, that God would work the same change in my heart.[25]

Personal confrontation has here passed the boundaries of its normal state and become a kind of total intercourse which, since it leaves out nothing which is an essential aspect of the self, cannot be successfully paraphrased or described but only repeated. Paradoxically, though it is given in a public context more open than the sermons of Whitefield and Wesley—in modern England the soldier would speak in Hyde Park from a soapbox—the soldier's confession so fills Nelson that he apparently does not even approach him after the speech for more personal counsel. It is obviously a model of what effective—and affective—confession should be, and immediately after his own conversion Nelson begins not only to rejoice in the Methodist style of life but to rehearse the style of discourse in which that life, at its fullest, issues. His landlord and landlady, noticing the change in his spiritual outlook, question him about it:

So I sat down with them, and told them of God's dealing with my soul, and prayed with them; soon after which they both went to hear Mr. Wesley preach, when the woman was made partaker of the same grace; and I hope to meet them both in heaven.[26]

In many ways, the antitype of the radical Protestant confession discussed here is the Roman- and Anglo-Catholic form of medita-

24. Ibid., p. 17.
25. Ibid., pp. 21–22.
26. Ibid., p. 25.

tion, which was current in England during the sixteenth and seventeenth centuries and which is discussed most completely in Louis L. Martz's *The Poetry of Meditation*. The comparison of the two forms, confession and meditation, serves greatly to clarify the salient characteristics of confession. In the matter of address as a constituent element of the religious work, Martz is especially helpful in his discussion of the part of meditation called *colloquy*. As meditation, in the view of most of the major writers of devotional manuals, directs itself to the "three parts" of the Platonic-Christian soul, the understanding, the memory, and the will, so is the typical process of a meditation tripartite: the composition of place, or setting of the imaginative scene; the reflection upon the theological and personal implications of that scene; and the colloquy, or individual prayer of thanksgiving and petition arising from what has been learned in the reflection.[27] In other words, as the whole art of meditation is directed toward the motivation of the will to praise God, so the prayer in which the meditation issues is necessarily a form of address highly structured and formalized—that is, definitively willed. It is a highly Catholic mode of speech, with significant overtones of the Counter-Reformation emphasis upon the efficaciousness of works, and imbued with a sense of the object of address—God—as irrevocably other. Spenser's use of Gloriana in *The Faerie Queene* is one important analogue for this technique, as I have already indicated. Another—as Martz's study makes pellucidly clear—is the poetry of the "metaphysicals" of the seventeenth century. George Herbert's lyrics, particularly, are most often subtle expansions of the meditative colloquy, evolving from private disruption toward the resolution of decorous prayer. Thus "Jordan (I)" and "The Collar," both poems about the religious duties of a priest-poet, develop respectively toward the decorum of full rhyme and regular meter.

Protestant confession, on the other hand, transforms the conscious will to praise into the compulsion to recount. The epigraph to Hester Ann Roger's *Short Account*, also quoted in Newton's confession, gives perhaps the archetypal pattern for confessional address:

27. Louis L. Martz, *The Poetry of Meditation* (New Haven, 1962), pp. 37–38.

Come and hear, all ye that fear God; and I will declare what he hath done for my soul. (Psalm lxvi. 16)[28]

Prayer as a willed, formal structure of address plays at best a minor role in the confession—because the confession, as personal record of salvation achieved, is precisely the personal and social fruit of prayer and strivings. The assumption, as in Nelson's encounter with his landlord, is always that the confessant's speech arises naturally and spontaneously from his joy in God, celebrating the healing of that gap between self and creator which makes willed prayer necessary to the unregenerate. John Bunyan's highly influential *Grace Abounding to the Chief of Sinners* makes it quite clear that his confession is in fact a distillation of the strivings of the will, transforming them into the sweetness of the full assurance:

I have sent you here enclosed, a drop of that honey, that I have taken out of the carcase of a lion (Judges xiv. 5–9). I have eaten thereof myself also, and am much refreshed thereby. . . . It is something of a relation of the work of God upon my own soul, even from the very first, till now; wherein you may perceive my castings down, and raisings up; for he woundeth, and his hands make whole. . . . Yet, it was for this reason I lay so long at Sinai (Deut. iv. 10, 11), to see the fire, and the cloud, and the darkness, that I might fear the Lord all the days of my life upon earth, and tell of his wondrous works to my children (Ps. lxxviii. 3–5).[29]

And George Fox's doctrine of the Inner Light provided a spiritual epistemology for the literary form Bunyan had perfected: an idea of the indwelling of the person of Christ at once intensely private with each individual and yet shared and celebrated by all the community of the elect, by—most Wordsworthian of phrases—the Society of Friends.

As opposed to the careful subordination and decorum of meditational style, then, confession is marked by a deliberate interplay between public and private modes of address, introspective com-

28. *A Short Account of the Experience of Mrs. Hester Ann Rogers* (New York, 1811).

29. John Bunyan, *Grace Abounding to the Chief of Sinners*, ed. G. B. Harrison (London, 1963), pp. 3–4.

position and other-directed prayer. It is the same kind of internalization of the audience which we have already seen at work in *The Prelude*, in Wordsworth's complex use of Coleridge in two important passages. Without asserting direct stylistic or intellectual influence, we may at least say this much: that the Protestant confessants' variation of Catholic and Anglo-Catholic prayer and Wordsworth's variation of conventional courtly address both involve the same linguistic, structural transformations. But this degree of parallelism is, in fact, an indication of an even deeper formal resemblance, one which involves the sense of audience not simply as a rhetorical trope but as a crucial means of imaginative mediation.

Much has been written in recent years about the importance of "mediation" in Wordsworth's poetry and in Romantic and post-Romantic poetry generally. Paul de Man's "Intentional Structure of the Romantic Image" and Geoffrey Hartman's *The Unmediated Vision* both indicate the ways in which, for the Romantic poet, language and imagery simultaneously facilitate and frustrate his desired confrontation with the "really real," the splendor of pure phenomena.[30] And certainly *The Prelude*, as an enthusiastic celebration and preparation for the "great philosophic poem" *The Recluse*, participates in this double sense of language:

> How strange that all
> The terrors, pains, and early miseries,
> Regrets, vexations, lassitudes interfused
> Within my mind, should e'er have borne a part,
> And that a needful part, in making up
> The calm existence that is mine when I
> Am worthy of myself! Praise to the end!
> Thanks to the means which Nature deigned to employ;
> Whether her fearless visitings, or those
> That came with soft alarm, like hurtless light
> Opening the peaceful clouds. . . .
>
> (1. 344–354)

The resemblance between the theme of these lines and some of the confessional passages we have examined is, of course, striking. But

---

30. Paul de Man, "Intentional Structure of the Romantic Image," in *Romanticism and Consciousness*, ed. Harold Bloom (New York, 1970), pp. 65–77; Geoffrey Hartman, *The Unmediated Vision* (New York, 1966).

the passage's subtle power arises, even more than from its announced theme, from the remarkable way in which the language seems to imitate the calm assurance of which it speaks. Here as so often, Wordsworth's genius consists largely in his acceptance and use of that inevitable mediating power of language which was so to torment such later Romantics as Shelley, Mallarmé, and Hart Crane. The enthusiastic center of the passage, the moment of confrontation with the immortal spirit (1. 340), is of course the salutation "Praise to the end!" But this brief burst of praise derives its energy, stylistic as well as autobiographical, precisely from the long and carefully prosaic sentence which precedes it. That is, the "means which Nature deigned to employ" for the blessedness of the poet must be taken not only as the "terrors, pains," and so on, of the poet's past but also as the "means"—the words for those experiences—which now allow him to articulate his gratitude to the spirit moving behind and within both mind and world. Immediately upon the utterance of "Praise to the end," then, the poet returns to the mediated narrative of Nature's visitations, but now in a sentence which is itself interfused with imagery and rhetorical cadence, a heightened recapitulation of the first sentence. One of Wordsworth's most fascinating and consistent habits is his avoidance of conventional metaphor. And as the present passage makes clear, one reason for that avoidance is simply that in an epistemological structure like *The Prelude*, whose polar terms are man's absolute self and the very existence of a world or a history, language itself assumes the role of metaphor (*translatio*, "carrying across"), or mediation.

Hartman, in *Wordsworth's Poetry*, discusses this sort of acceptance of—and even reliance upon—varieties of mediation as Wordsworth's impulse toward evasion of direct confrontation with the immortal spirit. In his highly suggestive terms, the mental warfare within the poet is between *apocalypse*, or the drive toward direct confrontation and transcendence, and *akedah* (Hebrew, "binding"), or the drive toward evasion, mediation, the world of everyday objects.[31] In his reading, then, the paradigmatic action of *The Prelude* is the continual displacement of apocalypse into akedah. What I wish to suggest here, however, is a significant revision of Hartman's schema, for seen in its confessional aspect, the drive of

31. Hartman, *Wordsworth's Poetry*, p. 225.

The Prelude toward mediation is not an evasion or refusal of visionary power but a means to that power.

We have already seen how the Protestant confessants, in transforming prayer into narrative, engage in a process much like the intentional structure of Wordsworth's "Praise to the end." In fact, Hartman's biblical terms for this process are even more appropriate to the confessants: in Nelson, Bunyan, and Fox the apocalyptic entry of Christ into the soul issues not in prophetic fury but in the very real binding of the convert to the church of the just. But in order fully to understand the nature of confessional mediation—and particularly the crucial role played in such mediation by the confessant's audience—it is helpful to turn to the book which literally invents the confessional form for Western culture, the *Confessions* of Saint Augustine.

It is nearly as correct, of course, to say that Augustine invents Western culture. At least, one can track so many later and seminal ideas and attitudes within the creations of his astounding spirit that any specific claim for his patronage is likely to seem suspiciously partial and suspect. But the *Confessions* are surely, on one level, radically individualist, Protestant, and "confessional" in the sense we have been discussing. They are addressed, not to the community of the elect, but to God himself: a temerity to which no seventeenth- or eighteenth-century confessant can quite steel himself. But in the very audacity of such address, the magnificent opening of the *Confessions* makes clear the function of auditor in confession as both means and end of mediation:

> Great art Thou, O Lord, and greatly to be praised; great is Thy power, and Thy wisdom infinite. And Thee would man praise; man, but a particle of Thy creation; man, that bears about him his mortality, the witness of his sin, the witness that Thou resistest the proud: yet would man praise Thee; he, but a particle of Thy creation. Thou awakest us to delight in Thy praise; for Thou madest us for Thyself, and our Heart is restless, until it repose in Thee. Grant me, Lord, to know and understand which is first, to call on Thee or to praise Thee? and, again, to know Thee or to call on Thee? for who can call on Thee, not knowing Thee? for he that knoweth Thee not, may call on Thee as other than Thou art. Or, is it rather, that we call on Thee that we may know Thee? but how

shall they call on Him in whom they have not believed? or how shall they believe without a preacher? and they that seek the Lord shall praise Him: for they that seek shall find Him, and they that find shall praise Him. I will seek Thee, Lord, by calling on Thee; and will call on Thee, believing in Thee; for to us hast Thou been preached. My faith, Lord, shall call on Thee, which Thou hast given me, wherewith Thou hast inspired me, through the Incarnation of Thy Son, through the ministry of the Preacher.

(1.1)

So powerful is the rush of this opening passage that the exuberance of its rhetoric cannot be muted even in translation. It need hardly be said that with such an explicit audience "edification" ceases to be a relevant description of the book's primary motivation. This complex eloquence, however, centers dynamically on two verbs, "to praise" (*laudare*) and "to call on" (*invocare*), which between themselves indicate an extraordinary dimension of this kind of address to God.

As the motive of praise dominates the first half of the paragraph, that of calling on God—literally summoning Him—dominates the second: the center of energy passes from the one verb to the other in the almost exactly centered question, "which is first, to call on Thee or to praise Thee?"—the only time these two verbs meet in the same sentence. Both acts, praising and calling, are normally willed but are here deprived of their willful implications through the supervening agency of grace ("Thou awakest us to delight in Thy praise. . . . I will seek Thee, Lord, by calling on Thee; and will call on Thee, believing in Thee . . ."), so that the *Confessions* become a long and quasi-spontaneous outpouring of thanks for Augustine's conversion. But that thanksgiving, like other confessions we have seen, is still a constitution of the confessor's audience: praise, for Augustine, necessarily becomes summoning, because it is only the converted soul, conscious of his salvation and his oneness with the grace of Christ, who can bridge the unbridgeable gap between God and man, "a particle of His creation," and make praise a fully meaningful human activity. "How shall they believe without a preacher?" Thus the passage quite literally moves from the object of praise, the Lord, through the subject of calling, the regenerate "I" of Augustine, to issue in the image of the nearly

divinized man who combines the two movements, the Preacher
(Ambrose, and by tactful implication, Augustine himself). The
movement, as with all confessions, is toward the complex inter-
relation of inner- and outer-directed speech: Kenneth Burke has
suggested that the great number of words in the first book with
the prefix *in-* may indeed amount to a subtle pun on the Latin *in*
of subjectivization and the privative *in* of objective moral negation.[32]

Edification—the conversion of others through the recitation of
one's own conversion—is of course present as a secondary effect, an
overflow, as it were, of the saint's address to God. The confessor
is here overheard by his human auditors.

It is through the exemplary transaction between God and the
Augustinian "I" that the public, the City of God, becomes transformed. But this transaction itself is made possible only by Augustine's assumption of the role of Preacher: a role which is literally a
dramatic performance, a kind of baptism of the saint's previous,
pagan enthusiasm for the theater. For while the Preacher's audience,
as eavesdroppers upon his prayer, mediate between him and the pure
confrontation of his divine auditor, so the Preacher himself mediates
between the congregation and the God whom he addresses, as their
human representative before the Throne. The audience saves the
Preacher from the sin of presumption, and he saves them from the
sin of idolatry.

This displacement of unmediated prayer through confessional
preaching, intimated in Augustine, becomes a central and explicit
technique in the works of the radical English Protestants. Stephen
Crisp, for example, one of the most intelligent and literate of the
early Quaker confessants, opens his journal with a passage which
closely parallels the opening of Augustine's *Confessions* but is much
more deliberately displaced:

> Oh! all ye Saints, and all ye Inhabitants of the Earth, let the Name
> of *Jehovah* be famous among you, for there is no God like unto
> him; and let his Mercies and Judgments be remembered and
> Recorded from Genration [sic] to Generation: For Infinit is his
> Goodness, and his Loving Kindness Unspeakable. And although
> no man can fully recount his Loving Kindness to him reached out,

32. Kenneth Burke, *The Rhetoric of Religion* (Boston, 1961), p. 53.

yet let all men Testify of his Goodness, and Declare of his Mercies, by which he is Engaging the Sons of Men to Himself. . . . And who can feel his Goodness, and partake of his Love, but it will constrain a Testimony to him? And in the sweet remembrance of his manifold Innumerable Mercies, I am even overcome.[33]

Significantly, the great age of religious confession in England coincides, in its beginnings, with the decline and fall of the Protectorate. As the hopes of the radical sects for a visible kingdom of God on earth were crushed, the need for an invisible church, a societal mediation with God to replace the lost political one, became all the more acute. Even the Quakers, who as a group were less concerned with the theology of mediation—actually, less Christ-centered—than their spiritual heirs the Methodists, demonstrate a high degree of conformity to public standards of confessional experience, as well as the usual insistence upon the private nature of revelation. As Luella M. Wright discusses it: "These confessions are unmistakeably dominated by a prevailing consciousness of the group mind. The dominance of the Society intervenes between the personality of the writer and the mind of the reader [and, we would further suggest, the mind of an omniscient God]. The Quaker memorandist constantly played a double role."[34]

Among the Romantics, the turn to inwardness upon the disappointment of political aspirations, especially the French Revolution, has been eloquently documented in such essays as M. H. Abrams's "English Romanticism: The Spirit of the Age."[35] But again, and especially in the case of Wordsworth, the Protestant confessional analogue helps rectify the partiality of this insight. For the turn was not to sheer inwardness, not to what some critics, after Keats, have called the "egotistical sublime," but to a myth of minimal but sympathetic community which, as audience, made possible that inwardness which the poetry so brilliantly achieves.

33. *A Memorable Account of the Christian Experiences, Gospel Labours, Travels and Sufferings of That Ancient Servant of Christ Stephen Crisp* (London, 1694), pp. 1–2.

34. Wright, *The Literary Life of the Early Friends*, p. 11.

35. M. H. Abrams, "English Romanticism: The Spirit of the Age," in *Romanticism and Consciousness*, ed. Harold Bloom (New York, 1970), pp. 91–119.

The specific kind of apocalypse against which Wordsworth's poetry is designed to mediate is the apocalyptic power of the eighteenth-century sublime. And Wordsworth's quarrel with the poetry of the sublime is probably best interpreted as a quarrel with madness—specifically, the madness attendant upon a vision which attempts to be purely, absolutely unmediated. "Resolution and Independence" is perhaps the central lyric of this quarrel, especially important since it subtly allies Coleridge himself with the unhealthy, presumptuous solitude of the earlier sublime poets:

VI

My whole life I have lived in pleasant thought,
As if life's business were a summer mood;
As if all needful things would come unsought
To genial faith, still rich in genial good;
But how can He expect that others should
Build for him, sow for him and at his call
Love him, who for himself will take no heed at all?

VII

I thought of Chatterton, the marvellous Boy,
The sleepless Soul that perished in his pride;
Of Him who walked in glory and in joy
Following his plough, along the mountain-side:
By our own spirits are we deified:
We Poets in our youth begin in gladness;
But thereof come in the end despondency and madness.

The last three lines of the passage are the most important, both for the poem and for Wordsworth's entire major period: the final alexandrine literally breaks out of regular meter and insists on being read as a series of spondees. It is a grim statement of despair, all the more moving since it is a statement, not a cry. The self-deification of the spirit, typified by the mad solitude of Chatterton, while it may be a precondition for the poetic act, condemns the poet himself to solitary confinement, with no one and nothing to talk to. It is like the vexing problem of overenthusiasm among some of the

Quakers and Wesleyans: a too literal acceptance of the Inner Light, leading to the terrible loneliness of the man who thinks he has become God.

It is difficult, furthermore, not to see the figure of Chatterton here as partly a polite displacement of the figure of Coleridge. For at the time of the poem's composition, the spring of 1802, Coleridge himself was experiencing some of his most profound difficulties with the experience of the sublime, difficulties reflected in the great but despairing power of his "Dejection: An Ode." Coleridge's own difficulties with the sublime, or the idea of the autonomous Romantic imagination, were further complicated by his growing opium addiction, as Wordsworth well knew, for the ecstatic but unproductive visions of opium, like the lonely eminence of sublime sensibility, are an important analogue for the distinctively modern theme of the self-trapped poet. And if Coleridge's predicament in "Dejection" derives from the experience of such as Chatterton and Cowper, it also anticipates such later varieties of drug-induced Romanticism as the work of De Quincey, Baudelaire, and Malcolm Lowry. Like the associationist and sensationalist sublime of the eighteenth century, the pharmacological sublime of the nineteenth and twentieth centuries raises radical new problems of communication which Wordsworth is perhaps the first man fully to understand.

One of the reasons why "Resolution and Independence," great lyric that it is, trembles so close to the verge of triviality and has been the most parodied of Wordsworth's poems is that it is about the possibility of communication at the most minimal, primary level. How does the mind full of itself speak? How does it listen? That it listens at all is miraculous, a recovery like the grace of God:

XVI

The old Man still stood talking by my side;
But now his voice to me was like a stream
Scarce heard; nor word from word could I divide;
And the whole body of the Man did seem
Like one whom I had met with in a dream;
Or like a man from some far region sent,
To give me human strength, by apt admonishment.

The poet is barely able to listen to what the old man says, but that "barely" is just enough. For the "far region" from which the old man is sent is, surely, the far region of *the world of other people*, that region whose deep and unbearable mystery has been the object of so much modern thought. And that such communication can take place between two people at all is the "strength" and the "admonishment" which the old man's muddled speech gives Wordsworth: a guarantee of the possibility of contact with others which saves the poet from the grim fate of the Chattertons, Cowpers, and Coleridges. "Resolution and Independence" is not itself a confessional poem, but it does represent a moment of conversion—a saving spot of time—which reinforces the poet's trust both in life and in his own gift. And it is significant that this conversion, too, is made possible through a careful management of the poet's relationship with his auditor, through a "socialization of the sublime."

But these energies find their fullest expression, of course, in *The Prelude* itself, where Wordsworth, recounting the career of his blessing, finds it possible to listen and to speak to other people with an assurance seldom found elsewhere in his, or any, poetry. Book 14 is, in large part, a hymn of thanks to both Dorothy and Coleridge for their restorative influence upon Wordsworth. And speaking to Dorothy, he again deals with the traditions of the sublime:

> For, spite of thy sweet influence and the touch
> Of kindred hands that opened out the springs
> Of genial thought in childhood, and in spite
> Of all that unassisted I had marked
> In life or nature of those charms minute
> That win their way into the heart by stealth
> (Still to the very going-out of youth),
> I too exclusively esteemed *that* love,
> And sought *that* beauty, which, as Milton sings,
> Hath terror in it. Thou didst soften down
> This over-sternness; but for thee, dear Friend!
> My soul, too reckless of mild grace, had stood
> In her original self too confident,
> Retained too long a countenance severe;
> A rock with torrents roaring, with the clouds
> Familiar, and a favourite of the stars:
> But thou didst plant its crevices with flowers,
> Hang it with shrubs that twinkle in the breeze,

And teach the little birds to build their nests
And warble in its chambers.

(14. 237–256)

The submerged metaphor here is that of "Paradise Regained": both of Milton's poem itself and of the whole concept of a new Eden. Somewhat in the manner of the passage from book 1 culminating in "a visible scene, on which the sun is shining," Wordsworth here constructs a pastoral landscape within the mode and syntax of personal address. Most interesting is the reference to Milton: that love and that beauty which have terror in them are spoken of by Satan in book 9 of *Paradise Lost*. Directly before the climactic moment of the poem, the temptation of Eve, Satan discovers her among the paradisiacal flowers and stands, momentarily, "Stupidly good, of enmitie disarm'd" (465) before the vision of innocence. He soon talks himself back into his purpose, however:

Shee fair, divinely fair, fit Love for Gods,
Not terrible, though terrour be in Love
And beautie, not approacht by stronger hate,
Hate stronger, under shew of Love well feign'd
The way which to her ruin now I tend.

(489–493)

This is of course a "Satanic" view of the possibilities of love and beauty—Satan always sees such things strategically, as more powerful for his divisive purposes than open hostility. But precisely because of its Satanic slant, the statement is a perfect type of one of the aspects of sublime beauty with which Wordsworth has a permanent quarrel. The beauty of the sublime odes is Satanic precisely in its insistence on an autistic imaginative experience, its heroic, exciting, but self-thwarting assertion that "The mind is its own place" (*PL.* 1, 254). Wordsworth would have been in fundamental agreement with the instinct which led Blake, in *Milton*, to identify Satan with that most well-meaning and most monstrously egocentric of sublime "appreciators," William Hayley. A further importance of the passage from *Paradise Lost* is that Satan's main reason for attacking Eve at this point is that she herself is separated, for the moment, from the company of Adam (479–488); and surely Wordsworth's address to

Dorothy is a suggestion, tactful but definite, that she has functioned rather as a "Second Eve" (the traditional nomination of the Virgin) who, by renewing his powers of human intercourse, has reunited him to the race and thence to the prelapsarian state of imagination.

But if this passage from book 14 is a gracious identification of Dorothy with the supreme Mediatrix of Christianity, it is also the only extended address to her in the poem and the sole attribution to her, in the poem, of the important title "Friend." Otherwise that title is Coleridge's alone, and it is to the importance of Coleridge as the confessional audience of *The Prelude* that we must now turn again.

As we have seen, the relationship between the confessor and his audience is an ambivalent one: the confessor, in the very act of writing a confession, sets himself as in some respect a mediator of grace to his audience; while the audience, as a displacement of psalmodic direct address to God, plays a mediatory role between the confessor and the full acceptance of his semidivine status. The audience, that is, is simultaneously a projection of the confessor's personality and a strict limit to that personality's expansion.

It is precisely such an ambivalent relationship which Wordsworth, in the years after the great collaborations of 1797–98, was coming increasingly to hold toward Coleridge. As Coleridge's poetic energies declined while Wordsworth's grew ever stronger, and as the personal misfortunes of Coleridge, his addiction and his unhappy marriage, seemed increasingly to mark his older friend as destiny's chosen, the mentor-disciple relationship which had held between them was being reversed.

The Prelude, certainly, could not exist in its present form had it not been for the growth of such an ambivalent but affectionate relationship. If anything, indeed, the importance of Coleridge for the poem seems to have increased with the years. The last lines of book 1 in the 1850 version:

> And certain hopes are with me, that to thee
> This labour will be welcome, honoured Friend!
>
> (645–646)

are not present in the 1805 text.

Another and more significant addition to the 1805 version occurs at the end of book 13: Wordsworth is speaking of his early poetic efforts (*Guilt and Sorrow*, specifically) and their favorable, flattering reception by Coleridge. I quote first the 1805 text:

> This for the past, and things that may be view'd
> Or fancied, in the obscurities of time.
> Nor is it, Friend, unknown to thee, at least
> Thyself delighted, who for my delight
> Hast said, perusing some imperfect verse
> Which in that lonesome journey was composed,
> That also then I must have exercised
> Upon the vulgar forms of present things
> And actual world of our familiar days,
> A higher power, have caught from them a tone,
> An image, and a character, by books
> Not hitherto reflected. Call we this
> But a persuasion taken up by Thee
> In friendship. . . .
>
> (12. 354–367)

The 1850 text, however, adds the following lines:

> Call we this
> A partial judgment—and yet why? for *then*
> We were as strangers; and I may not speak
> Thus wrongfully of verse, however rude,
> Which on thy young imagination, trained
> In the great City, broke like light from far.
>
> (13. 360–365)

De Selincourt remarks that, since Wordsworth and Coleridge were indeed not strangers when Coleridge encountered *Guilt and Sorrow*, Wordsworth must be confusing, in the added passage, *Guilt and Sorrow* with his first publication, *Descriptive Sketches*.[36] The conjecture is perhaps accurate, but it is difficult, in the present context, to regard Wordsworth's activity as a confusion: he had, after all, as de Selincourt himself points out, Coleridge's own account in *Biographia Literaria*, chapter 4, to aid his memory of what particular poem had first brought him to Coleridge's attention. The passage—

36. Wordsworth, *The Prelude*, ed. de Selincourt and Darbishire, p. 618.

which on the face of it is certainly a strong argument for Wordsworth's overweening egotism—is best taken as a deliberate conflation of his early work *in general*, in order to clarify and consolidate both the permanently efficacious, "chosen" nature of his poetic genius and the edifying design upon Coleridge which is so central to *The Prelude*. The fact that the passage is a product of later years may be an indication, not of a lapse of memory, but rather of the power with which the motive of confessional address enables the poet to control memory, to use it rather than be used by it.

It is interesting that Wordsworth refers to Coleridge's "young imagination, trained / In the great City": Coleridge, when he encountered *Descriptive Sketches*, was not in London but in his last year of studies at Cambridge (1793). The description of Coleridge as reared far from Nature in the "great City" is one of Wordsworth's favorite modes of reference to his friend in *The Prelude* (cf. 2. 452; 6. 265; 8. 435); it is probably influenced by Coleridge's own description of himself in "Frost at Midnight":

> For I was reared
> In the great city, pent 'mid cloisters dim,
> And saw nought lovely but the sky and stars.
>
> (51–53)

But the source of the motif is undoubtedly *Paradise Lost*, again in the crucial narration preceding Satan's temptation of Eve in book 9. As Satan stands "stupidly good" in Paradise, momentarily liberated from the devouring energies of his egotism, Milton remarks that he is

> As one who long in populous City pent,
> Where Houses thick and Sewers annoy the Aire,
> Forth issuing on a Summers Morn to breathe
> Among the pleasant Villages and Farmes
> Adjoynd, from each thing met conceaves delight,
> The smell of Grain, or tedded Grass, or Kine.
>
> (445–450)

The sentiment itself is a conventional version of pastoral release, dating at least from Vergil's Tenth Eclogue (Gallus); applied to

Satan himself, however, it represents the remarkable extension and transfiguration of the powers of pastoral which is going on throughout *Paradise Lost*. And Wordsworth uses the allusion, consciously or not, as a subtle and pervasive undercurrent to the major movements of *The Prelude*. The distinction between himself as country-bred and Coleridge as city-bred is at once a way of determining the source of his natural powers of imagination (the audience as mediator) and a way of verifying their force for good in liberating Coleridge from the specter of his own doubts (the confessor as mediator):

> Thou, my Friend! wert reared
> In the great city, 'mid far other scenes;
> But we, by different roads, at length have gained
> The self-same bourne. And for this cause to thee
> I speak, unapprehensive of contempt,
> The insinuated scoff of coward tongues,
> And all that silent language which so oft
> In conversation between man and man
> Blots from the human countenance all trace
> Of beauty and of love. For thou hast sought
> The truth in solitude, and, since the days
> That gave thee liberty, full long desired
> To serve in Nature's temple, thou hast been
> The most assiduous of her ministers;
> In many things my brother, chiefly here
> In this our deep devotion.
>
> (2. 451–466)

The Prelude, in its assured and complex use of audience, represents a personal assurance and technical skill even greater than that of the lyrics of the major period. For these lyrics, too, especially "Tintern Abbey," "Stepping Westward," and "The Solitary Reaper," depend upon a named or implied personal audience for much of their distinctive power. But often their invocation of audience seems to be a *plea* for the ratification of human company rather than the triumphant assertion of community which is *The Prelude*. This quality in the lyrics, in fact, has led John Edward Hardy, in a little-known but important essay on "Tintern Abbey," to remark that the quality of Wordsworth's imagination is that "he was actually terrified of being alone—in a world without meaning."[37]

Hardy's description, though, applies better to Coleridge than it does to Wordsworth, particularly the Coleridge of the Conversation Poems. Many critics have remarked the importance of these poems for understanding Wordsworth's own career. But in the context of a confessional reading of *The Prelude*, their importance becomes crucial, for if Wordsworth set himself the task of mediating between Coleridge and the universal power of imagination, it was at least partly because Coleridge himself was predisposed toward such an act of mediation. And a poem like "The Eolian Harp" demonstrates how and why that mediation failed in Coleridge's own career: it actually appears to be a kind of confessional lyricism manqué. Carefully building, on the pretext of idle conversation with his "pensive Sara," toward the magnificent vision of the universal Harp, Coleridge suddenly pulls himself back from this full imaginative confrontation, through the agency of his audience:

> And what if all of animated nature
> Be but organic Harps diversely fram'd,
> That tremble into thought, as o'er them sweeps
> Plastic and vast, one intellectual breeze,
> At once the Soul of each, and God of all?
>   But they more serious eye a mild reproof
> Darts, O beloved Woman! nor such thoughts
> Dim and unhallow'd dost thou not reject,
>   And biddest me walk humbly with my God.
>   Meek Daughter in the family of Christ!
>   Well hast thou said and holily disprais'd
>   These shapings of the unregenerate mind;
>   Bubbles that glitter as they rise and break
>   On vain Philosophy's aye-babbling spring.
>   For never guiltless may I speak of him,
>   The Incomprehensible!
>
> (44–59)

Confession as a mode of address, of course, has as its purpose precisely to allow one, though guiltless, to speak of the Incompre-

---

37. John Edward Hardy, *The Curious Frame* (South Bend, Ind., 1962), pp. 79–80.

hensible; but here the mediating function of the audience has gone too far. Coleridge has let his "pensive Sara" act as a block between himself and his own powers rather than as a medium through which to achieve them more fully. Coleridge, always a more consciously Christian poet than Wordsworth, uses a set of terms ("the family of Christ," "unregenerate," "guiltless") which are the stock-in-trade of the religious confessants. But the confessional stance—its concentration upon an auditor—in Coleridge occludes that celebration of self and world which is, after all, the prime motive of confession. "The Eolian Harp" is a brilliant poem, but it is a poem of renunciation, of the conscious choice not to risk all that might be risked.

In *The Prelude*, of course, Coleridge is most frequently addressed as "O Friend!" Most such addresses, to be sure, are simply unembellished apostrophe, supporting the constant undercurrent of confessional speech necessary to the poem's momentum. But in a number of cases, Wordsworth addresses his Friend at sustained length. And these passages bring the elements of confessional address we have been discussing to their highest pitch of self-consciousness, both in Romantic poetry and in the religious confessions of the time. It is to these I now turn. The most important sustained address to Coleridge occurs in book 6—in the original version, the center of *The Prelude*, and in the 1850 version, still in many ways its imaginative center.

Book 6, "Cambridge and the Alps," is remarkable for two important acts of naming. In the Simplon Pass episode, Wordsworth confronts and names for the first and only time

> Imagination—here the Power so called
> Through sad incompetence of human speech,

> (592–593)

the direct, unmediated, apocalyptic power of the creative intellect. But earlier in the book, he also confronts and names for the first time the Friend who is his central auditor. He is speaking of his summer vacations, 1787–91:

> Another maid there was, who also shed
> A gladness o'er that season, then to me,
> By her exulting outside look of youth

And placid under-countenance, first endeared;
That other spirit, Coleridge! who is now
So near to us, that meek confiding heart,
So reverenced by us both. . . .

                                                    (224–230)

The reader who has followed *The Prelude* to this point cannot help hearing a certain ring of triumphant recognition, a sudden access of affection, in the proper name. (Whether for this reason, or simply to clarify the syntax, Wordsworth changes the comma after "Coleridge" in the 1805 text to a mark of exclamation.) At any rate, the naming of Coleridge and consequent change from the "me" of line 225 to the "us" of 230 is the signal for a pause in the narration and reflection upon its memorial structure—an afterthought-afterimage construction closely anticipating the Simplon Pass section:

O Friend! we had not seen thee at that time,
And yet a power is on me, and a strong
Confusion, and I seem to plant thee there.
Far art thou wandered now in search of health
And milder breezes,—melancholy lot!
But thou art with us, with us in the past,
The present, with us in the times to come.
There is no grief, no sorrow, no despair,
No languor, no dejection, no dismay,
No absence scarcely can there be, for those
Who love as we do. Speed thee well! divide
With us thy pleasure; thy returning strength,
Receive it daily as a joy of ours;
Share with us thy fresh spirits, whether gift
Of gales Etesian or of tender thoughts.

                                                    (237–251)

The by now familiar pattern of confessional address is retraced here, but with a higher degree of self-consciousness than is usual, even for Wordsworth. The next sixty-five lines are a further elaboration on this passage and perhaps the most explicit separation in *The Prelude* of the two complementary functions of address to Coleridge. Coleridge organizes the aim of the poem, i.e., therapy,

> Throughout this narrative,
> Else sooner ended, I have borne in mind
> For whom it registers the birth, and marks the growth,
> Of gentleness, simplicity, and truth,
> And joyous loves, that hallow innocent days
> Of peace and self-command. Of river, fields,
> And groves I speak to thee, my Friend! to thee,
> Who, yet a liveried schoolboy, in the depths
> Of the huge city, on the leaded roof
> Of that wide edifice, thy school and home,
> Wert used to lie and gaze upon the clouds
> Moving in heaven . . .
>
> (259–270)

and its means, the sense of present time-in-nature which allows Wordsworth to place such high hopes in the power of memory:

> Through this retrospect
> Of my collegiate life I still have had
> Thy after-sojourn in the self-same place
> Present before my eyes, have played with times
> And accidents as children do with cards,
> Or as a man, who, when his house is built,
> A frame locked up in wood and stone, doth still,
> As impotent fancy prompts, by his fireside,
> Rebuild it to his liking.
>
> (286–294)

It is worth noting that Wordsworth uses the term "narrative" for the poem considered as edifying and the term "retrospect" for the poem considered as mediating: the distinction is a very precise one. Retrospect both arises from and controls narrative by implying a definite now, an end point, which gives a meaningful shape to narration.

The alternative to this sort of retrospect-narrative Wordsworth has already made clear, in book 2 (again addressing Coleridge):

> But who shall parcel out
> His intellect by geometric rules,
> Split like a province into round and square?
> Who knows the individual hour in which

His habits were first sown, even as a seed?
What that shall point as with a wand and say
"This portion of the river of my mind
Came from yon fountain?" Thou, my Friend! art one
More deeply read in thy own thoughts; to thee
Science appears but what in truth she is,
Not as our glory and our absolute boast,
But as a succedaneum, and a prop
To our infirmity.

. . . .

Hard task, vain hope, to analyse the mind,
If each most obvious and particular thought,
Not in a mystical and idle sense,
But in the words of Reason deeply weighed,
Hath no beginning.

(203–215; 228–232)

It is difficult, reading these lines, not to think of *Tristram Shandy*. Indeed, Wordsworth very probably has *Shandy* in mind here; for Tristram begins his story *ab homunculo* and in many ways never gets past, never escapes from, that beginning:

I wish either my father or my mother, or indeed both of them, as they were in duty both equally bound to it, had minded what they were about when they begot me; had they duly consider'd how much depended upon what they were then doing;—that not only the production of a rational Being was concern'd in it, but that possibly the happy formation and temperature of his body, perhaps his genius and the very cast of his mind . . . might take their turn from the humours and dispositions which were then uppermost . . . I am verily persuaded I should have made a quite different figure in the world, from that, in which the reader is likely to see me.[38]

The importance of Sterne's book for Wordsworth is interesting. As a young man, if we can trust his own statement, it would have literally formed his conception of "contemporary literature": asked by his friend William Mathews, in 1791, to comment on some aspects of modern literature, he replied, "God knows my incursion

38. Laurence Sterne, *Tristram Shandy*, ed. James A. Work (New York, 1940), p. 4.

into the fields of modern literature—excepting in our own language three volumes of Tristram Shandy, and two or three papers of the Spectator, half subdued—are absolutely nothing."[39] The relevance of *Shandy* in the present context should be obvious. For *Shandy* is itself an antitype of the Romantic confession: an attempt at confession which, imprisoned in a surrealistic structure of Lockean epistemology and associationism gone mad, of "that false secondary power / By which we multiply distinction" (2. 216–217), can never break through narrative into retrospect, never fully establish the *present* personality of Sterne-Tristram. Thus, as Victor Shklovsky indicates in his remarkable essay on the novel, conversation—both between characters and between Sterne and his audience—becomes a technique not of communication but of "defamiliarization."[40] What has been called the "continuous present" experience of the art of the sublime is perhaps, in this respect, misnamed.[41] For the present which is truly continuous simply annihilates time— which is tantamount, furthermore, to the annihilation of human personality. Thus Tristram, desperately promising to write two volumes of his story in every year, is in a frantic race with his own life, for by definition, when the time of the narrative coincides with the "real" time of Tristram's present, his life is at an end. This is life-in-death in its distinctively Enlightenment permutation. Tristram is like Gray's Bard, to whom all things are present and who, because he cannot relate meaningfully to any conceivable audience, ends his prophecy with unmediated self-confrontation and suicide:

"Enough for me: With joy I see
"The different doom our Fates assign.
"Be thine Despair, and scept'red Care,
"To triumph, and to die, are mine."
He spoke, and headlong from the mountain's height
Deep in the roaring tide he plung'd to endless night.

(139–144)[42]

39. *The Early Letters of William and Dorothy Wordsworth*, ed. Ernest de Selincourt (Oxford, 1935), pp. 55–56.

40. Victor Shklovsky, "Sterne's *Tristram Shandy*," in *Russian Formalist Criticism*, trans. Lee T. Lemon and Marion J. Reis (Lincoln, Nebr., 1965), p. 53.

41. Frye, *Fables of Identity*, p. 133.

42. *The Poems of Gray and Collins*, ed. Austin Lane Poole (London, 1961).

We have already seen the manner in which Wordsworth, through the invoked presence of Coleridge, avoids such confrontation with and assimilation into his literary *doppelgänger*. That he was fully aware of the poetic necessity of his technique is indicated in the famous passage in book 3 where he first "discovers" his true theme:

> And here, O friend! have I retraced my life
> Up to an eminence, and told a tale
> Of matters which not falsely may be called
> The glory of my youth. Of genius, power,
> Creation and divinity itself
> I have been speaking, for my theme has been
> What passed within me.
>
> (170–176)

Wordsworth here, through the mediary of the Friend, discovers another, more efficient title for his great retrospect. And returning to the idea of title as paradigm for action, we may now attempt a large—and admittedly rather freehand—sketch of *The Prelude* as a whole. This sketch witnesses the paradigmatic act of conversation at three points, all three of which are, in a sense, the same narrative present of the poem. We will be tracing Wordsworth's address to Coleridge, of course, under two confessional aspects: edification and mediation. The subtle interplay of these aspects is, in fact, an important principle of the poem's unity.

Most of the primarily edifying addresses to Coleridge are in the middle and most heavily storied books of *The Prelude*. Certainly, at the opening of book 7, which consciously resumes the materials of book 1 in a fresh beginning, Wordsworth explicitly identifies his resumption of the poem with his concern for his friend:

> Six changeful years have vanished since I first
> Poured out (saluted by that quickening breeze
> Which met me issuing from the City's walls)
> A glad preamble to this Verse: I sang
> Aloud, with fervour irresistible
> Of short-lived transport, like a torrent bursting,
> From a black thunder-cloud, down Scafell's side
> To rush and disappear. But soon broke forth

(So willed the Muse) a less impetuous stream,
That flowed awhile with unabating strength,
Then stopped for years; not audible again
Before last primrose-time. Beloved Friend!
The assurance which then cheered some heavy thoughts
On thy departure to a foreign land
Has failed; too slowly moves the promised work.

(1–15)

Here, Wordsworth's expectations for *The Prelude*—and beyond that, *The Recluse*—are indistinguishable from his hopes for Coleridge's recovery, and the very affecting line, "too slowly moves the promised work," transvalues the work of Coleridge's imaginative and personal reconstitution—a transvaluation strengthened by the change of the line from its 1805 version: "for slowly doth this work advance."

Symmetrically at either end of *The Prelude* from this central vision of the poem as life-giving to Coleridge are the other two points of the sketch. In book 1, after the so-called preamble of 45 lines, faced with the occlusion of his imaginative power, Wordsworth turns to Coleridge for the first time:

Thus far, O Friend! did I, not used to make
A present joy the matter of a song,
Pour forth that day my soul in measured strains
That would not be forgotten, and are here
Recorded. . . .

(46–51)

The sudden—and radically innovative—leap from an indeterminate "present joy" to a present defined by memory and the mediatory presence of an auditor is heightened in the 1850 version. The 1805 reads:

. . . measur'd strains
Even in the very words which I have here
Recorded.

It is the extreme case of mediacy, as the preamble is the extreme case of nonmemorial lyricism. Coleridge is here giving life to

Wordsworth, making it possible for the work of composition to go on at all. And from the juxtaposition of these two limiting cases of imaginative activity, *The Prelude* begins its long work of integration.

The last passage to be examined here, like the second of the triad, is one in which the mediatory impulse in address predominates over the edifying. It is Wordsworth's last speech to Coleridge, at the end of book 14:

> Oh! yet a few short years of useful life,
> And all will be complete, thy race be run,
> Thy monument of glory will be raised;
> Then, though (too weak to tread the ways of truth)
> This age fall back to old idolatry,
> Though men return to servitude as fast
> As the tide ebbs, to ignominy and shame
> By nations sink together, we shall still
> Find solace—knowing what we have learnt to know,
> Rich in true happiness if allowed to be
> Faithful alike in forwarding a day
> Of firmer trust, joint labourers in the work
> (Should Providence such grace to us vouchsafe)
> Of their deliverance, surely yet to come.
>
> (430–443)

The triumphant sweep of this remarkable passage is built on images of minimal hope, the most startling of which is certainly the projection of Coleridge's own death. As Coleridge realized, in "To William Wordsworth," though in a rather different sense, *The Prelude* finally involves his dissolution. And, as always, Wordsworth uses the precise term for this death: "complete." For this death is a completion and perfection of Coleridge's role as auditor, a perfection necessitated by his function as mediator of that imaginative Eternity which is "first, and last, and midst, and without end."

Wordsworth again, as in book 1, looks to the future and the great work to come. But this time, with full assurance of his past blessings and present power, he envisions also the end of his address to his friend—that is, a friend who has been reconverted to the glory of the imagination and who now defines the present and future of the narrator by himself passing into a memorial timelessness.

If we wish to be graphic about the three pivot points discussed, coordinating the time of Wordsworth's narrated experience with the time period of Coleridge's life to which that experience is related, the scheme is as follows:

Wordsworth

Past	Present	Future
1	7	14
Present	Future	Perfected (Memorial) Past

Coleridge

The final passage, from book 14, is structurally necessary as the last term in a set of tense permutations which exhausts the possibilities of narrative versus auditory versus "real" time for *The Prelude*. This again is a phenomenon reminiscent of *Shandy*, for it is a brilliant inversion and solution of the problem which threatens silence and extinction for Tristram, that of bringing the book finally up to date. More importantly, however, as a macroscopic analogue of the act of confessional address, it shows marked similarities to the general movement of almost all the enthusiastic confessions of the seventeenth and eighteenth centuries, developing from an exhortation to the worship of God on the basis of past trials and blessings, through the kerygmatic narration of the speaker's career, and culminating in a final forward-looking, implicitly apocalyptic praise of Providence or, more simply (and effectively), in a single "Amen" committing narrator, audience, and text to their definitive and timeless constellation in the Divine Field of Being.

With this much said about the nature of *The Prelude*'s mode of address, we can proceed to a discussion of its other confessional qualities—the first of which is the complex problem of the daemonic and the strategies for overcoming or circumventing it.

CHAPTER TWO

❦

THE
SENSE
OF THE
HUMAN

I know not whether my reader is aware that many children, perhaps most, have a power of painting, as it were, upon the darkness, all sorts of phantoms; in some that power is simply a mechanic affection of the eye; others have a voluntary or semi-voluntary power to dismiss or summon them, or, as a child once said to me when I questioned him on this matter, "I can tell them to go, and they go; but sometimes they come when I don't tell them to come."

Thomas De Quincey, *Confessions of an English Opium-Eater*

That good and delightful affection, which you sometimes feel, is the effect of present grace, and a sort of foretaste of your heavenly country. You ought not to lean too much upon it, because it comes and goes.

Thomas a Kempis, *Of the Imitation of Christ*

The central motive of this study is to locate some of the guiding principles of unity in *The Prelude*. To attempt this is, of course, to take part in a critical debate which has been going on almost since the poem's first publication—a debate which, in its way, is one of the marks of *The Prelude*'s continuing importance for the modern imagination.

While *The Prelude*'s influence upon later English poetry and thought is amply documented, it remains, formally, one of the most difficult and strangest poems of the last two centuries. Partly this is a simple result of the sheer bulk of the work: few readers, even on a second or third reading, could really claim to hold the whole development of the poem clearly in memory. But the difficulty is qualitatively different even from that presented by other long poems, such as *Hyperion, The Ring and the Book*, or—unlikely though it may seem at first blush—*The Bridge*. In these other poems there is at least an objective plot—the Titanic myth, a murder trial, the history of America—a "public" structure upon which one can batten. And this, at the simplest level, is what we normally understand by the literary term *form*: a mnemonic, a handle with which to grasp the core of a work.

In *The Prelude*, however, such an objectively verifiable structure is only fleetingly present. What was said in the last chapter about the interchange of public and private in its mode of address applies equally to its method of dealing with history, so much so that the French Revolution itself, the traumatic core of Wordsworth's mental life and of English Romanticism generally, is almost completely assimilated into a series of personal responses which frequently obscure what is being responded to. Autobiography naturally tends to be circumstantial and rambling, of course. But *The Prelude*, as a confession, is an autobiography of states of consciousness rather than of facts, so that the problem of locating a form—even a private one—becomes much more challenging. It is understandable, then, why critics from Matthew Arnold to T. S. Eliot have found the poem a mélange of sporadic lyrical brilliance, flat autobiography, and second-rate metaphysical speculation. And it is equally understandable why critics arguing for the poem's unity have sometimes been led into formulations whose subtlety greatly exceeds their accuracy. Hartman's analysis of *The Prelude* as the warfare of apocalypse and akedah, to which I have already alluded, is perhaps the best example of this kind of criticism. For while his analysis is strikingly original and illuminating for certain aspects of the Wordsworthian spirit, it tends to transform *The Prelude* into an allegory. And as I shall attempt to indicate in this and the following chapter, *The Prelude* derives its distinctive power and most profound unity precisely from its transformation of allegorical or daemonic forms of consciousness.

In discussing *The Prelude* as a confessional form, then, I am attempting to describe what I feel to be the poem's essential unity in terms that are less recherché than those of many recent approaches to Romanticism but which still indicate the innovative role of the poem in the forming of the modern consciousness. We have seen how Wordsworth's original sense of personal address provides one basic unifying structure for the poem. And having explored the importance of confessional art as speech to someone, we now turn to an examination of what, exactly, the confessant has to speak about.

The basic subject of confession is easy to name. Paul in 1 Corinthians and Wordsworth at the end of *The Prelude* are in remarkable agreement about it:

> But when that which is perfect has come, that which is imperfect will be done away with. When I was a child, I spoke as a child, I thought as a child. Now that I have become a man, I have put away the things of a child.
>
> (13: 10–11)

> And now, O Friend! this history is brought
> To its appointed close: the discipline
> And consummation of a Poet's mind,
> In everything that stood most prominent.
> Have faithfully been pictured; we have reached
> The time (our guiding object from the first)
> When we may, not presumptuously, I hope,
> Support my powers so far confirmed, and such
> My knowledge, as to make me capable
> Of building up a Work that shall endure.
>
> (14. 302–311)

Both men are concerned with describing to themselves and to others the nature and quality of their maturity, their achievement of spiritual manhood. And the ability to perceive, in one's own self, the complex interrelationship and the great difference between childhood and maturity is, for the confessant, a serious test of his powers. Wordsworth's discovery of childhood for literature has, of course, become almost a critical cliché; but it should be equally obvious that, like Paul, like Augustine, and even like Freud, he invents the state of childhood primarily to realize its development into a responsible prophetic maturity.

The confessant's full realization of maturity, though, is made difficult precisely by that childhood which is its precondition. Wordsworth, in "Tintern Abbey," speaks of his youth as a time when Nature was

> An appetite; a feeling and a love,
> That had no need of a remoter charm,
> By thought supplied, nor any interest
> Unborrowed from the eye.
>
> (80–83)

But this is childhood imagined as more than simply a time of life: it is a state of consciousness and not necessarily one which disappears in later life. It is, to be exact, the state of mind we all have experienced, of exalted joys, exalted despairs, exalted terrors, which needs no thought and no language because it is an immediate time-annihilating presentness. And Wordsworth, here as at the beginning of the *Intimations Ode*, laments not so much the disappearance of this state in adulthood as the terrible nostalgia of adulthood which leads a man to long for youth's constant excitement rather than to accept growth into something different but greater. We need to include Freud in the catalog of Wordsworth's confessional analogues, for Freud, too, realized that childhood is another of our names for the magical, the sublime, and the daemonic which persist within us. And the concern of this chapter will be with seeing how Wordsworth came to confront the daemonic child within him and to integrate that disruptive vision into the fabric of his myth of maturity, *The Prelude*.

Before turning to *The Prelude*, however, I would like to

examine the previous growth of the problem in Wordsworth's own verse and in the poems which were his imaginative patrimony. An especially important version of the quest for imaginative maturity—and one cast in archetypal terms of religious conversion—is the epic I have already alluded to in connection with *The Prelude*, Milton's *Paradise Regained*. It, too, is a poem about the growth from childhood into adulthood—specifically, the childhood of the Son of God. And it will help clarify the way in which this problem of growth is actually a special case of the major problem of the daemonic.

Paradise Regained is, to paraphrase John Crowe Ransom's designation of *Lycidas*, "a poem nearly confessional." Louis Martz, in his valuable commentary on the poem, writes:

> In such a poem we are bound to hear throughout a personal voice.
> . . . That is why the poem never shows any extended effort to
> present a drama of characters in the usual sense. Satan and the Son
> of God in this poem speak within the mind of one who hopes to
> be himself a Son of God; both these actors use the human voice
> that this particular possible Son of God, John Milton, possesses. . . .[1]

The epic is written in middle style—*sermoni propriora*—the exultant energies of the line of *Paradise Lost* being here chastened and subdued for a theme which is, paradoxically, far greater than that of the earlier and longer story:

> Thou Spirit who ledst this glorious Eremite
> Into the Desert, his Victorious Field
> Against the Spiritual Foe, and broughtst him thence
> By proof the undoubted Son of God, inspire,
> As thou art wont, my prompted Song else mute,
> And bear through highth or depth of natures bounds
> With prosperous wing full summ'd to tell of deeds

---

1. Louis L. Martz, *The Paradise Within* (New Haven, 1967), p. 191.

Above Heroic, though in secret done,
And unrecorded left through many an Age,
Worthy t' have not remain'd so long unsung.

(1. 8–17)

This middle style of narration, in its constant pressure against the more than heroic theme of the myth itself, is a source of tension throughout the poem. More significantly, however, it is a strategy on the part of the narrator to contain and discipline his own Satanic or non-Christian self. Such containment, furthermore, is surely related to Milton's refusal to admit that the soul can live on, separated from the body. The theme of the poem is Eden restored, but more specifically,

Eden rais'd in the wast Wilderness.

(1. 7)

This is an impulse which is shared by the early Wordsworth, who believed firmly that man's paradise, if it is to be built at all, is to be built

Not in Utopia,—subterranean fields,—
Or some secreted island, Heaven knows where!
But in the very world, which is the world
Of all of us,—the place where, in the end,
We find our happiness, or not at all!

(*Prel.* 11. 140–144)

We have already spoken of the importance of mediation in the typical religious confession and of the sense of audience as one method of achieving this mediation. Without such saving mediation, the perversion of confession is the sin of presumption, the sin which Christ explicitly rejects at the outset of His ministry during His temptation in the wilderness. And when Milton, as a poet, attempts to discover through the figure of Christ his own sonship to God, he sees this temptation as an analogue to the problems of his own poetry: the penultimate resource of the tempter becomes epic style. In a moment which must have had enormous poignance for John Milton the humanist, when all temptations but the last have failed,

Satan extends to the Son the prospect of all that was best and noblest in the ancient world:

> There thou shalt hear and learn the secret power
> Of harmony in tones and numbers hit
> By voice or land, and various-measur'd verse,
> *AEolian* charms and *Dorian* Lyric Odes,
> And his who gave them breath, but higher sung,
> Blind *Melesigenes* thence Homer call'd,
> Whose Poem *Phoebus* challeng'd for his own.
>
> (4. 254–260)

The Son's reply is immediate and surprisingly acerbic, an impassioned defense of the superiority of biblical style over classical fable:

> All our Law and Story strew'd
> With Hymns, our Psalms with artful terms inscrib'd,
> Our Hebrew Songs and Harps in *Babylon*,
> That pleas'd so well our Victors ear, declare
> That rather *Greece* from us these Arts deriv'd;
> Ill imitated, while they loudest sing
> The vices of thir Deities, and thir own
> In Fable, Hymn, or Song, so personating
> Thir Gods ridiculous, and themselves past shame.
> Remove their swelling Epithetes thick laid
> As varnish on a Harlots cheek, the rest,
> Thin sown with aught of profit or delight,
> Will far be found unworthy to compare
> With Sion's songs, to all true tasts excelling,
> Where God is prais'd aright, and Godlike men. . . .
>
> (4. 334–348)

Martz discusses the way Milton qualifies this repudiation of Hellenism through the Son's final speech in book 2 (457–483); but this qualification is itself a subordination of Socrates, the most "Christian" figure of the Golden Age, to the type of the Christian metahero, showing "how the Socratic reliance on the inner man . . . leads onward into the Christian concept of highest kingship. . . ."[2]

2. Ibid., pp. 188–89.

The definition of style in *Paradise Regained* is central to that poem's movement as a fundamental gesture toward mediation and human wholeness in much the same way as the development of a viable mode of conversation functions for the myth of recall and renewal in *The Prelude*. The crucial Miltonic theme of temptation has here undergone a transformation beyond even the subtlety of its presentation in *Paradise Lost* or in the great passages on Christian moral empiricism in the *Areopagitica*. For here temptation is not only of a moral intellect but of the typological moral intellect of the Son of God, who is, by implication, all the Sons of God. The temptation, accordingly, is more complex than ever before in Milton's poetry or prose, for the choice is not between good and evil:

> What doubts the Son of God to sit and eat?
> These are not Fruits forbidden, no interdict
> Defends the touching of these viands pure,
> Thir taste no knowledge works, at least of evil,
> But life preserves, destroys life's enemy,
> Hunger, with sweet restorative delight.
>
> (2. 368–373)

The choice lies, rather, between different ways of affirming the good:

> To whom thus Jesus temperately reply'd:
> Said'st thou not that to all things I had right?
> And who withholds my pow'r that right to use?
> Shall I receive by gift what of my own,
> When and where likes me best, I can command?
>
> (2. 378–382)

Presumption is one of the nastiest of sins precisely because it is a sin committed only by men convinced—almost rightly—of their own justice.

But given this much about the moral and poetic energy of *Paradise Regained*, it may be asked, How does the mediation of style ensure the narrator's safety from presumption? What, exactly, is being mediated against? which is the same thing as asking, What *are* the different modes of affirming the good between which one has a choice? The answer to these questions is crucial for understanding the more fully confessional "Paradise Regained" of *The Prelude*. To discover that answer, one more question must be asked, the question which, in many ways, is the creative impulse of Milton's poem: Who is the Son of God?

This is Satan's question from the beginning to the end of the poem, and it is answered not so much in terms of any direct reply of the Son or of the narrator as by Satan's continually asking it. We see who the Son is by seeing Satan's inability to cope with Him:

> His Mother then is mortal, but his Sire,
> He who obtains the Monarchy of Heav'n,
> And what will he not do to advance his Son?
> His first-begot we know, and sore have felt,
> When his fierce thunder drove us to the deep;
> Who this is we must learn, for man he seems
> In all his lineaments, though in his face
> The glimpses of his Fathers glory shine.
>
> (1. 86–93)

Satan is unable to connect the various and accurate pieces of information he has at his command; his ignorance, that is, is the result of a deeper flaw, stupidity. And Satan's stupidity about the Son is the effect of his existence as an antinatural, discontinuous force trying to inhabit a poem about continuity and dominated by an antitype—the Son—who is the incarnation of universal process. This interpretation of the Son is substantiated by Milton's own exposition, in *The Christian Doctrine*, of his complex interpretation of the Trinity. He refuses to accept the generation *ab eterno* of the Son from the Father, and his refusal is, in its simplest terms, an argument for the personality of the Son as process, a literal *natura naturans*:

> Thus the Son was begotten of the Father in consequence of his decree, and therefore within the limits of time, for the decree itself must have been anterior to the execution of the decree, as is sufficiently clear from the insertion [in Heb. 1:5] of the word to-day.[3]

3. *John Milton: Complete Poems and Major Prose*, ed. Merritt Y. Hughes (New York, 1957), p. 934.

The Son *is*, then, in an important way, history itself. For while Milton insists that the Father's act of generating the Son is not determined by necessity but is a free act of the will, nevertheless that generation, once committed, necessitates of and by itself the processes of the natural universe. The Son is the fact of mediation whereby the unknowable and eternal Father confronts His intelligible and historical emanation. And it is this historicity, the unity-in-time of the Son, which Satan cannot possibly comprehend. His questioning of the Son is a constant demand to be shown, *outside* historical process, the identity of the being who is mediatory history itself. His final questioning, immediately before the last temptation, is an extraordinary performance: the picture of a mind which, with full awareness of discrete historical facts, cannot translate them into meaningful historical events:

> Then hear, O Son of *David*, Virgin-born;
> For Son of God to me is yet in doubt,
> Of the Messiah I have heard foretold
> By all the Prophets; of thy birth at length
> Announc't by *Gabriel* with the first I knew,
> And of the Angelic Song in *Bethlehem* field,
> From that time seldom have I ceas'd to eye
> Thy infancy, thy childhood, and thy youth,
> Thy manhood last, though yet in private bred;
> Till at the Ford of *Jordan* whither all
> Flock'd to the Baptist, I among the rest,
> Though not to be Baptiz'd, by voice from Heav'n
> Heard thee pronounc'd the Son of God belov'd.
> Thenceforth I thought thee worth my nearer view
> And narrower Scrutiny, that I might learn
> In what degree or meaning thou art call'd
> The Son of God, which bears no single sence;
> The Son of God I also am, or was,
> And if I was, I am; relation stands;
> All men are Sons of God; yet thee I thought
> In some respects far higher so declar'd.
>
> (4. 500–520)

"If I was, I am; relation stands": it is the same Satan speaking as in the defiant speeches of *Paradise Lost* 1, with his absolute refusal to concede the power of the temporal within the context of the eternal. The paratactic construction of his speech is worth noting. He refuses to admit the possibility of time leading into time, and he sees the career of Jesus, His growth into His messianic role, much as a series of newsreel scenes, juxtaposed without sense of subordination or development. (The only time words in the whole passage—"From that time," "till," "Thenceforth"—refer to Satan's own self-perception, and he, of course, assumes his character to be constant and immutable.)

His sense of time, that is to say, is demonic—and the inevitable pun is highly instructive—for the demonic is precisely the realm in which "terms for order" become separated by an incalculable gulf from "terms for narrative."[4] The demon (or daemon, since this discussion applies to the *eudaemonic* also) is pure potentiality, frozen and obsessively fixated. It can define itself only in schematic opposition to another equally daemonic and contrary power. For it, "relation [and relationship] *stands*" as rigid and determined but does not move or progress in any human manner.

The daemonism of Satan in *Paradise Regained*, furthermore, seems to be the chief reason for what Martz has called the poem's lack of dramatic energy. For the poem makes explicit the daemonic qualities inherent in classical drama and tests these qualities by a standard which is antidaemonic, more than heroic. Thus it becomes a kind of predrama, a ritual contest which finally transcends ritual forms for a more fully human perspective on man's fate. Satan, prisoner of his style, behaves as if he were in a dramatic situation; while the Son, developing instead in the direction of a growing self-knowledge which is beyond the inherent daemonism of drama, never meets him on these terms:

> . . . hee unobserv'd
> Home to his Mothers house private return'd.
>
> (4. 638–639)

---

4. These phrases are from Kenneth Burke's Introduction to *The Rhetoric of Religion* (Boston, 1961).

Milton's poem, besides placing the problem of the daemonic in a Protestant theological context, also helps demonstrate its permanence in human thought and imagination. For the daemonic and its contrary, the unitary, are more than simply alternative modes of vision which carry on an everlasting psychic war. They need each other and, in mature minds as in mature cultures, they generate and support each other in that higher complexity which is, precisely, "maturity." Claude Lévi-Strauss has written of the way in which primordial ideas of "opposite" and "same"—myths of daemonism and myths of consubstantiality—reduce "to a particular fashion of formulating a general problem, viz., how to make opposition, instead of being an obstacle to integration, serve rather to produce it."[5] One impulse or the other, daemonic or unitary, may predominate at a given time; but the critic always deals, as does the poet, with both. In terms that are by now familiar, Wordsworthian apocalypse and Wordsworthian akedah must be seen not as canceling each other but as developing, mutually and naturally, toward that full vision of manhood which *The Prelude* seeks to record.

Wordsworth's growth toward the integration of the daemonic, however, was not an easy one. And his intense self-consciousness about the path he followed is important not only for *The Prelude* but for the history of English Romanticism. For the precise version of the daemonic which he sought, in his career, to humanize, involved not only the tyranny of the sublime over the human but the mutual tyrannies of phenomenal reality over the intellect and the intellect over phenomenal reality. Both, for him, merged and became one monstrous error in the system of Godwin; it was Godwin's revolutionary necessitarianism, coupled with his own disappointment in the French Revolution, which led Wordsworth into what he describes in *The Prelude* as the most abject intellectual and poetic despair of his life:

> This was the crisis of that strong disease,
> This the soul's last and lowest ebb; I drooped,

5. Claude Lévi-Strauss, *Totemism* (Boston, 1963), p. 89.

Deeming our blessed reason of least use
Where wanted most: "The lordly attributes
Of will and choice," I bitterly exclaimed,
"What are they but a mockery of a Being
Who hath in no concerns of his a test
Of good and evil; knows not what to fear
Or hope for, what to covet or to shun;
And who, if those could be discerned, would yet
Be little profited, would see, and ask
Where is the obligation to enforce?
And, to acknowledged law rebellious, still,
As selfish passion urged, would act amiss;
The dupe of folly, or the slave of crime."

(11. 306–320)

The process of Wordsworth's disaffiliation with Godwin has been mapped many times, though never perhaps with more clarity and conviction than in Arthur Beatty's pioneering study.[6]

It is interesting to note here, however, that the two classes of men Wordsworth bitterly envisions existing under the philosophy of Godwin, "the dupe of folly" and "the slave of crime," are characters inevitably suggestive of the main characters Marmaduke and Oswald in Wordsworth's early play *The Borderers*, a work which Beatty first identified as the poet's definitive break from the ideas of *Political Justice*.

The Borderers (1795–96) is far from a great play, although not nearly so bad as some of Wordsworth's commentators have made it out to be. It is, furthermore, nearly an anatomy of that "strong disease" from which Wordsworth was in process of recovering at the time and against which he was to struggle with growing confidence and grace during his great years.

Coleridge, in *Biographia Literaria*, notes that Wordsworth's greatest strength does not lie in the dramatic. It is a significant remark, especially in the light of what has been said concerning *Paradise Regained* about drama as a form with strong daemonic overtones. The story of Christ's temptation by Satan, we have suggested, may be called a predrama or a metadrama in that it implies a standard of humanity beyond the daemonism of the

---

6. Arthur Beatty, *William Wordsworth* (Madison, 1962), chapter 2.

conventional tragic hero. In the same fashion, *The Borderers* might best be described as a hyperdrama, for it contains no projection of a transcendent human form reconciling the daemonic oppositions of its plot—that, in Wordsworth's life as well as his verse, was to come later. But the very ferocity of those oppositions finally breaks down the dramatic structure itself in a kind of exhausted expectation of something better, fuller, and more integrated to come. The tragedy of *The Borderers*, then, fails not through a weakness of the dramatic sense but rather through a fierce concentration of dramatic elements which amounts to a criticism of the form. As a cure from the strong disease, the disease of obsessive rationalism and obsessive revolutionism, it is homeopathic and a fascinating exercise in self-analysis and self-criticism through traditional, non-confessional literary forms.

The plot itself is somewhat feverishly muddled: Marmaduke, the virtuous and innocent leader of an outlaw band of borderers, is persuaded by his sinister lieutenant, Oswald, that Baron Herbert, the father of Idonea (whom Marmaduke loves), is in reality not her father at all but an evil old lecher planning to sell Idonea's chastity for preferment. Marmaduke and Oswald meet with the blind Herbert and offer to conduct him along his road; Oswald urges Marmaduke to kill the old man, but Marmaduke, unable to overcome his scruples, decides to abandon him instead to the elements as a trial by ordeal of his honor. Naturally, the old man dies; but not before Oswald has revealed his treachery to Marmaduke. In the denouement, Oswald is outlawed by all the band, and Marmaduke, having revealed his part in the action to Idonea, resolves on a lifelong and silent journey of penance.

It all sounds very much like a conflation of *Othello* and *King Lear*; but in fact, it is an even more unusual combination of motifs—as if Iago had corrupted Robin Hood while a sinless Oedipus Coloneus died separated from Antigone. And this sense, pervasive throughout *The Borderers*, that all manner of dramatic archetypes have become jumbled together is an essential part of what I regard as its remarkable power. It is not merely that Oswald, the most vivid character in the play, is an incarnation of Godwinian necessitarianism and hence a single daemonic character in a world of milder spirits. In the beginning, Marmaduke, too, is a tacit allegory of Godwinianism, of that part of the system which holds, paradoxically contrary to the necessitarian ideal, that man can effect a real and total change in the injustices of the political world. That both men are paralyzed by their own excessive energy is the daemonic point of the tragedy.

The only speech of the play frequently quoted in studies of Wordsworth is Oswald's in act 3, when he thinks Marmaduke has killed Herbert:

> Action is transitory—a step, a blow,
> The motion of a muscle—this way or that—
> 'Tis done, and in the after-vacancy
> We wonder at ourselves like men betrayed:
> Suffering is permanent, obscure and dark,
> And shares the nature of infinity.
>
> (1539-1544)

It is a striking passage with important links to the vision of man and nature in other early poems, such as the Convict's tale in *Guilt and Sorrow* and *The Old Cumberland Beggar*. It is also highly daemonic in a necessitarian way, suggesting a kind of Satanic commitment to action despite all action's senselessness. But we must set against this passage an equally important one earlier in the play in which Marmaduke, beginning to feel the first effects of Oswald's deception, suddenly realizes the hidden nature of his own benevolent revolutionary activity and sees the waste which lies beneath all efforts at renovation:

> Lacy! we look
> But at the surfaces of things; we hear
> Of towns in flames, fields ravaged, young and old
> Driven out in troops to want and nakedness;
> We grasp our swords and rush upon a cure
> That flatters us, because it asks not thought:
> The deeper malady is better hid;
> The world is poisoned at the heart.
>
> (Act 2, ll. 1029-36)

While Oswald's purpose in the drama is to bring Marmaduke from this despair of meaningful action to the Satanic energy he himself enjoys, he fails to do more than simply destroy Marmaduke's trust in direct and purposeful political action. And this failure—the fact that Marmaduke never really acts, since the only alternative actions allowed him are all daemonic to some degree—is a marginal salvation for Marmaduke. He cannot be said to be fully humanized at the end of the tragedy, but his suffering and self-isolation—which adumbrate the figure of the Wanderer in *The Excursion*—present, literally, a path out of the world of the drama into the possibility of a more fully human experience:

> A hermitage has furnished fit relief
> To some offenders; other penitents,
> Less patient in their wretchedness, have fallen,
> Like the old Roman, on their own sword's point.
> They had their choice: a wanderer *must I* go,
> The Spectre of that innocent Man, my guide.
> No human ear shall ever hear me speak;
> No human dwelling ever give me food,
> Or sleep, or rest: but over waste and wild,
> In search of nothing that this earth can give,
> But expiation, will I wander on—
> A Man by pain and thought compelled to live,
> Yet loathing life—till anger is appeased
> In Heaven, and Mercy gives me leave to die.
>
> (Act 5, ll. 2340–2353)

This is still a vision of compulsion, of course, but of a compulsion which arises, ironically, out of an awareness of guilt and of the inhumanity of his previous attitudes to experience. It is like the first conviction of sin in Quaker or Methodist religious typology, which is essentially a daemonic self-accusation of having acted daemonically. And to make a leap which is not as abrupt as it may seem, it is with essentially the same sort of figure that *The Prelude* begins—a figure who is experiencing not compulsive guilt but compulsive joy at his release into nature but who faces the same basic problem of humanization: how to reconcile the elements of will and necessity in one's relationship to the natural and human world, and how to achieve a stance toward experience which fulfills the internal requisites for complete integration; how, in other words, to become truly a son of the difficult god of this universe.

In *The Borderers*, Wordsworth splits the obsessive, self-contradictory energy of Godwinian radicalism into the contrary figures of Oswald and Marmaduke. This split itself, as much as the system it seeks to dramatize, is daemonic. For, as we have intimated, the daemonic is definitively the realm of two-ness, of Manicheanism, of morality as psychomachia, while its contrary is the realm of spiritual autonomy and of morality as decision.

In this context, the common epithet for those enigmatic figures of Wordsworth's later poetry—his "solitaries"—takes on new meaning as a sign of the poet's growing command over the chaotic, divisive energies of his youth. Figures like Michael, the Old Cumberland Beggar, the Leech-gatherer, and the Solitary Singer are mysteriously solitary in their unification of such dramatic opposites as simplicity and profundity, ignorance and enlightenment, the quotidian and the supernatural. In many cases, in fact, one can even imagine Wordsworth consciously transforming dramatic dialogue into the distinctive form of mediating address we have already discussed at length. This process, whereby what would normally be a dramatic interlocutor becomes a curiously admonitory auditor, has already been spoken of in relation to "Resolution and Independence." And in a poem like "We Are Seven," at once moving and ludicrous, it can be seen in an even more crudely incipient state, as the poet argues of life and death with the solitary little girl for whom arithmetic is an intimation of immortality. Wordsworth is experimenting not with form but with a *release* from form, a mode which will allow him to fuse memory and imagination in a language whose "intent . . . is to originate like the flower, [in] that it strives to banish all metaphor, to become entirely literal."[7]

It is useful to see how, in the mode of personal address, the unitary language of *The Prelude* differs from the similar, but ultimately nonunitary, speech of Coleridge in a Conversation Poem like "The Eolian Harp." The contrast in that poem between the exalted,

7. Paul de Man, "Intentional Structure of the Romantic Image," in *Romanticism and Consciousness*, ed. Harold Bloom (New York, 1970), p. 68.

visionary Coleridge and his orthodox, humble Sara is a version of daemonic opposition which itself undercuts the all-embracing expansiveness of the "universal harp" theme. The development of Coleridge's own thought, in fact, once again offers an illuminating contrast to Wordsworth's growth during roughly the same period. Particularly, it helps highlight the next, post-*Borderers* stage of his quarrel with the daemonic, a stage achieved as early as *Lyrical Ballads* but reaching full maturity in *The Prelude*.

Coleridge, like Wordsworth, wrote some of his most powerful poetry out of a distaste for the mechanistic, hyperrationalist beliefs of his youth. In the case of Coleridge, however, this reaction against a materialist absolutism was coupled with a faith in the (for Coleridge) ironically named doctrines of Unitarianism. And his reaction against such beliefs, while striving toward a unitary vision both of man-in-nature and of his own past, inevitably and frustratingly fell back into varieties of opposition, two-ness, and the daemonic. A number of critics have cited Coleridge's continual uneasiness with his early tenets of faith. James D. Boulger writes:

> There was one area in which the theory [mechanism] continued to be important for him, to awaken in him the most violent annoyance, and that was in its connection with Socinianism and Unitarianism. In attacking Unitarianism and mechanism with such violence . . . he exhibited a *mea culpa* attitude not unlike that of anticommunists who were fellow travelers in the 1930's.[8]

And J. B. Beer indicates a complementary, even more significant aspect of this difficulty: that Coleridge, even during the height of his commitment to Unitarianism, was drawn strongly to more mystical, less thoroughly rationalistic religious systems.[9] The opposition itself, between reason and mysticism, would have imposed an inevitable dichotomy in his later questionings. *Religious Musings*, written during Coleridge's disenchantment with Unitarianism (1794–96), makes this divisiveness agonizingly clear. Beer cites the description of Christ in the poem:

8. James D. Boulger, *Coleridge as Religious Thinker* (New Haven, 1961), p. 13.

9. J. B. Beer, *Coleridge the Visionary* (New York, 1962), p. 89.

> Holy with power
> He on the thought-benighted Sceptic beamed
> Manifest Godhead, melting into day
> What floating mists of dark idolatry
> Broke and misshaped the omnipresent Sire. . . .
>
> (29–33)

These lines are a good deal more christological than orthodox Unitarianism would find comfortable. And the lines that follow, which Beer does not cite, emphasize yet more strongly Coleridge's attraction to an explicitly numinous Christ:

> And first by Fear uncharmed the drowsed Soul.
> Till of its nobler nature it 'gan feel
> Dim recollections; and then soared to Hope.
> Strong to believe whate'er of mystic good
> The Eternal dooms for His immortal sons.
> From Hope and firmer Faith to perfect Love
> Attracted and absorbed: and centered there
> God only to behold, and know, and feel,
> Till by exclusive consciousness of God
> All self-annihilated it shall make
> God its Identity: God all in all!
> We and our Father one!
>
> (34–45)

As the last line indicates, this passage too, like *Paradise Regained*, is an attempt to answer the crucial question, Who is the Son of God? Notably, however, the dim recollections of line 36 strike a chord which is Wordsworthian and not really consistent with the movement of the passage as a whole. The saving memory of a better self is a myth of human continuity in time. But it is set in precarious equilibrium with the twin daemonisms of skepticism (identified, in a Blakean way, with "dark idolatry") and the *via negativa* of self-annihilation.

Indeed, this passage from *Religious Musings* is almost an unintentional allegory-in-small of the course of Coleridge's imaginative and religious career. It moves from an uneasy materialism and associationism to what Carlyle calls a "centre of indifference" in which the poet recognizes the contradictions of that earlier commitment and then into a new orthodoxy which becomes itself increasingly daemonic with the years. It is to the period of the centre of indifference—distinctively, the period of the Conversation Poems—that Coleridge's closest poetic approach to Wordsworth can be assigned; and conversely, it is during this period that Wordsworth's poetic differences from Coleridge can be most profitably examined. The final passage of *Religious Musings*, for example, offers a striking contrast with Wordsworth in the matter of animism—Christian or otherwise:

> Contemplant Spirits! ye that hover o'er
> With untired gaze the immeasurable fount
> Ebullient with creative Deity!
> And ye of plastic power, that interfused
> Roll through the grosser and material mass
> In organizing surge! Holies of God!
> (And what if Monads of the infinite mind?)
> I haply journeying my immortal course
> Shall sometime join your mystic choir! Till then
> I discipline my young and novice thought
> In ministeries of heart-stirring song,
> And aye on Meditation's heaven-ward wing
> Soaring aloft I breathe the empyreal air
> Of Love, omnific, omnipresent Love,
> Whose day-spring rises glorious in my soul
> As the great Sun, when he his influence
> Sheds on the frost-bound waters—The glad stream
> Flows to the ray and warbles as it flows.
>
> (402–419)

The immediate analogue, of course, is the famous passage from "Tintern Abbey":

> And I have felt
> A presence that disturbs me with the joy
> Of elevated thoughts; a sense sublime
> Of something far more deeply interfused,
> Whose dwelling is the light of setting suns,
> And the round ocean and the living air,
> And the blue sky, and in the mind of man:
> A motion and a spirit, that impels
> All thinking things, all objects of all thought,
> And rolls through all things. Therefore am I still

A lover of the meadows and the woods,
And mountains; and of all that we behold
From this green earth; of all the mighty world
Of eye, and ear,—both what they half create,
And what perceive; well pleased to recognise
In nature and the language of the sense
The anchor of my purest thoughts, the nurse,
The guide, the guardian of my heart, and soul
Of all my moral being.

(93-111)

    The first notable thing about the two passages—something whose larger implications have been discussed in the preceding chapter—is, of course, that Coleridge's passage is an apostrophe in the manner of the sublime ode, while Wordsworth's is in the middle mode of address. In fact, it immediately precedes the poet's sudden and daring importation of an auditor into the lyric, his address to Dorothy. More important for our present concerns is the way in which Wordsworth, with remarkable subtlety, skirts the elements of religious and materialistic daemonism which are so pervasive in the Coleridge passage. The "Monads of the infinite mind" of Coleridge's poem become "something far more deeply interfused" with Wordsworth; the refusal to give the "something" a more definite name and also the compression of plurality into singularity are crucial.

    The animizing power of names in both primitive religions and Western allegory is by now an anthropological and critical truism. What has not yet been made clear, at least in criticism, is the extent to which the magic act of naming, as a kind of semantic daemonism or fixation, is tinged with the ambivalence of all daemonism. To name an object is not only to exert a certain control over it but also irrevocably to sacrifice a certain amount of autonomy in return for that control. An example is the common practice in primitive societies of making magic against an enemy by destroying an article of his clothing or clippings from his nails or hair or by destroying a doll or artifact with his name written on it.

    This is a psychic and linguistic problem which does not appear to become fully realized until the advent of Romanticism, and the passage cited from *Religious Musings* must be one of its earliest and most graphic presentations. It will be noted that Coleridge seems almost to try not to give a name to his nature daemons—

they are first addressed as "ye of plastic power"—and that he slips into the animizing epithets "Holies of God" and "Monads," as is symptomatic of his weaker poetry, out of a kind of desperation: a failure of the will toward the fully human. The two epithets are syntactically outside the structure of the thought; they are appendages in the most unfortunate sense. Wordsworth, on the other hand, by positioning the "presence" and the "something" within the past of his experience ("And I have felt"), avoids apostrophe. And in doing this, he tactfully contains the daemonic energies inherent in the concept within a dense syntax whose chief energy is that of imaginative unification. "A sense sublime / Of something far more deeply interfused" is impossible to read logically—or should be, since worrying out the grammatical reference of "more" militates against the real purpose of the phrase, which is, as Carl Woodring says, "intensive . . . not toward limited comparison, but toward the unlimited."[10] It is a placing of energy in a frame which avoids the oppositions inherent in Coleridge's differentiation of "plastic power" and the "grosser and material mass." Syntax imitates meaning here and imitates it brilliantly. The "something" is "far more deeply interfused" not only throughout the material universe but, by the absence of a clear reference for the word "more," throughout the verbal universe of the sentence itself. Lacking such a clear reference, the word can only refer back to the entire sentence, including the light of setting suns, the round ocean, the living air, the blue sky, and even the mind of man in a unitary image. Such an image makes the projection of a daemonic nature, a two-ness in mind and phenomenal world, at once impossible to affirm and yet strongly suggested as an undertone of the poem. This is the "language of the sense" in a highly original and self-conscious formulation, one which can meaningfully articulate the poet's "purest thoughts" and "moral being" simultaneously within and beyond "the mighty world / Of eye, and ear."

The antitype of this vision of nature is the conclusion of Coleridge's passage. Here the final natural image—"The glad stream / Flows to the ray and warbles as it flows"—is an affecting but uneasy return to natural process, but only after a spiraling vision of the beatified soul in which natural symbols, such as the day-spring, the sun, and the melting waters, function as more or

10. Carl Woodring, *Wordsworth* (Boston, 1965), p. 62.

less conventional mystical analogues for a fundamentally antinatural, nonhistorical eternity. Indeed, comparing the use of names in the two passages from Coleridge and Wordsworth, suggests what Donald Davie has already described as the characteristic syntax of *The Prelude*: concrete verb forms coupled with abstract, indeterminate substantives.[11] And it enables us to see how this stylistic habit is, for Wordsworth, an important way of integrating opposites and, as such, a necessary precondition for the unified narrative of *The Prelude*.[12]

It is *The Prelude*, of course, which represents Wordsworth's fullest triumph over the daemonic, as it is his fullest release from the exigencies of conventional narrative form. The two victories are the same, for Wordsworth, in *The Prelude*, integrates and unifies the daemonic elements of his personality precisely by narrating how he has come, through severe psychic trials, to integrate and unify the daemonic elements of his personality. In other words, the "iconic" imitation of meaning by language which we saw operating in "Tintern Abbey" has become more than a tour de force; it is now a central principle of the poetry, annihilating even that most primal and perennial of literary daemonisms, the opposition between form and content.

Such an effect is an inevitable result, to be sure, of the fully confessional mode. For the religious confessant, too, demonstrates to himself and his audience—and his God—that he has integrated the indwelling of Christ with his daily life by narrating the process of that integration. Furthermore, both "Christ" for the confessants and "imagination" for Wordsworth appear, in retrospect, in the natural and highly traditional image of a light shining into the darkness of earthly life, but unusually, a light originating within the human self embedded in time. Both the confessants and Words-

11. Donald Davie, *Articulate Energy: An Inquiry into the Syntax of English Poetry* (London, 1955).

12. Cf. Harold Bloom on Shelley's *Mont Blanc*, in *Shelley's Mythmaking* (New Haven, 1959), p. 25.

worth speak in very similar terms of this assurance of divinity-within-humanity:

> A plastic power
> Abode with me; a forming hand, at time
> Rebellious, acting in a devious mood;
> A local spirit of his own, at war
> With general tendency, but, for the most,
> Subservient strictly to external things
> With which it communed. An auxiliar light
> Came from my mind, which on the setting sun
> Bestowed new splendour; the melodious birds,
> The fluttering breezes, fountains that run on
> Murmuring so sweetly in themselves, obeyed
> A like dominion, and the midnight storm
> Grew darker in the presence of my eye:
> Hence my obeisance, my devotion hence,
> And hence my transport.
>
> (2. 362–376)

This "auxiliar light"—which achieves perhaps its most magnificent articulation in the final lines of the *Intimations Ode*—is both necessary and highly dangerous to the fully human imagination. For while it ensures the unity-in-time and unity-in-place of the human experience, its very insistence on the ability of unassisted human power to make a livable world can easily become a new version of daemonism which turns the human faculty into a divisive, world-devouring force.

This history of radical Protestantism offers a number of examples of the potentially destructive, daemonic force of the Inner Light of private revelation. The most notorious example—and one which continually embarrassed radical Protestants of the seventeenth and eighteenth centuries—was probably James Nayler, whose literal acceptance of Fox's doctrines led him finally to an inability to distinguish between himself and Christ as historical personages.[13] Such sensational events as Nayler's garish heresy trial and his terrible public mutilation helped give the word *enthusiasm* the disreputable tinge it had indelibly acquired by Wordsworth's day.

The great confessants of the Society of Friends and the

13. See appendix 1.

Wesleyan Movement, of course, were very careful in their narratives to avoid the excesses implied by the vulgar term *enthusiasm*. And it was the technique of narrative itself, the anchoring of personal revelation in the story of a developing personality-within-history, which was their chief resource in this integration of the transcendent. E. D. Hirsch, whose book *Wordsworth and Schelling* is a valuable exploratory study in the relationships we are discussing here, writes of the integrative imagination of the eighteenth-century reformers:

> Sometimes, indeed, Enthusiasm may experience a mystical fusion with the beyond, but this is merely a moment within its experience as a whole. . . . The subject is always faced with distinctions to be overcome, distinctions like that between life and death, the ideal and the real. Yet, at the same time, the task of overcoming distinctions is already implicitly accomplished by the beyond. The both-and motif underlies every aspect of experience.[14]

One student of autobiography, disparagingly contrasting the confessants with Gibbon and Hume, has spoken of their "static representation of the personality."[15] Precisely. But it is a stasis dynamic rather than inert, necessitated by the exigency of taming the daemonic and readjusting and integrating the past. Such stasis is not merely a prerogative but a sine qua non for the radical confessant. We shall now examine one such confession and its startling similarity to narrative procedures in *The Prelude*.

George Fox, certainly one of the most "enthusiastic" and numinous of all confessors, relates throughout his journal strange and apparently unmotivated urgings of an inner voice. With equal thoroughness, however, the journal seeks to contain these urgings within a context of freedom of development. In 1656, for example, preaching to the people of Wales, he projects a Christology purified of its atemporal types and figures:

> I opened also to them the types, figures, and shadows of Christ, in the time of the law; and showed them that Christ was come, and had ended the types, shadows, tithes, and oaths, and put down

14. E. D. Hirsch, *Wordsworth and Schelling* (New Haven, 1960), p. 16.
15. Roy Pascal, *Design and Truth in Autobiography* (Cambridge, Mass., 1960), p. 8.

swearing; and had set up yea and nay instead of it, and a free ministry. For He was now come to teach the people Himself, and His heavenly day was springing from on high.[16]

Fox's awareness of the danger of a daemonic Christology is apparent, of course, in his estrangement from Nayler and the careful tact of his own christological references to his career in the journal. Even more striking than this, however, is a remarkable passage early in the journal where Fox faces and overcomes the contrary version of daemonism, the temptation to believe in an absolutely determinative and possessive natural universe:

> One morning, as I was sitting by the fire, a great cloud came over me, and a temptation beset me; and I sat still. It was said, "All things come by nature"; and the elements and stars came over me, so that I was in a manner quite clouded with it. But as I sat still and said nothing, the people of the house perceived nothing. And as I sat still under it and let it alone, a living hope and a true voice arose in me, which said, "There is a living God who made all things." Immediately the cloud and temptation vanished away, and life rose over it all; my heart was glad, and I praised the living God.[17]

It would of course be a violence to the text to call this passage "Wordsworthian"; but it seems undeniable that the shape of the experience Fox undergoes is very like that progressive assimilation of daemonic attitudes which forms the general narrative shape of *The Prelude*—a shape of experience which Fox and his followers were to make commonplace in Protestant belief and which Wordsworth was to articulate in a purely secular poetic form.

A final example from Fox will suffice for our present point; it is one of the most surprising and subtle uses of narrative in the journal. In 1652 Fox was on his way to Westmoreland, the territory where he was to make his most faithful converts, meet the woman who was to become his wife, and establish Quakerism as a full-fledged movement. In retrospect, he sees it as a portentous moment, perhaps the most portentous in his career as a preacher. On the way

---

16. *The Journal of George Fox*, ed. Rufus M. Jones (New York, 1963), p. 274.
17. Ibid., p. 94.

there, he had climbed Pendle Hill, and he begins the story with
that incident. What follows must be quoted at length:

> As we travelled we came near a very great hill, called Pendle
> Hill, and I was moved of the Lord to go up to the top of it; which
> I did with difficulty, it was so very steep and high. When I was
> come to the top, I saw the sea bordering upon Lancashire. From
> the top of this hill the Lord let me see in what places he had a great
> people to be gathered. As I went down, I found a spring of water
> in the side of the hill, with which I refreshed myself, having eaten
> or drunk but little for several days before.
>
> At night we came to an inn, and declared truth to the man of
> the house, and wrote a paper to the priests and professors, declaring
> the day of the Lord, and that Christ was come to teach people
> Himself, by His power and Spirit in their hearts, and to bring
> people off from all the world's ways and teachers, to His own free
> teaching, who had bought them, and was the Saviour of all them
> that believed in Him. The man of the house spread the paper abroad,
> and was mightily affected with the truth. Here the Lord opened
> unto me, and let me see a great people in white rainment by a river
> side, coming to the Lord; and the place that I saw them in was
> about Wensleydale and Sedbergh.[18]

We may accurately describe this narrative as apocalypse turned
into akedah through the very process of matter-of-fact narrative.
But it is even subtler than that. The central experience of the
passage is the vision of that key motif of Revelations, the gathering
of the peoples. This apocalyptic sight begins to appear on the top
of Pendle Hill (the mountaintop being the archetypal place for such
a revelation) but is thwarted, with a definite narrative wrench, as
Fox turns aside to his descent from the mountain and to the
strangely vivid detail of the spring (which is still called "George
Fox's well"). The night at the inn is then described as one of
especially productive evangelical excitement. Then, and only then,
is the apocalyptic vision allowed to complete itself in the "people
in white rainment." It seems, by implication, to be a visionary
dream of Fox's rather than a waking vision, but this is not finally
important. What is important is that the vision has been deliberately

18. Ibid., pp. 150–51.

embedded in narrative process and that, even in its second and fuller articulation, it is once more anchored to the naturalistic world by the reference to "Wensleydale and Sedbergh."

The unmistakable analogue to this experience in *The Prelude* is, surely, the Simplon Pass episode. It is, of course, with the possible exception of the ascent of Mount Snowdon in book 14, the single most intricate moment of the poem and inexhaustible by any amount of commentary or analogy. But here we may notice that the whole episode takes its energy from Wordsworth's original desire to ascend to the top of the Alps and confront the natural world at its most sublime—which is to say, its most important. It is a daemonic

> . . . under-thirst
> Of vigour seldom utterly allayed.
> And from that source how different a sadness
> Would issue. . . .
>
> (6. 558–561)

Lost in the dark, however, Wordsworth and his companion wander along the mountain roads until they meet a peasant and learn from him that they have already crossed the Alps. What follows the realization that *"we had crossed the Alps"* (591) is a very important bit of textual reorganization.[19] In the initial composition, line 591 led directly into the downward-moving vision published in 1845 as "The Simplon Pass (composed about 1799), the vision of an ongoing apocalypse within nature in recompense for the poet's own thwarted will:

> Tumult and peace, the darkness and the light—
> Were all like workings of one mind, the features
> Of the same face, blossoms upon one tree;
> Characters of the great Apocalypse,
> The types and symbols of Eternity,
> Of first, and last, and midst, and without end.
>
> (635–640)

In composing the sequence for *The Prelude*, however, Wordsworth breaks the narrative time of the episode to describe his present reaction to the memory of the experience. But the famous apostrophe

---

19. See Geoffrey Hartman, *Wordsworth's Poetry, 1797–1814* (New Haven, 1964), pp. 45–48.

to Imagination, following line 591, is very easy to misread, as R. A. Foakes has pointed out, as referring to the past time of the experience itself.[20] The imagery is precisely that of the poet's wandering over the Alps:

> Imagination—here the Power so called
> Through sad incompetence of human speech,
> That awful Power rose from the mind's abyss
> Like an unfathered vapour that enwraps,
> At once, some lonely traveller. I was lost;
> Halted without an effort to break through;
> But to my conscious soul I now can say—
> "I recognize thy glory". . . .
>
> (592–599)

That the final collation of the episode seems inevitable rather than patchy is partly due to this deliberate imagistic connection. But more meaningfully, it is a result of the fact that Wordsworth, like Fox in the Pendle Hill story, is utilizing narrative and time sense to discipline the daemonic tendencies of his experience. Both the description of the autonomous power of Imagination and the description of the great Apocalypse of natural decay and regeneration are, from the vantage of the present-tense narrator, versions of the daemonically complementary extremes of experience: limits of human existence. The poet in his descent from the mountain and in his retrospective coupling of these two extremes does not impose, but rather *extrapolates*, a narrative sequence out of them—a sequence which enriches the sense of his present humanity without annihilating it in the face of either experience. For if the Imagination section, as a rupture in the narrative time, radically qualifies the inhuman vision of the natural apocalypse, that vision itself serves as a qualification to the vision of Imagination, following it in the "spoken" time of the passage.

In a passage like the Simplon Pass episode, ideas of form have found a definition which provides the poet with, simultaneously, total release from one kind of history and total bondage to another. For the principle of formal organization by this point has become at once the most primal and most tenuous of principles—the poet's own sense of his remembering, reflecting, speaking self. It is a

---

20. R. A. Foakes, *The Romantic Assertion* (London, 1958), p. 63.

method of integrating the timeless, daemonic energies of inspiration which succeeds by pretending to be no method at all but simply the casual reminiscences of an inspired mind whose inspiration is already assimilated into the daily processes of living and speaking. Wordsworth is never clearer about his own sense of this method than in the brilliant conclusion to book 5 of *The Prelude*:

> Visionary power
> Attends the motions of the viewless winds,
> Embodied in the mystery of words:
> There, darkness makes abode, and all the host
> Of shadowy things work endless changes,—there,
> As in a mansion like their proper home,
> Even forms and substances are circumfused
> By that transparent veil with light divine,
> And, through the turnings intricate of verse,
> Present themselves as objects recognised,
> In flashes, and with glory not their own.
>
> (595–605)

To make "forms and substances"—the substratum of our common world—"circumfused" with the glory of the sublime, but yet to make them remain "as objects recognized," is surely the fully articulated goal not only of the passage but of the whole poem. And the "turnings intricate of verse"—a phrase which, by the poetic transposition of adjective and noun, does exactly what it says —are crucial in this transformation and transfiguration. For the memorial verse of the poet localizes and embeds the sublime "mystery of words" in the convolutions of his confessional narrative. And at the same time, the phrase describing the "turnings intricate," interposed between the two phrases describing the resplendence of the numinous in the everyday, enforces a pause in the narration which perfectly imitates the mediating, integrative power of language which is being spoken of.

This is an approach to imaginative form which, by asserting the constitutive centrality of the self in history, is itself monumentally constitutive of the modern temper. Robert Langbaum, in a perceptive essay on "The Evolution of Soul in Wordsworth's Poetry," has compared the method of *The Prelude* to the investigations of twentieth-century information theory and mathematical linguistics. Wordsworth, Langbaum argues, is trying to assert the

continuity and independence of *human* speech against the impinge-
ments, which we would call daemonic, of associationism and
mechanism.[21] And surely he is right in seeing this assertion as
fundamentally the one made by contemporary "mathematical"
grammarians, whose systematization of language is designed explicitly to isolate and affirm the unsystematized, integrative role
of human will in the act of speech.[22] In much the same way F. A.
Pottle has demonstrated that the much-vaunted "fidelity to the
object" of Wordsworth's descriptions is actually a fidelity not to
the object as such but to the process whereby the object *comes to
be perceived*.[23] And it is difficult not to see in this aspect of Wordsworth's imagination an anticipation of another distinctively modern
reaction against daemonism, Wolfgang Köhler's refutation of be-
haviorist theories of perception: "Instead of reacting to local stimuli
by local and mutually independent events, the organism responds
to the *pattern* of stimuli to which it is exposed; and . . . this answer
is a unitary process, a functional whole, which gives, in experience,
a sensory scene rather than a mosaic of local sensations."[24] Köhler's
phrase for the unitary process of gestalt perception is, in fact,
startlingly Wordsworthian: "a sensory scene."

The following chapters will extend this description of the
formal principle of *The Prelude* into a more specific analysis of its
narrative structure and language. But for the present, it will be
useful to examine in detail one incident of the integration of the
daemonic in the poem, both as a way of concluding the description
of Wordsworth's experiments with form which we have been
tracing and as itself a prelude to the discussion to follow.

Perhaps the most celebrated "daemonic" moment in *The Prelude*
is the episode of the Stolen Boat in book 1. It is an important

21. Robert Langbaum, *The Modern Spirit* (New York, 1970), chapter 2.
22. E.g., Noam Chomsky, *Language and Mind* (New York, 1968).
23. F. A. Pottle, "The Eye and the Object in the Poetry of Wordsworth,"
in *Romanticism and Consciousness*, ed. Harold Bloom (New York, 1970),
pp. 273–87.
24. Wolfgang Köhler, *Gestalt Psychology* (New York, n.d.), p. 62.

moment in the poem, for in it Wordsworth relates not only one of his earliest visitations by a sublime power beyond nature but also one of his earliest—and most permanently refreshing—intimations of how to integrate that power into a myth of human continuity. The introduction of the episode has already been discussed in the last chapter: in it Wordsworth, through the medium of address to his Friend, channels the prophetic energy of "Praise to the end!" into a sustained and poised autobiographical discourse. The sequel to this address, the episode itself, achieves the same effect, but on the much greater scale of the poet's unity with his own remembered experience of nature, the divine, and himself. I quote the episode in full.[25]

> Praise to the end!
> Thanks to the means which Nature deigned to employ:
> Whether her fearless visitings, or those
> That came with soft alarm, like hurtless light
> Opening the peaceful clouds; or she may use
> Severer interventions, ministry
> More palpable, as best might suit her aim.
>
> One summer evening (led by her) I found
> A little boat tied to a willow tree
> Within a rocky cave, its usual home.
> Straight I unloosed her chain, and stepping in
> Pushed from the shore. It was an act of stealth
> And troubled pleasure, nor without the voice
> Of mountain-echoes did my boat move on;
> Leaving behind her still, on either side,
> Small circles glittering idly in the moon,
> Until they melted all into one track
> Of sparking light. But now, like one who rows,
> Proud of his skill, to reach a chosen point
> With an unswerving line, I fixed my view
> Upon the summit of a craggy ridge,
> The horizon's utmost boundary; far above
> Was nothing but the stars and the grey sky.
> She was an elfin pinnace; lustily

25. For much of my information concerning this episode, I am indebted to an absorbing and suggestive conversation with Professor Ephim G. Fogel of Cornell University.

I dipped my oars into the silent lake,
And, as I rose upon the stroke, my boat
Went heaving through the water like a swan;
When, from behind that craggy steep till then
The horizon's bound, a huge peak, black and huge,
As if with voluntary power instinct
Upreared its head. I struck and struck again,
And growing still in stature the grim shape
Towered up between me and the stars, and still,
For so it seemed, with purpose of its own
And measured motion like a living thing,
Strode after me. With trembling oars I turned,
And through the silent water stole my way,
Back to the covert of the willow tree;
There in her mooring-place I left my bark,—
And through the meadows homeward went, in grave
And serious mood; but after I had seen
That spectacle, for many days, my brain
Worked with a dim and undetermined sense
Of unknown modes of being; o'er my thoughts
There hung a darkness, call it solitude
Or blank desertion. No familiar shapes
Remained, no pleasant images of trees,
Of sea or sky, no colours of green fields;
But huge and mighty forms, that do not live
Like living men, moved slowly through the mind
By day, and were a trouble to my dreams.

(350–400)

This great passage is easy to interpret as what Edward E. Bostetter
calls "Wordsworth's basic experience, stripped of its civilized
abstractions . . . an elemental primitive rite in which he absorbs
nature into himself. . . ."[26] It is one of nature's "severer interventions"
in the education of the poet, and the huge black peak, "as if with
voluntary power instinct," certainly seems a nature daemon of
some sort, a disruption of the natural order of things by a higher
and "other" power. Robert Langbaum, in *The Poetry of Experience*,
gives a cogent version of this reading, locating the daemonic element
primarily in the sense of landscape perspective:

26. Edward E. Bostetter, *The Romantic Ventriloquists* (Seattle, 1963),
p. 14.

The revelation proceeds from an optical illusion which, by disrupting the ordinary appearance of things, allows the imagination to transform them into significance. The effect of the revelation is to make us feel that so extraordinary a perspective is no less true to the reality of the object than an ordinary perspective, that it is even in a sense truer.[27]

To what extent, however, is the vision an optical illusion? Wordsworth is an unusually careful observer not of natural phenomena as they appear but as they come to be perceived—an important distinction which should make us wary, in any passage, of assuming that Wordsworth means more than he describes. In the present case, the crucial fact to remember—one which Langbaum, among others, does not develop—is that as he rows Wordsworth is facing away from the direction of the boat's movement and thus sees, during the entire incident, only the shore he is leaving. Like a rower striving to reach a fixed point in a straight line, he sights not over his back at the direction in which he is rowing but at the highest point of the receding horizon. As he gets farther and farther from the shore, his view of "the horizon's utmost boundary" becomes more panoramic, and the black peak begins to appear over the craggy ridge. It is huge, growing still in stature not in itself but precisely in relation to the ridge on which the rower has taken a fix. Far from being, as Langbaum implies, a violation of natural perspective, this is an effect so common as to be normally unnoticeable. What brings it into consciousness for the rower—and for anyone who will take the trouble to focus on two close objects, the taller behind the shorter (e.g., a telephone pole in front of a house), and then walk backward away from them for twenty steps—is that the vision is fixed on the shorter and closer of the two objects rather than ranging freely over the horizon. Hence the relative heights of the objects are seen to vary abruptly with each stroke of the oar rather than gradually with the general recession of the horizon.

It is important not to misunderstand what Wordsworth means when he says that the stature of the peak grows steadily. For *stature* is a carefully relative term for size and means precisely what

27. Robert Langbaum, *The Poetry of Experience* (New York, 1963), p. 42.

it says. Thus everything on the horizon, perceived singly, is becoming smaller; but in configuration, with the craggy ridge as the center of the pattern (not the peak itself), the peak's relative stature over the ridge grows ever more impressive. When the peak is said to tower between the rower and the stars, we must not assume that it is in any way blacking out the heavens. The stars involved must be those along the angle of vision which had originally included the craggy ridge as the biggest thing in sight. In fact, Wordsworth skillfully ensures this interpretation by all but describing the critical angle of vision at the beginning of the narration.

In saying this much about the episode, however, we have not denied the presence of a strong animistic or daemonic element in the narration. We have only discovered that, if it is to be located and understood fully, it must be interpreted in a context more complex than the primitivism of either Wordsworth the narrator or Wordsworth the boy rower. Reading the poet's vision of the pursuing cliff as a kind of gestalt perception is in no way a domestication of the passage; it is simply an attempt to get the terms of the problem in a clearer perspective than, it seems, they have often enjoyed. Returning again to the stages of the episode, we notice that the carefully schematic outline of the rower's experience—his angle of vision, the configuration of his objects of sight—is deeply involved with another, subtle movement that can only be described as psychophysical.

We have already mentioned that the most important visual component of the rower's experience—what actually lifts the black peak into its threatening predominance over his field of vision—is the act of fixing his sight on the craggy ridge. This establishes the angle of vision upon which the peak impinges. The fixing of this angle of vision, however, is accompanied by a shift in the rower's purposiveness and in his whole muscular sense of the boat in the water. The base line is also and necessarily the leisurely, unpurposive movement of the boat toward no particular point at all. The "small circles glittering idly in the moon" which describe the line of the boat's movement at this stage are the small circles caused by barely dipping the oars in the water, letting it have its own way. And Wordsworth, at this point, studiously avoids using the word *I*; it is the boat itself which moves to the sound of mountain echoes.

With the fixing of the second line of the angle, however, a

new sense of purposiveness enters the narration, changing the whole feeling of the episode. The rower behaves like one who strives to reach a goal with unswerving line. It is important that he actually has no such goal in mind but is rather performing strenuous activity in, as it were, a logical vacuum, with no motivation outside the activity itself. Now the narrator's I becomes explicit; and Wordsworth seems to emphasize the disjunction between this and the previous leisurely vision with the "But now, like one who rows . . ." of the 1850 text (1805 has "And now . . ."). What is really remarkable, and distinctively Wordsworthian, about this sudden shift is the way all the modulations of tone form an instantaneous and unified movement. One is not aware of a change of perspective, followed by a playful adoption of mock purpose (as boys will run an imaginary race with themselves downhill), increased muscular exertion, and stronger muscular imagery in the narration. Rather, the boy's raising his eyes to the craggy ridge is so presented as to constitute, rather than occasion, his adoption of mock purpose. And the grammatical frame of the whole action ("But now . . . I fixed my view"), especially after the calm anonymity of the preceding sentence, syntactically suggests the increased exertion of this part of the episode. The act of rowing is exertive, willful, disruptive. But it is here contained by a retrospective narrative form which subtly asserts the identity of intent and action in a movement which is not disruptive but unifying.

It has been necessary to spend so much time on one section of the Stolen Boat episode, in order to develop as fully as possible the complexities of Wordsworth's handling of his daemonic experience. But now we reverse our context, for if the episode is not animistic or primitive in the sense we have presented, neither is it a case of subconscious projection, later recognized as such by the narrator himself. Wordsworth is not saying, that is, that as a boy he once went rowing and thought he saw a mountain peak come alive with mysterious force but that now he recognizes that it was all an illusion fostered by the concurrence of his guilt at stealing the boat and his sudden access of physical energy in rowing. Such an interpretation simply substitutes for the primitive, Lawrentian Wordsworth of some interpretations another equally unsatisfying Wordsworth who, like a contemporary armchair Freudian, assumes that to examine and explain the workings of the dark daemonic self is also somehow to explain away or at least render harmless its existence.

The lines of the passage we are considering which most lend themselves to such interpretation are, of course, those describing the growth of the black peak:

> I struck and struck again,
> And growing still in stature the grim shape
> Towered up between me and the stars, and still,
> For so it seemed, with purpose of its own
> And measured motion like a living thing,
> Strode after me.

From what we have already seen of the operation of perspective in this vision, it is easy to read these lines as a powerful conflation of the rower's own muscular energy ("I struck and struck again") and the apparent "measured motion" of the growth of the daemonic peak. It is an image nearly Dantesque in its precision, for in the situation Wordsworth describes, the increase in stature of the peak would follow not only the linear movement of the boat away from the horizon but also the steady pulse of the boat's rise and fall in the water. But is this, in the final analysis, simply projection? Surprisingly, the effect of the lines is not to diminish but rather to make more oppressive the sense of a substantive, "other" presence in the very act of describing its correlation to the nervous system of its observer. It seems that the peculiar terror of the episode— and it is, we should note, a very terrifying experience—is neither in the animism of primitive nature-worship nor in the intellectualism of sense analysis. Rather, it is in the startling recognition that they are fundamentally the same thing, fundamentally both daemonic ways of experiencing the world.

The recognition, of course, is that of Wordsworth the narrator; Wordsworth the boy rower and subject of the episode does not take time to worry whether his fright is the result of a pursuing nemesis or of his own subjective guilt feelings but rather reacts like a boy, turning his boat around and heading for shore. This is not, however, to dismiss the boy's own experience as secondary to the episode. If the boy does not bother to separate the natural-daemonic and the rational-daemonic, he nevertheless inevitably feels both these drives in an instinctive way; he must, of course, for the mature Wordsworth to be able to look back on the episode and shape it in the way he has. But more significantly, the boy's very reaction to the frightening vision is an indication of his confused sense of the two complementary daemons who are pursuing him. He turns around (i.e., turns his back to the apparition) and "with trembling oars" makes for the shore. Either action alone would have stopped the terrifying effect: ceasing to look at the threatening peak or slowing down the precipitate motion of the boat. That the boy does both indicates his intuitive awareness of the twin sources, visual and muscular, of his experience.

For days afterward, we are told, the boy's perception of nature was transformed into an unfamiliar, disturbing sense of "unknown modes of being" and "mighty forms, that do not live / Like living men." Harold Bloom writes of this final section of the episode: "This is a fundamental paganism, so primitive that it cannot yield to any more sophisticated description without distortion. It is like the Titanism of Blake, with its Giant Forms like the Zoas wandering in a world substantially our own."[28] But surely this is too simple. It is true that, as the young Wordsworth's earliest intimation of visionary power behind his normal perception of nature, the incident of the boat necessarily issues in a sense of the life force as world annihilating. It might reasonably be called a sensory magic, with the "unknown modes of being" operating rather like *mana*, destroying, in their constant transaction between the mind's imaginings and the nature behind nature, the ordinary world of sight and hearing, of familiar forms. I do not think it a distortion of this moving passage, however, to note that its necessary assertion of the daemonic principle is carefully combined within what we have been describing as the fundamentally antidaemonic movement of the whole episode. The "huge and mighty forms" bear a recognizable relationship to the "Huge peak, black and huge" of the experience proper—but a recognizable relationship of abstraction.

Wordsworth implies a strong disjunction between the experience on the lake and its aftereffect: a disjunction which is itself another narrative device for containing and channeling the energies released. The Stolen Boat episode apparently had tremendous importance for the young Wordsworth: he seems to have regarded it poetically somewhat as we have been regarding it critically, as

28. Harold Bloom, *The Visionary Company* (New York, 1963), p. 157.

a paradigm for handling certain crucial problems in his narration. An examination of Wordsworth's Goslar notebook—de Selincourt's MS "JJ" of *The Prelude*[29]—reveals two versions of the episode. In the first version, one can feel the poet wrestling with the daemonic implications of the experience as he repeats obsessively the striking lines:

> And growing still (in) stature the huge (cliff)
> With measured motion like a living thing
> Strode after (me)
> Rose up between me & the stars & still
> With measured motion like a living thing
> Strode after me.
>
> (JJ, p. S *verso*)

In this first version, furthermore, the narration of the effect of the experience precedes the narration of the rower's return to shore: the pagan and animistic implications of the experience on the lake are unabsorbed into the episode and literally break through the narrated sequence of the incident. The return itself, both as a completion of the story and as a necessary breaking of the spell of the daemonic—the way out of the experience—is correspondingly truncated and uncertain:

> with trembling hands I turn'd
> And through the silent water stole my way
> Back to the cavern of the willow
> And to my [age] in
>
> (JJ, p. T *verso*)

The second version follows the final order of the episode, narrating the return to the shore before the aftereffect of the experience, with one curious difference. In this version we are told how the boy returned to shore, then how the experience exercised its apocalyptic effect on his perception for days afterward, and then how, after returning to the shore, the boy made his way homeward through the meadows (JJ, p. R *verso*). Wordsworth is still having trouble, that is, containing the aftereffect within the narrative time of the episode. Shortly after these entries in the Goslar notebook,

---

29. William Wordsworth, *The Prelude*, ed. Ernest de Selincourt and Helen Darbishire (Oxford, 1959), pp. 633-42.

however, the episode seems to have achieved nearly its final form; it is included, along with two Lucy poems, "Nutting," and the Skating episode from *Prelude* 1 in a letter of William and Dorothy's to Coleridge,[30] with only slight variations from the 1805 version.

There is one last adjustment in the episode, however, as it appears in the 1850 text: the smallest and yet most important of changes. The 1805 text has:

> There, in her mooring-place, I left my Bark,
> And, through the meadows homeward went, with grave
> And serious thoughts; and after I had seen
> That spectacle, for many days, my brain
> Work'd with a dim and undetermin'd sense
> Of unknown modes of being. . . .
>
> (1805, 415–420)

In 1850, the only variation from this text is that the second "and" of the third line is changed to "but." This change provides the ultimate narrative control over the daemonic energy of the Stolen Boat episode, precisely because, in replacing the alogical and paratactic "and," it strengthens the disjunction between experience and aftereffect. Thereby Wordsworth implies more strongly a present narrator who absorbs the timeless and world-destroying "blank desertion" into a retrospective process. "But," as used here, is far from simply the logical equivalent of "and" and farther still from its common implication of strong parataxis. Since it points to a present-tense, fully humanized narrator who can *see* the disjunction it implies, it is the strongest of connectives: it establishes the unity and maturity of the narrator himself not in the grammar of causality but precisely in the grammar of confession.

There is, as I suggested at the beginning of this chapter, no mnemonic formula for the profound narrative unity of *The Prelude*. But, on the basis of the Stolen Boat episode, we may locate at least two crucial elements of remembered and narrated experience for Wordsworth's fiction of continuity. They are the memory of obsessive vision and the integrating, reminiscent speech which disciplines that memory, that vision.

30. *The Early Letters of William and Dorothy Wordsworth*, ed. Ernest de Selincourt (Oxford, 1935), no. 89.

CHAPTER THREE

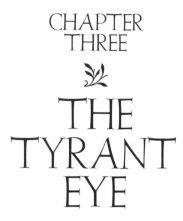

THE TYRANT EYE

Mit deinen Augen, welche müde kaum
von der verbrauchten Schwelle sich befrein,
hebst du ganz langsam einen schwarzen Baum,
und stellst ihn vor den Himmel: schlank, allein.
Und hast die Welt gemacht.

Rilke, "Eingang"

And if thy eye is an occasion of sin to thee, pluck it out! It is
better for thee to enter into the kingdom of God with one eye,
than having two eyes, to be cast into hell fire.

Mark 9:47

The memory of vision, disciplined by narrative speech, is a formula
which conceals a fascinating history, both in Wordsworth's own
development and in the long tradition of self-analysis and self-
definition which is so crucial for understanding Wordsworth. The
present chapter will concentrate on the first part of the phrase:

the shape of remembered experience, the scenes of the past, what was seen as opposed to what is said. But of course we will be dealing with the memory of vision precisely through the mediating language of the poet's present speech—the speech of *The Prelude*—so that the concerns of this and the following chapter will, quite naturally, tend to merge as the discussion proceeds.

We have already seen, from a number of passages, that the daemonic in Wordsworth's poetry tends almost exclusively to take the form of the visual rather than the other senses. And, correspondingly, we have been examining for some time now the mediating, unitary function of speech in *The Prelude*: how the visual is overcome by the aural, by what radical Protestants before Wordsworth had referred to as the life-giving, *in*visible manifestation of the Word. We shall examine, shortly, the curious development of this visual-aural distinction in the history of radical Protestant thought, for that development throws particularly clear light upon Wordsworth's own way of defining "the visual" in *The Prelude*.

But before this general survey of the problem, I wish once again to examine the peculiar development of Wordsworth's own imagination. For, from *The Borderers* onward, we can observe the poet defining and reworking his ideas about the nature and meaning of the sense of sight until, about the time of *The Prelude*, he comes upon the critical distinction between "sight" and "vision," a distinction about which we shall have much to say.

If sight for Wordsworth is the daemonic sense par excellence, it is so because of the power that beautiful or gigantic or terrifying sights have to rivet our attention, taking us out of ourselves in that transport which so fascinated the eighteenth-century theorists of the sublime. For Wordsworth, however, such experience comes to represent a paralysis of the imagination, a freezing of natural mental growth which, as we saw in the Stolen Boat episode, is intimately connected with the idea of "fixing" the sight on a particular object. The next stage of this argument, quite natural from Wordsworth's special point of view, is to assert that the fixation of the eye, obsession with the visual scene, is in fact a form of blindness, both because overreliance upon any sense transforms that sense into a limitation of the spirit, and because such over-reliance blocks the apparition of the inner vision, the "auxiliar light" so central to the poetry of the great decade. We shall now examine three Wordsworthian pictures of "blind" characters, in order to graph the development of his complicated and original attitude toward the faculty of sight.

Baron Herbert in *The Borderers* is blind. Abandoned to his trial by ordeal in the wilderness, he wanders through a storm toward what he thinks is the tolling of a chapel bell to signal a refuge for wanderers:

> That Chapel-bell in mercy seemed to guide me,
> But now it mocks my steps; its fitful stroke
> Can scarcely be the work of human hands.
> Hear me, ye Men upon the cliffs, if such
> There be who pray nightly before the Altar.
> Oh that I had but strength to reach that place!
> My Child—my Child—dark—dark—I faint—this wind—
> These stifling blasts—God help Me!
>
> (Act 4, ll. 1651–58)

Ironically, we discover that the chapel is deserted and that it is only the wind, in a cruel parody of the aeolian-harp theme, which lures the old man to his exhaustion and death. This blindness is fully "natural," then. Its pathetic overtones for the tragedy do not arise from the quality of blindness itself but rather from the barbaric use which Herbert's sighted persecutors make of it.

Counterpointing Herbert's blindness, though, is a series of implications about the relationship of the visible to the true, as befits a tragedy whose jealousy motif derives so strongly from *Othello*. As Oswald plots the corruption of Marmaduke, he reflects:

> I have left him
> To solitary meditation;—now
> For a few swelling phrases, and a flash
> Of truth, enough to dazzle and to blind,
> And he is mine for ever. . . .
>
> (Act 2, ll. 561–65)

The flash of truth is provided by a Female Beggar whom Oswald hires to impersonate a ruined mother betrayed by Herbert. It is a figure reminiscent of the Mad Mother or the Margaret of later poems but, like every typical "Wordsworthian" element in *The*

Borderers, diabolically inverted. Later, as Marmaduke describes the fabricated sins of Herbert to his band, one of them is led to exclaim with an irony the rest of the play bears out:

> The whole visible world
> Contains not such a Monster!
>
> (Act 2, ll. 1056–7)

I have already indicated that *The Borderers* is an important document in the history of Wordsworth's general quarrel with the daemonic. It is equally important in the crucial area of his handling of the sense and the imagery of sight, because it organizes itself around the pathetic image of the sightless man preyed upon by daemonic characters. Such characters, ironically, so trust visual evidences and the whole world of the visual that they become possessed (either as manipulators or gulls) by its prejudices and thus destroy any truly human behavior or relationship. Lacy is right that the visible world cannot contain such a monster as the Herbert fabricated by Oswald; but it is precisely the visible world which allows Oswald to fabricate him, and the visible world which becomes for the unhappy Marmaduke "poisoned at the heart," incapable of sustaining evidences of its own benevolence or transcendence.

The Borderers, of course, represents a dead-end version of experience for Wordsworth, a bitter revision of his necessitarianism which holds out the possibility of only a marginal salvage. But its central dramatic element, the figure of the blind man in the wilderness, is one which continues to hold a fascination for the poet and develops into one of his most suggestive images of man in *The Prelude*.

The next time he appears is in the fascinating, disturbing shape of *The Old Cumberland Beggar*. Here the wilderness solitary is stripped of his royal rank, of his power of articulate speech, and most subtly, of his blindness itself:

> He travels on, a solitary Man;
> His age has no companion. On the ground
> His eyes are turned, and, as he moves along,
> *They* move along the ground; and, evermore,

Instead of common and habitual sight
Of fields with rural works, of hill and dale,
And the blue sky, one little span of earth
Is all his prospect.

(44–51)

As has often been remarked, this is a minimal humanity, so totally alien to our normal assumptions as to appear almost, but not quite, fantastic. Unlike Herbert, the Beggar need not be physically blind, since he is so far down the scale of human intelligence as not to desire sight in any conventional manner. What in *The Borderers* had been an external deformation of the senses, and served to reveal the intrinsic viciousness of one kind of character, becomes here something quite different. It is a way of examining the limits of the human, whose effect is to enrich the visual and spiritual perception of the more normally sighted people in the neighborhood:

. . . all behold in him
A silent monitor, which on their minds
Must needs impress a transitory thought
Of self-congratulation, to the heart
Of each recalling his peculiar boons,
His charters and exemptions; and perchance,
Though he to no one give the fortitude
And circumspection needful to preserve
His present blessings, and to husband up
The respite of the season, he, at least,
And 'tis no vulgar service, makes them felt.

(122–132)

We have not read the poem correctly if we are not shocked by these sentiments. Our own age is in fundamental agreement, at least, with Blake that

Pity would be no more,
If we did not make somebody Poor;
And Mercy no more could be,
If all were as happy as we.

and such a frankly egocentric celebration of feelings of benevolence is distasteful. But thinking of *The Borderers*, we can see that the

old beggar represents a considerable advance in Wordsworth's
ethics of vision. He is moving toward his great theme of continuity,
toward a poetry in which the visible world is robbed of its tyrannous
and divisive power and is interfused with a unitary perception:

> And let him, *where* and *when* he will, sit down
> Beneath the trees, or on a grassy bank
> Of highway side, and with the little birds
> Share his chance-gathered meal; and, finally,
> As in the eye of Nature he has lived,
> So in the eye of Nature let him die!
>
> (192–197)

The "eye of Nature" here is a new formulation for Wordsworth
and one which he might have developed into a very different mature
vision than the one we have in *The Prelude*. It is an approach to an
absolutely minimal poetry, testing a lower limit for the transforming
power of imagination and memory. The beggar is not transformed
in himself or in the sensibility of the observer; nor is the operation
of the natural world redeemed in any perceptible way, since the
eye of nature continues to manifest itself in the winds that will
blow against the old man and the rains that will beat against him.
We need only compare this uncompromising conclusion to the
end of *Resolution and Independence*, where the poet feels compelled to state a personal, memorial profit from the experience, to
understand the radical change in Wordsworth's vision of man's fate
around the time of *Lyrical Ballads*.

What is important in *The Old Cumberland Beggar*, however,
what does continue into the later poetry and especially *The Prelude*,
is the peculiar articulation of the act of sight which Wordsworth
gives us. Seeing is a block to vision in this poem in a much more
radical way than in *The Borderers*. For here the life of sight, of
everyday trust in the visual, is not simply deceptive but what a
psychologist would call overdetermined. The sight of the beggar,
a customary phenomenon in the villages, tends to be emptied of
its high significance exactly because it is so clearly and fully seen
by all the inhabitants—including the poet. Roughly the first half
of the poem is a series of images of the old man of startling clarity,
made the sharper for their intense matter-of-factness. The progress
of the poem is really an attempt by the observer to get beyond this

fullness of visualization, not to a generalization about the human condition, but to a vision, a way of seeing, which can bear such generalization. The poles of the poem are the statement that the beggar "travels on, a solitary Man" (44) and the statement that "we have all of us one human heart" (153). Between these poles the speaker struggles to transvalue the world of the visual without ever transcending it or denying its tyrannical primacy.

A third version of blind solitude, this one from *The Prelude*, will show what I take to be Wordsworth's fully mature handling of the visual sense. Toward the end of book 7 Wordsworth narrates one of his most striking experiences in London:

As the black storm upon the mountain top
Sets off the sunbeam in the valley, so
That huge fermenting mass of human-kind
Serves as a solemn back-ground, or relief,
To single forms and objects, whence they draw,
For feeling and contemplative regard,
More than inherent liveliness and power.
How oft, amid those overflowing streets,
Have I gone forward with the crowd, and said
Unto myself, "The face of every one
That passes by me is a mystery!"
Thus have I looked, nor ceased to look, oppressed
By thoughts of what and whither, when and how,
Until the shapes before my eyes became
A second-sight procession, such as glides
Over still mountains, or appears in dreams;
And once, far-travelled in such mood, beyond
The reach of common indication, lost
Amid the moving pageant, I was smitten
Abruptly, with the view (a sight not rare)
Of a blind Beggar, who, with upright face,
Stood, propped against a wall, upon his chest
Wearing a written paper, to explain
His story, whence he came, and who he was.
Caught by the spectacle my mind turned round
As with the might of waters; an apt type
This label seemed of the utmost we can know,
Both of ourselves and of the universe;
And, on the shape of that unmoving man,

His steadfast face and sightless eyes, I gazed,
As if admonished from another world.

(619–649)

This beggar, like the Old Cumberland Beggar, is "a sight not rare" in the city, a common inhabitant of the visible world; but his everyday nature is set off here by the crowd of sights among which he moves—or rather, does not move—like a single ray of light against a black cloud. Sight, in fact, through the medium of memory, is being used to baffle sight: the beggar, who would normally be invisible through his very obviousness, is rendered surrealistically clear by the swarm of life which surrounds him—and more importantly, by the alien sensibility of the rural narrator, for whom the whole vision is a moment of conversion. It is a union of the matter-of-fact and the wonderful in a single vision and represents for Wordsworth a way of approaching the visual which can include both antitheses of the paradox of seeing. "I was smitten / Abruptly, with the view (a sight not rare)," he says, and the distinction between view (or vision) and sight is operative at the heart of the passage (a distinction not explicitly present in the parallel lines from the 1805 version and which Wordsworth obviously felt compelled to point up). It is the same dialectic we have already seen operating in the Stolen Boat episode, with the narrator simultaneously aware of the naturalistic workings of his perception and of the usurping, daemonic power of that perception. Here, though, the perception is more complicated: it is not simply of motion—sight and muscular effort combined—but of perception itself—sight *as* motion and effort.

The lines leading up to the apparition of the beggar, interestingly, remind one of the technique known to film viewers as a pan: a rapid camera survey of a broad scene—literally, a panorama—coming to rest in a single shot. The parallel, indeed, is more than coincidence, for the movie—a rapid series of still photos not qualitatively different from the magic lantern of the late nineteenth century—is a mechanical analogue of Wordsworth's narrative problem: how to bring continuity and change out of a universe which at every instant tends to congeal into the frozen, fixed, and daemonic. A succession of fixed images, speeded up enough, becomes truly "a second-sight procession, such as . . . appears in dreams," but only

by continually triumphing over its own inertia, its own tendency
to settle into the frozen image.

Something very like this trompe-l'oeil—an appropriate name
for Wordsworth's attitude toward the eye—occurs in the movement
of the passage as a whole. For the panorama of city sights comes
to rest, startlingly and fixedly, on the image of the blind beggar.
And *this* image becomes even more fixated, more obsessively visible,
in the written paper on his chest: man with label takes on the
reductive, minimal identity of man as label. But at this last fixation,
the moment of maximum inertia in the passage, the narrator shifts
to the aural image of the "might of waters"—always an intimation
of life and grace in Wordsworth. And the beggar himself begins
to be transformed, through the narrator's consciousness, into a force
beyond the phenomenal, an energy which is not daemonic because
it manifests itself as the obliteration of daemonic imagery.

It is an unpleasant but undeniable fact of human nature that
the blind man among the sighted is more visible because of his
privation. It is necessary for the sense of the passage that we understand the beggar as being rendered more fixed but not more eternal
for his blindness. Geoffrey Hartman is right in seeing the passage
as an event "that enters through, yet overpowers, the eye."[1] The
written paper, which is almost a magic talisman for the beggar,
actually does represent "the utmost we can know, / Both of ourselves and of the universe." The mystery within the beggar, the
intimation of a power beyond sight, eternal like the apocalyptic
might of waters, is the gift not of his own condition but of the
radical change that has taken place within the vision of the observer.
The beggar himself is "fixed," a word we have seen Wordsworth
use before to suggest the sense of the visual as obsessive, imprisoning:
he is "propped against a wall," unmoving only because of the
precarious imbalance of his sightless condition. It is Wordsworth
the observer who translates this fixedness into the very different
kind of stillness of the last lines, a translation which is like grace
in that it follows the exhaustion of the powers of the visual world.
Wordsworth changed the final description of the beggar's face
from "fixed" in 1805 to "steadfast" in the 1850 text; and we must
not miss the irony of this word, in its root meaning, contrasted to

1. Geoffrey Hartman, *The Unmediated Vision* (New York, 1966), p. 132.

the earlier description of the beggar's precarious "stead," leaning against a wall.

What I am suggesting is that the blind beggar passage, as a kind of terminal point in Wordsworth's treatment of blindness—and metonymically, of the sense of sight—represents both a radical advance over the formulation in his earlier poetry and also the peculiar, confessional strength of *The Prelude* as Wordsworth's necessary form for his mature vision. For it is the confessional voice of the observer which effects the final liberation of the image from sight into vision. That liberation is the direct result of a narrative poise (lacking, in any full sense, in *The Old Cumberland Beggar*) which makes it possible for the observer to *look back* from the label on the man's chest to the whole "shape of that unmoving man." The vision, finally, is "mediated" precisely by the mediatory, confessional voice itself. Or, as Wordsworth himself has it in the lines immediately following the passage:

> Though reared upon the base of outward things,
> Structures like these the excited spirit mainly
> Builds for herself. . . .

> (650–652)

The distinction between the "structures" of the mind and the supporting "base" of outward things expands the difference between the old beggar as "propped" or "prop" and the mind's earned vision of a "steadfast" shape and intimation of eternity.

Wordsworth's original, epoch-making attitude toward the sense of sight has, of course, been discussed frequently by his commentators. Probably the most important discussion, Basil Willey's "Wordsworth and the Locke Tradition" in *The Seventeenth Century Background*, presents the poet's handling of the visual as an inheritance from and reaction against the epistemology of Locke and his school. The Lockean doctrine regards "primary qualities" of objects—length, weight, etc.—as the *really* real and "secondary qualities"—color, texture—as illusory. Such a doctrine, according to Willey, left the natural world devoid of its former sensual vitality, thus preparing the ground for Wordsworth's poetry as a way of regaining a sense of that vitality without restoring an unquestioning trust in the images of the eye.

In fact, however, the radical mistrust of the eye—or at least of the blandishments of the visible world—is at least as old as the saying of Christ I have used as an epigraph to this chapter. And the specifically Protestant, confessional version of that mistrust lies not only behind the mature Wordsworth's poetry but in some ways even behind the "Locke tradition" identified by Willey (Berkeley, for one, seems to have been quite aware of the connection).

St. Augustine, in the *Confessions* (10, 54), names the thirst for earthly knowledge at the expense of the divine "the lust of the eyes," "sight being the sense chiefly used for attaining knowledge." In Augustine's own experience, furthermore, this lust after knowledge is indissolubly linked to his early love of the daemonic and hypervisual astral imagery of the Manichaeans:

> Yet they still set before me in those dishes, glittering fantasies, than which better were it to love this very sun (which is real to our sight at least), than those fantasies which by our eyes deceive our mind. . . .
>
> (3. 10)

Augustine's conversion to the true God, it will be remembered, is phrased in terms of his learning to listen to the invisible voice of the spirit within him, turning away from the soul-freezing images of his early deceivers.

For the confessant Augustine, then, the visual is defined as an intellectual error, leading man to fixation on the things of this world rather than upon the God within him. This is nowhere more apparent than in the famous description of the corruption of Alypius at the Circus. Alypius, Augustine's friend (and surely his surrogate here as elsewhere in the *Confessions*) enters the Circus determined not to watch the carnage and closes his eyes piously. But aroused to curiosity by the shouts of the crowd, he begins to look—and is lost:

> For so soon as he saw that blood, he therewith drunk down savageness; nor turned away, but fixed his eye, drinking in frenzy, unawares, and was delighted with that guilty fight, and intoxicated with the bloody pastime.
>
> (6. 13)

Here again the motif of fixing the eye is both central and disastrous. In fact, Alypius, who is led to fix his eye because of what he has previously heard, represents an exact daemonic inversion of the rhythm of salvation (sight overcome by pure sound) we have seen at work in both Augustine's conversion and the Blind Beggar passage in *The Prelude*.

What Augustine and Wordsworth—and the Lockean tradition—have in common here is not simply a sense that appearances may deceive or even the more serious sense that they may corrupt. Referring to the "sense of the human" discussed in the last chapter, we can see that these thinkers all use the sense of sight as a type, and a crucial type, of intellectual and spiritual rigidity which undermines the fluid, dynamic life of the mature soul. For Augustine, that maturity is defined primarily as the consciousness of the living God; for Locke, it is the very different consciousness of one's own perceptive processes; and for Wordsworth, it is the complex sense of poetry and life which he seeks to describe in his poem. But for all three, it involves the deep awareness that a man, to achieve vision, must sometimes turn away his eyes from what he thinks is this world. Modern, phenomenological descriptions of the tyranny of object-consciousness—Heidegger's *Existenz* or Sartre's *être en soi*—are in this way not so much discoveries as rediscoveries of an ancient and radical wisdom about human life as becoming-and-being in one.

The continuity of this wisdom is nowhere stronger than in the writings of the Protestant confessants, whose lack of epistemological sophistication is more than compensated for by their sheer narrative power. Two passages from the English confessants particularly enrich not only the historical background but the reading of the "visual-daemonic" sense we have seen in Wordsworth's poetry.

We have already marked, in George Fox's journal, the conscious deflection of visual revelation in the ascent of Pendle Hill. But perhaps the most powerful example of the tyranny of the eye in Fox's narrative is his experience at Lichfield in 1651. It is a famous passage, cited by William James at the opening of *The Varieties of Religious Experience*. For our purposes, the most important part of it is its beginning, where Fox feels himself literally attacked by the church spires of Lichfield—what Fox always called and abomi-

nated as "steeple-houses," visual incarnations of the presumption
and "towering" pride of the English Church:

> As I was walking with several Friends, I lifted up my head and saw
> three steeple-house spires, and they struck at my life. I asked them
> what place that was. They said, "Lichfield." Immediately the Word
> of the Lord came to me that I must go hither. . . . As soon as I
> was got within the city, the Word of the Lord came to me again,
> saying, "Cry, 'Woe to the bloody city of Lichfield!' " So I went
> up and down the streets, crying with a loud voice, "Woe to the
> bloody city of Lichfield!" . . . As I went thus crying through the
> streets, there seemed to me to be a channel of blood running down
> the streets, and the market-place appeared like a pool of blood.[2]

We cannot help but remark, as with an earlier passage from Fox,
the similarity between the shape of this experience and the shape
of the Blind Beggar passage. The form of the "steeple house,"
surely an imposing visual image, is the immediate cause of the whole
action—and leads directly to a compensatory revelation to the
aural sense. The Word of God serves here the same apocalyptic
and transforming function as the sound of the "might of waters"
for Wordsworth. This oral-aural formula, furthermore, leads to
Fox's second "sight" of Lichfield as a bloody trough of martyrs: a
vision *sub specie aeternitatis* after the manner of Wordsworth's
transforming the blind beggar from "fixed" to "steadfast" avatar
of another more permanent world.

John Bunyan, in *Grace Abounding to the Chief of Sinners*,
gives another powerful example of the malign ambience of the
sense of sight. At the first stage of his conversion to Christ, the
stage usually described as the "conviction of guilt," he tells us how
he had delighted in ringing the bells at his local church:

> But my conscience beginning to be tender, I thought such practice
> was but vain, and therefore forced myself to leave it, yet my mind
> hankered; wherefore I should go to the steeple house, and look
> on it, though I durst not ring. But I thought this did not become
> religion neither, yet I forced myself, and would look on still; but
> quickly after, I began to think, How, if one of the bells should

2. *The Journal of George Fox* (New York, 1963), pp. 132–33.

fall? Then I chose to stand under a main beam, that lay overthwart the steeple, from side to side, thinking there I might stand sure, but then I should think again, should the bell fall with a swing, it might first hit the wall, and then rebounding upon me, might kill me for all this beam. This made me stand in the steeple door; and now, thought I, I am safe enough; for, if a bell should then fall, I can slip out behind these thick walls, and so be preserved notwithstanding.

34. So, after this, I would yet go to see them ring, but would not go farther than the steeple door; but then it came into my head, How, if the steeple itself should fall? And this thought, it may fall for aught I know, when I stood and looked on, did continually so shake my mind, that I durst not stand at the steeple door any longer, but was forced to flee, for fear the steeple should fall upon my head.[3]

This remarkable passage may, of course, be viewed simply as a version of the psychopathology of religious belief. For the experience Bunyan is describing is one we have all had: the illusion, looking up at a tall object from very close to it, that the object is actually beginning to fall toward us. And we can easily see how this common optical trick is transvalued by Bunyan's latent guilt feelings at being near the now "sinful" steeple bells. But to do this is, I think, to approach the text from exactly the wrong end of an argument. For while this certainly is projection in the strict psychoanalytic sense of that word, it is also projection within confession, within explicit and firm narrative control over the experience. The point is, in fact, that Bunyan employs such an exclusively visual set of sensations as the basis of the episode. Nowhere does he describe himself as pursued by the sound of the steeple bells—an alternative certainly as natural to simple projection—but only by the obsessive, accusing vision of them.

Between Augustine and the seventeenth century confessants, however, another radically innovative theologican complicates even farther the daemonism of the "lust of the eyes." Martin Luther has been identified by many critics as crucial to the growth of the modern self: J. H. van den Berg is particularly revealing as he

3. John Bunyan, *Grace Abounding to the Chief of Sinners* (London, 1963), p. 15.

traces Luther's discovery of private revelation to his terror at the sight of sacramental Catholicism:

> Luther said: The robes, candles, and relics are matter, nothing else; anything else that is said about it is a human creation, vanity. Luther did not know the word, projection. . . . Did Luther transfer things to a hastily constructed area called the "inner self," because his contemporaries were escaping from an all-embracing totality and were threatening to come adrift? One remembers how much against a rupture he was. "Do not leave each other," was what, after all, his aversion towards candles and robes meant. "Let the objects become poor—so long as we can stay together."[4]

For Luther, that is, the visual-daemonic is no longer simply the seductive world of matter or even the idolatry of false religions: it has penetrated within the sanctuary of the true church itself, as an overreliance upon the visible sacraments and allegories of liturgy. The "inner self" which Luther discovers for European culture, then, while Augustinian in parentage, quests for an even subtler, even more difficult discrimination between its proper humanity and the daemonic temptations which impede its progress. Sacrament, ceremony, even the most apparently certain signs of grace—all of these may now deceive, may lead the believer into unwilling but poisonous idolatry.

There is another name, of course, for the daemonism discovered and abominated by Luther. It is, simply, the allegorical temperament. And the radical Protestants of the eighteenth century are as opposed to allegory as they are to sacramentalism or to conventional evidences. Almost invariably, in Quaker and Methodist confessions, allegorical passages are also passages describing lapses into a sacramental mentality, an overreliance on the power of human will, or simply a state of divided consciousness. Here is Stephen Crisp, for example, describing his brief relapse into reliance on human will:

> So I took up that Ordinance . . . of *Water Baptism*, expecting then to have found more Power than before. And my will wrought strongly to Bridle and keep down that Airy part and sinful nature. . . . But these Reasons held but for a Season, before the Temptation

4. J. H. van den Berg, *The Changing Nature of Man* (New York, 1964), p. 230.

grew too strong for my Will, and the Devil entred [*sic*] his own
Ground, and prevailed upon me. . . .[5]

Or Frances Paxton, describing how at the urgings of her family
before her conversion, she

> passively gave way to the persuasions of my intimates, to try if the
> strictest life in the way of the Church of England would not excuse
> me in the sight of my Maker and meet with his approbation. O the
> forbearance of a merciful Father to me in that time of probation,
> that He did not consume me by the breath of His displeasure! . . .
> *Sacrifice and meat offerings thou wouldest not accept.* . . .[6]

These confessants avoid the sacramental, the allegorical, and
the visual—even in a Christian form—as fervidly as they would
outright sin or the Devil himself. Not to do so would be to betray
not only their own souls but the form in which they write. For
the confession is the confessant's evidence of election; and to rely
upon another kind of proof would be to demonstrate how little the
speaker actually has acquired the Inner Light, which, for both
Fox and John Wesley, must ratify itself or not be ratified at all.
This is the point of Wesley's famous dialogue with the Moravian
Peter Böhler, in which Böhler uttered the counsel which was
finally to save Wesley: "Preach faith till you have it; and then,
because you have it, you will preach faith."[7] One remembers
Augustine's decision, at the opening of the *Confessions*, that to
call upon, know, and praise God is a single verbal act. If reliance
upon visible evidences implies a daemonic fixation of the will, the
confessant's speech overcomes such fixation by its insistence on
continuity: by insisting that to choose grace is already to be in
the state of grace (even if unconsciously), and to be in the state
of grace is necessarily to confess that state.

    We have already seen many of the same attitudes at work in

---

5. *A Memorable Account of the Christian Experiences, Gospel Labours,
Travels and Sufferings of that Ancient Servant of Christ Stephen Crisp*
(London, 1694), p. 13.

6. In Stephen Hobhouse, *William Law and Eighteenth Century Quakerism*
(New York, 1928), p. 28.

7. John Wesley, *The Journal of John Wesley.* 4 vols. (London, 1930),
1: 84.

The Prelude. But an especially illuminating working-out of the problem is "The Solitary Reaper," a lyric composed in November 1805, perhaps six months after the completion of *Prelude* 11 and Wordsworth's articulation of his central myth of recovery and continuity, the "spots of time."

"The Solitary Reaper" has always had a special fascination for readers of Wordsworth. Geoffrey Hartman, for example, builds much of the argument of his book *Wordsworth's Poetry, 1797–1814* upon the insights of his particularly fine reading of the lyric. But in terms of the present study, that reading deserves some qualification. Hartman writes of Wordsworth's minute examination of his own emotional responses:

> . . . Its only real justification . . . was that it carried the Puritan quest for evidences of election into the most ordinary emotional contexts. Wordsworth did not himself talk of election or salvation but . . . of renovation (regeneration), and he did not seem to be directly aware of his Puritan heritage, although the *Poems* of 1807 . . . shows a heightened intimacy with seventeenth-century traditions.[8]

The use of the word "regeneration" inevitably brings to mind the poetry of Henry Vaughan, who is frequently cited as a seventeenth-century anticipation of Wordsworth. But Vaughan's central poem, "Regencration," is valuable here precisely as an indication of the gulf between the later poet and the quest for evidences. In Vaughan's poem, in the heart of a natural chapel on a mountaintop, the soul-sick speaker hears the Pentecostal wind of God:

> I turn'd me round, and to each shade
>   Dispatch'd an Eye,
> To see, if any leafe had made
>   Least motion, or Reply,
>   But while I listning sought
>   My mind to ease
> By knowing, where 'twas, or where not,
>   It whisper'd; *Where I please*.

---

8. Geoffrey Hartman, *Wordsworth's Poetry, 1797–1814* (New Haven, 1964), p. 5.

Lord, then said I, *On me one breath,*
And let me dye before my death!

(73–82)

But compare the end of Vaughan's poem with the last stanza of
"The Solitary Reaper":

Whate'er the theme, the Maiden sang
As if her song could have no ending;
I saw her singing at her work,
And o'er her sickle bending;—
I listened, motionless and still;
And, as I mounted up the hill,
The music in my heart I bore,
Long after it was heard no more.

(25–32)

Vaughan, in a way, is looking for precisely the correspondent
breeze in nature which will constitute an evidence of election; the
wind's "*Where I please*" is a nearly literal translation of God's "I
am that I am" or "I will be wherever I choose to be"—*eyeh asher
eyeh*—in *Exodus*. But Vaughan does not find the breeze and therefore prays for a death to the natural world, which will save the
soul from the second death in a fallen universe. For the orthodox
Protestant, the search for evidences of election is itself penitential,
an admission of banishment into an unfamiliar world where the
road signs are necessary but painful reminders of the distance from
home; "Regeneration" is a grimly and touchingly ironic title, since
it is just what the speaker does not and cannot attain in a pastoral
context. The wind, simply, is spiritually not at home in the heavily
visual and allegorical world in which Vaughan finds it.

Wordsworth, on the other hand, is recording, not a quest for
evidences, but a real renovation of a peculiar sort. Vaughan and
Wordsworth both show the radical Protestant predilection for
aural experience, but Wordsworth is prepared to trust it to a
much greater degree. For him, the sound is an image neither of
phenomenal experience nor of apocalyptic visitation; in traditional
terms, indeed, although it behaves deceptively like the conceit of
a metaphysical poem, it is hardly an image at all. It is a unit of
continuity, for if "the Maiden sang" in the past "As if her song

could have no ending," one of the functions of the poem is to demonstrate the still unending quality of it as present music. The shifting of verb tenses in the poem has been often enough remarked; but note that, in the movement from present in the first three stanzas to past in the final stanza, the last two lines define what is really another—and the most important—time frame. This is the characteristic confessional tense. Wordsworth says he "bore" the music in his heart long after he ceased to hear it. But of course he is still bearing it in his heart, since his poem itself is not merely inspired by but is a real reincarnation in time of the song whose anonymity is so strongly suggestive. The reason he can put this climactic and exquisitely understated formula in a past tense is that the whole song has by this time become both the maiden's and his own, demonstrating not only the ability of the past to determine the present (the natural order of experience) but the ability of the present to penetrate and make meaningful the past (the classical strategy of confession). The Wordsworth who says "bore" is really neither the Wordsworth who long ago heard the lass singing, nor yet the Wordsworth who has just completed "The Solitary Reaper," but a Wordsworth who, from the vantage point of his regeneration in and through history, can observe both the other time experiences as interpenetrating and continuous.

Wordsworth, working through a purely aural experience (since he cannot understand the Maiden's language), has reduced the experience to the minimal condition of recorded, printed fact and thereby transcended fact for an experience on a higher level, that of imaginative salvation. And the terms of that salvation are the terms of his ability to control memorial time, to remake the experiential world.

In this connection, our own most important fact about "The Solitary Reaper" is the well-known one that Wordsworth did not really have the experience but cribbed it from Wilkinson's "Tour of Scotland": "The last line," Wordsworth says in his note to the 1807 edition, "being taken *verbatim*." And it is precisely the last line of the poem, as I have just discussed it, in which the confessional, unifying force of the lyric chiefly resides. Wordsworth's audacity and genius allow him to take a line from a minor prose piece and transform it into the very fabric of *his own* vision. Such daring is made possible by a sense of writing we have seen operating also in the Simplon Pass episode. For with both experiences, Wordsworth is able at a point in the narration (the "Imagination" passage, the last line of "The Solitary Reaper") to translate memory into the present experience of writing, of trying to write, or of quoting another's writing. What we have said about the mediating power of confessional speech, then, is here operating at its most basic level: first denuding remembered experience of its separate daemonic energy by reducing it to the lowest common denominator of written matter and then informing that lifeless, written matter with the new, unitary power of the narrator's present health and wholeness.

This technique—which is also foreshadowed in the use of the "written paper" in the Blind Beggar episode—depends, furthermore, upon yet another definition of the visual. It is a sense of the visual, which, like the antisacramental, seems to achieve its first full articulation in the work of Luther and which, as we shall see, is intimately connected with the progress of *The Prelude*. From the idea of the "tyranny of the eye," then, we now move to examine its most important corollary, "the tyranny of the book."

Luther's revolutionary insistence upon private interpretation of Scripture is famous. The complexity of this idea and its relation to Luther's experience of "The Book" is nowhere more fully documented than in his polemic against Erasmus, *The Bondage of the Will*. It is a passionately antischolastic book, written in Luther's most exuberant style. But it becomes apparent early in the work that Luther and Erasmus have, really, no chance of beginning to understand each other.

In terms recently popularized by communications theorists, *The Bondage of the Will* represents a baffled confrontation between a man of "manuscript culture" (Erasmus) and a man of "print culture" (Luther). Erasmus had asserted in *The Freedom of the Will* that Luther's theology failed to take account of the frequent difficulty and ambiguity of Scripture. Luther's reply goes to the heart of the whole problem:

Here is my distinction (for I am going to do a little lecturing—
or chop a little logic, should I say?): God and His Scripture are
two things, just as the Creator and His creation are two things.
Now, nobody questions that there is a great deal hid in God of
which we know nothing. . . . But the notion that in Scripture some
things are recondite and all is not plain was spread by the godless
Sophists (whom you now echo, Erasmus)—who have never yet cited
a single item to prove their crazy view. . . . I certainly grant that
many *passages* in the Scriptures are obscure and hard to elucidate,
but that is due, not to the exalted nature of their subject, but to
our own linguistic and grammatical ignorance; and it does not in
any way prevent our knowing all the *contents* of Scripture. For
what solemn truth can the Scriptures still be concealing, now that
the seals are broken, the stone rolled away from the door of the
tomb, and that greatest of all mysteries brought to light . . . that
Christ suffered for us, and will reign for ever?[9]

I quote this passage at some length, since it foreshadows a
sensibility that will be seen to have enormous importance for
Wordsworth's poetry. Luther here is actually redefining "Scripture"
as a working term and giving a new answer to that basic question
of all critical activity, theological or literary: "Where is the book?"
This is the same fundamental question raised by René Wellek's
influential essay "The Mode of Existence of a Literary Work of
Art": "What is the 'real' poem; where should we look for it; how
does it exist?"[10] And as Wellek's essay makes abundantly clear, the
answer we give to such a question determines the characteristic
shape of our insight into the text.

Now in a culture oriented around the book as manuscript, which
was a highly aural version of text (*grammatica* arising originally
from the pedagogical device of learning by taking down dictation),
the answer to this question tends to involve a strong sense of the
text *as* the Word—of the book as literally speaking to the reader.
And this is the sense in which Erasmus criticizes Luther. But Luther
himself, a denizen of the Gutenberg galaxy, makes a distinction
between text and Scripture, between *grammatica* and meaning,

9. *Martin Luther: Selections* (New York, 1961), p. 172.
10. In René Wellek and Austin Warren, *Theory of Literature* (New
York, 1956), p. 129.

which is like, he says, the distinction between Creator and Creation—and which generates, finally, a split between visual and aural. The visual text is not the Word—not, finally, the "Scripture" upon which Lutheran Christianity relies so strongly.

To the question, "Where is the book [or The Book]?" a Lutheran critic's reply would be something like this: "Certainly not in the text in any important sense. For while the Book, the efficient Word of God, is crystal clear to any reader with a well-formed heart, nevertheless the text may still present 'grammatical'—i.e., visual—difficulties of interpretation; these, however, have nothing to do with the essential meaning of the Book, being simply surface encumbrances to the transmission of its pure spirit. So though Book and text are 'substantially' one, by the very paradox of the word *substance* the Book cannot be the text."

What Luther discovers for exegesis and Wordsworth discovers for poetry is the simple and astounding fact, in the post-Gutenberg era, of the omnipresence of print. If there is a primary from which the visual-daemonic takes for the last four book-ridden centuries, it is surely the fixity and rigidity of the printed word. And for both Luther and Wordsworth, that rigidity must at all costs be liberated into the fluid vitality, spoken and heard, of words and images as aural.

Wordsworth's sense of his past has been so universally spoken of by critics as a memory of Nature that even to invoke the cliché seems a cliché itself. But the memory of Nature, at least as described and epitomized in *The Prelude*, is equally a memory of literary ideas of Nature, a highly self-conscious narrative of stylistic development—a *biographia literaria* at least as subtle as Coleridge's. Before proceeding to a general discussion of the "history of the eye" in *The Prelude*, then, I wish to examine those passages in which Wordsworth most explicitly deals with the existence of his own manuscript and the act of writing itself as varieties of the visual-daemonic to be confronted and overcome. They form a crucial backdrop to the larger history of the poet as man in *The Prelude*. And the first of them, the first passage to deal with "writing the book" as a form of—and possible liberation from—the daemonic, is also the first passage in the poem.[11]

11. See appendix 2.

We have already written of the opening of book 1 of *The Prelude*—the "preamble"—in connection with the mediatory function of the audience in confession. It is an equally important example of the radical sense of the book as visual and therefore to be overcome. The recovery from the preamble, lines 46–58, continually proves one of the most inexhaustible passages in the whole of *The Prelude*:

> Thus far, O Friend! did I, not used to make
> A present joy the matter of a song,
> Pour forth that day my soul in measured strains
> That would not be forgotten, and are here
> Recorded: to the open fields I told
> A prophecy; poetic numbers came
> Spontaneously to clothe in priestly robe
> A renovated spirit singled out,
> Such hope was mine, for holy services.
> My own voice cheered me, and, far more, the mind's
> Internal echo of the imperfect sound;
> To both I listened, drawing from them both
> A cheerful confidence in things to come.

In the light of what has been discussed in the last two chapters, we can see so many confessional strains operating here that it is difficult to begin sorting them out. For the present, working exclusively with the idea of the visible, we can note that the violent reversal of the first lines—from present rapture into memorial verse and from lyric outpouring to specific second person address—is poetically identical with a shift from the quasi-sublime vista of the agitated landscape to the astringent visibility of the printed lines. "Are here / Recorded" is one of those retroactive shifts of perspective which is so characteristic of Wordsworth's lyricism. It asks us, through Coleridge, effectively to translate the vicarious sight of the landscape in the first 45 lines into its minimal terms, literally, our sight of the lines on the page—surely one of the most brutally honest self-reductions in the history of lyric. Its poignancy and its relevance, of course, loom even greater when we consider the peculiar circumstances of *The Prelude*'s "mode of existence as a literary work of art": a life-long, continually revised manuscript straining for the condition of printed book. Furthermore, the reduction from paean to memorial "recording" prepares us for the slow decline of poetic fervor and will which is documented in the section immediately following his passage.

"To the open fields I told / A prophecy" has a special subtlety here, since it both carries over the mood of ebullience from the opening and, under pressure of the bookish transvaluation, contains an inevitable hint of one of the most despairing of prophecies to "the open fields." Jeremiah, most compulsive of the prophets, in his despair at the ignorance of the people and of the King of Judea, is moved to address the stones themselves:

> Why are they cast out, he and his seed, and are cast into a land which they know not? O earth, earth, earth, hear the word of the Lord. Thus saith the Lord: Write this man barren, a man that shall not prosper in his days. . . .
>
> (Jeremiah 22:28–30)

Here the sense of the visual and another aspect of confessional verse, the sense of an auditor, inevitably coincide. For the prophecy told to the open fields carries an undeniable weight of reflexive irony. It is both an overreliance on the visual and a speech without the mediation of an auditor; assigning logical primacy to either error is impossible since each, really, is the cause of the other.

In fact, as we have already intimated, we can see here one of the most subtle methods of unification in *The Prelude*: Wordsworth's drive toward the state of book, toward the minimal visual-literary experience, thence to transcend the state of bookishness in the same way we have seen the printed religious confessions striving to transform themselves from public commodity into effectual ways of salvation.

The book of *The Prelude* entitled "Books" (book 5) is, of course, notorious for having very little at all to do with books—a common estimate which we shall have occasion later to disagree with. But for the present we can accept it provisionally and proceed from book 1 to book 8, "Retrospect," which is the most explicitly bookish section of *The Prelude*. Book 8 is a retrospect, in fact, in a curiously reflexive way: a retrospect within the great retrospect which is the whole poem. The poet literally looks back upon his written book and tries to evaluate it, and naturally, images of the book present themselves to him. Reflecting on what he has said of the mysterious idyll of childhood, he pauses to address the hypothetical skeptics in his audience:

> Call ye these appearances—
> Which I beheld of shepherds in my youth,
> The sanctity of Nature given to man—
> A shadow, a delusion, ye who pore
> On the dead letter, miss the spirit of things;
> Whose truth is not a motion or a shape
> Instinct with vital functions, but a block
> Or waxen image which yourselves have made,
> And ye adore!
>
> (8. 293–301)

Wordsworth is not usually remarkable for his use of *irony* in the complex and highly punning sense given that term by the New Critics. But it is impossible not to notice here, in the context we have been sketching, the weight of the word *block* in this passage; coming as it does at the crucial end point of the line, it may suggest a block of wood from which one would carve an idol (a visual and solipsistic daemonism), a block in the sense of an occlusion of vision (in the way we have seen that, for Wordsworth, sight can block vision), or finally, referring back to the "dead letter" of the printed book, a block of type. And, as we have seen, all three overtones are necessary and inevitable ones to Wordsworth's imagination.

This sense of the dead letter is continued and elaborated a few lines later when Wordsworth describes his first poetic efforts— which he here regards as a false, "sublime" lyricism, explicitly linking it to a "bookish" Muse. His soul, he says,

> Ventured, at some rash Muse's earnest call,
> To try her strength among harmonious words;
> And to book-notions and the rules of art
> Did knowingly conform itself; there came
> Among the simple shapes of human life
> A wilfulness of fancy and conceit;
> And Nature and her objects beautified
> These fictions, as in some sort, in their turn,

They burnished her. From touch of this new power
Nothing was safe: the elder-tree that grew
Beside the well-known charnel-house had then
A dismal look: the yew-tree had its ghost,
That took his station there for ornament:
The dignities of plain occurrence then
Were tasteless, and truth's golden mean, a point
Where no sufficient pleasure could be found.
Then, if a widow, staggering with the blow
Of her distress, was known to have turned her steps
To the cold grave in which her husband slept,
One night, or haply more than one, through pain
Or half-insensate impotence of mind,
The fact was caught at greedily, and there
She must be visitant the whole year through,
Wetting the turf with never-ending tears.

(8. 368–391)

It is doubtful that Wordsworth could have given us, as retrospect upon his half-completed confession, a more convincing or
intelligent analysis of his poetic progress. We begin again with
the reference to "book-notions" of a compulsively overblown Muse;
and the crude folksiness of "book-notions" (a substitute for 1805's
"The notions and the images of books") is certainly deliberate.
From this center the poet proceeds in widening generalizations to
describe not only his own earlier poetry but his critical sense of
the poetry of the sublime. The feeling is strong that the sublime
(and here, of course, Wordsworth is obviously including such poems
as *Guilt and Sorrow* and *The Borderers*), through its exaggeration
of the visual image, involves a daemonic fixation of human fate
which is egocentric and debasing. It is a charge to which Wordsworth himself has often been liable from almost the first criticisms
of his work; and his awareness of its terms here is the best refutation
of the charge.

And finally, at the end of the section, we see the visual-
daemonic attitude as a disfigurement of one of Wordsworth's most
permanent symbols, the bereaved widow. This is a significant development in the passage, furthermore, bearing out what was said in
the previous chapter about the daemonic as an occlusion of continuity. For as Wordsworth describes the phenomenon, it is pri-

marily a fixation of the eye and the sensibility militating against story: a fixation insisting that the hypothetical widow's grief be of such an overweening and unconsolable variety as to prevent her ever doing anything except feed it. It is a reduction of the widow's history to the conditions prescribed by a bookish muse, a conversion of story into text; and Wordsworth, after the manner of Luther, will insist that the story is of, but not in, the text.

The final book passage to be discussed here is the most subtle and far-reaching: it can serve as a reunification of our concern for the visible text with the more general problem of the visible world in *The Prelude*. And, since it occurs in the "Retrospect" as a reflection on the poet's first sojourn in London, it can also tie the argument back to the episode with which we began this chapter, the blind beggar incident in book 7. Wordsworth again, as in book 7, is talking about the experience of looking at a panorama until the eye defeats itself and becomes a "second-sight procession" of objects.

> The curious traveler, who, from open day,
> Hath passed with torches into some huge cave,
> The grotto of Antiparos, or the Den
> In old time haunted by that Danish Witch,
> Yordas; he looks around and sees the vault
> Widening on all sides; sees, or thinks he sees,
> Erelong, the massy roof above his head,
> That instantly unsettles and recedes,—
> Substance and shadow, light and darkness, all
> Commingled, making up a canopy
> Of shapes and forms and tendencies to shape
> That shift and vanish, change and interchange
> Like spectres,—ferment silent and sublime!
> That after a short space works less and less,
> Till, every effort, every motion gone,
> The scene before him stands in perfect view
> Exposed, and lifeless as a written book!—
> But let him pause awhile, and look again,
> And a new quickening shall succeed, at first
> Beginning timidly, then creeping fast,
> Till the whole cave, so late a senseless mass,
> Busies the eye with images and forms
> Boldly assembled,—here is shadowed forth

From the projections, wrinkles, cavities,
A variegated landscape,—there the shape
Of some gigantic warrior clad in mail,
The ghostly semblance of a hooded monk,
Veiled nun, or pilgrim resting on his staff:
Strange congregation! yet not slow to meet
Eyes that perceive through minds that can inspire.

                                                    (8. 560–589)

This, much like Bunyan's illusion that the church spire was falling on him, is a more or less common visual occurrence raised to the level of the numinous. The eye observing the walls of the cave passes through a kind of "centre of indifference," exhausting itself through its automatic attempts to focus until it does indeed perceive the "perfect view / Exposed, and lifeless as a written book." Perfect, we might add, in almost the same sense Wordsworth envisions the perfection of his auditor Coleridge at the end of *The Prelude*: unchanging and hence dead. Once through this experiential center, however, the second-sight procession of visual images presents itself, not as an imposition of the mind on reality but rather as a real interaction. The cave "busies the eye" and, in busying the eye rather than fixing it, allows latitude for the inspiring mind to impregnate and be impregnated by the structure of outward things. This is a microscopic version, in fact, of the suspension of the will to creation which will be seen to play such a crucial part in the Wordsworthian imaginative synthesis. For what Wordsworth had earlier called a "wilfulness of fancy and conceit"—the will, literally, to excite the mind through the agency of the sublime imagination—is here suspended. And the magic show of ghostly figures, far from being daemonic, comes upon the mind and the eye as a free and unexpected gift. In the same way, the "Retrospect" of book 8 and *The Prelude* as a whole may be seen as a written book studiously avoiding imaginative finality in order to prepare itself for the gift of imaginative wholeness which is its completion. In other words, what we have before described as *The Prelude*'s "straining for the condition of printed book" is equally a straining away from that condition—Wordsworth never being quite ready to stop revising and commit the book to the press—since it finally repudiates the visuality of the printed book and opts for an aural, antivisual, confessional mode of existence.

An enlightening countertype to Wordsworth's use of the book as symbol is found in Blake's *Milton*—in many ways Blake's own prelude to the final articulation of his myth in *Jerusalem*. Blake, fundamentally a more "traditional" moralist and stylist than Wordsworth, envisions at the end of *Milton* the descent of Milton's emanation Ololon, her imaginative reunion with Milton-Blake, and the subsequent apparition of the "true" Jesus of Blake's revolutionary imagination:

> . . . with one accord the Starry Eight became
> One Man Jesus the Saviour. wonderful! round his limbs
> The Clouds of Ololon folded as a Garment dipped in blood
> Written within & without in woven letters: & the Writing
> Is the Divine Revelation in the Litteral expression:
> A Garment of War, I heard it named the Woof of Six Thousand
>   Years.
>
> (plate 42, 10–15)

The Garment of Ololon, unmistakably, becomes here the literal expression which is the book, *Milton* itself; that is, the poem, on one level, is an attempt to transform the physical prop into the poetry which it contains and to challenge Luther's answer to the question, "Where is the Book?" Blake, as visual allegorist, painter, and above all, engraver of his own poetry, has a much more sympathetic—or at least, more ambiguous—attitude toward the sublime than does his great contemporary. We shall return to this important distinction between the two pioneers of English Romanticism in the next chapter, when we examine Wordsworth's formation of a distinctive language and linguistic mythology of human continuity.

But at this point it seems appropriate to examine, over the expanse of the whole *Prelude*, Wordsworth's growth in understanding of and control over the visual.

In tracing the history of the eye in Wordsworth's imaginative growth, we will actually be describing two movements of thought, one narrat*ed*, one narrat*ive*. For if *The Prelude* as exemplary history is the story of how Wordsworth was once freed from enslavement to the daemonic and visual, *The Prelude* as confession is a present-tense imitation, a single long metaphor for that very process of enslavement and release. *The Prelude*, that is, is in a profound way an image of its own theme, self-referential in the way only the most radical acts of creation can be. Such a reading of the poem is quite in accordance with Wordsworth's own distinction between the confessional "now" and the recorded "then"—if only we remember that it is the then which is the only available, necessary *image* of the liberated now:

> A tranquillising spirit presses now
> On my corporeal frame, so wide appears
> The vacancy between me and those days
> Which yet have such self-presence in my mind,
> That, musing on them, often do I seem
> Two consciousnesses, conscious of myself
> And of some other Being.
>
> (2. 27–33)

We will be looking, then, for both a series to describe the progressive enslavement of the imagination to the power of the "tyrant eye" and a series to describe the present, redeemed imagination's transcendence of that power for a higher kind of vision. And furthermore, since both these series finally refer to a single exemplary person (and since *The Prelude* is in every sense "one" poem), we shall look for a point of transcendence, or what the Christian imagination would call an access of grace, in which the two consciousnesses become in some sense one. This involves, in all, seven passages. I begin with the past-tense series describing the enslavement of the eye, since its content is the basic, raw material of Wordsworth's experience in *The Prelude*.

The first stage of the series has already been implied: it is roughly traceable, on Wordsworth's own authority, to his sojourn at Cambridge and the beginnings of a bookish or traditional eighteenth-century attitude toward nature. It is a time of waning imagination and increasing vacillation of the creative will:

> It hath been told, that when the first delight
> That flashed upon me from this novel show

Had failed, the mind returned into herself;
Yet true it is, that I had made a change
In climate, and my nature's outward coat
Changed also slowly and insensibly.
Full oft the quiet and exalted thoughts
Of loneliness gave way to empty noise
And superficial pastimes; now and then
Forced labour, and more frequently forced hopes;
And, worst of all, a treasonable growth
Of indecisive judgments, that impaired
And shook the mind's simplicity.

(3. 205–216)

In spite of the young student's joyous discovery of the majesty of
English literary history—most pleasantly realized in the picture of
the young Wordsworth getting slightly tipsy drinking to the
memory of Milton—something is beginning to go wrong here,
something not wholly corrected by his visit back home over
"Summer Vacation" (book 4).

The pivotal point in this series, however, is book 5, "Books";
and referring back once more to what we have said about Wordsworth's acute sense of the book as minimum visibility, I think we
can see this section of *The Prelude* as being very much about its
announced subject, in spite of frequent protestations about its
rambling character. The most striking segment of book 5, of course,
is the dream with which it opens. This passage has been subjected
to exhaustive examination by Geoffrey Hartman. According to him,

> Wordsworth's dream transcends the subject it is supposed to
> illustrate. The perishability of books contrasted with the imperishable
> character of nature (the book of God) is at most its occasional
> cause. Read in the context of *The Prelude* as a whole, rather than
> in the frame of its own preface and epilogue, it shows its kinship
> with experiences by which imagination reveals its distinctness from
> nature.[12]

For Hartman, that is, the implications of the dream are fundamentally benign: it represents one of the poet's few confrontations

12. Hartman, *Wordsworth's Poetry*, p. 228.

with the autonomous, antinatural power of his imagination and
therefore the permanent possibility of apocalypse as a constant
undertheme of the poem.

But to say that the dream transcends the subject of books runs
counter to one of the main assumptions of this study: that the
printed book has a crucial imaginative importance for Wordsworth's
mature poetry. And indeed the subject, "books," is intimately involved with the immediate narrative context of the dream. That
context is Wordsworth's description of the perishability of imagination's repositories—books, paintings, temples—and his closest approach to a central theme of later Romantic poetry:

> But all the meditations of mankind,
> Yea, all the adamantine holds of truth
> By reason built, or passion, which itself
> Is highest reason in a soul sublime;
> The consecrated works of Bard and Sage,
> Sensuous or intellectual, wrought by men,
> Twin labourers and heirs of the same hopes;
> Where would they be? Oh! why hath not the Mind
> Some element to stamp her image on
> In nature somewhat nearer to her own?
> Why, gifted with such powers to send abroad
> Her spirit, must it lodge in shrines so frail?
>
> (5. 38–49)

Implicitly, this is a vision of the end of the world, inextricably
intertwined with a sense of the disparity between imagination and
the products of imagination—an exaggerated summary of the
"treasonable growth / Of indecisive judgments" we had seen growing in book 3. It also represents the real and immediate content of
the dream that is to follow; the poet is here bracing himself to
confront the dream, which is obviously one of his most unsettling
experiences. But this is not the only strategy of containment and
purification involved in presenting the dream. We must take note
of the curious chinese-box narrative in which the dream itself is set:

> One day, when from my lips a like complaint
> Had fallen in presence of a studious friend,
> He with a smile made answer, that in truth
> 'Twas going far to seek disquietude;

But on the front of his reproof confessed
That he himself had oftentimes given way
To kindred hauntings. Whereupon I told,
That once in the stillness of a summer's noon,
While I was seated in a rocky cave
By the sea-side, perusing, so it chanced,
The famous history of the errant knight
Recorded by Cervantes, these same thoughts
Beset me, and to height unusual rose,
While listlessly I sate, and, having closed
The book, had turned my eyes toward the wide sea.

(5. 50–64)

The present Wordsworth relates how an earlier Wordsworth related how an earlier Wordsworth had the dream. It is an extremely careful placement of the experience in the memorial time of the book, very like that reduction of lyricism to print we have seen operating at other points in *The Prelude*. The reason is obvious, for the dream is, indeed, "a *spot* of eternity,"[13] a usurpation of the imagination which would be dangerous if it were any closer to everyday consciousness. But whether it is a usurpation of the naturalistic imagination is doubtful. The progress of the dream is fairly straightforward: the dreamer, on a desert plain, encounters an Arab on a camel who reminds him of Don Quixote and who is carrying a stone and a bright shell. The Arab explains that the stone is "Euclid's Elements" and that the shell is a book of apocalyptic poetry:

An Ode, in passion uttered, which foretold
Destruction to the children of the earth
By deluge, now at hand.

(5. 96–98)

The Arab is going to bury these two "books" against the destruction foretold. The dreamer wishes to accompany him, but the Arab flees, and as he flees, the dreamer, looking behind him, sees the gathering waters of catastrophe:

He left me: I called after him aloud;
He heeded not; but, with his twofold charge

13. Ibid., p. 227.

Still in his grasp, before me, full in view,
Went hurrying o'er the illimitable waste,
With the fleet waters of a drowning world
In chase of him; whereat I waked in terror,
And saw the sea before me, and the book,
In which I had been reading, at my side.

(5. 133–140)

The final lines are another strategy of placement, of immediate contextualization, and they present a brilliant reversal of the dream image: the pursuing sea now before the dreamer, the obsessive and threatened book now resting at his side.

This reversal, furthermore, as an important change in the perspective of the dream, should weigh heavily in any attempt to interpret the dream. What does the sea in the dream represent, and how does it differ from the sea outside the dream, the sea Wordsworth confronts upon waking? Hartman feels that the sea in the dream is "Wordsworth's recognition of a power in him (imagination) which implies and even prophesies nature's death."[14] I think, however, we shall do better with the more straightforward interpretation of R. A. Foakes that "the sea here represents that necessary involvement in the life of the world from which it is impossible to preserve inviolate truth and poetry."[15] For the sea in this dream is not the apocalyptic "might of waters" so frequent in Wordsworth's poetry but rather a symbol of another order altogether. It is not an image of sound at all, in fact, but a hard, bright visual image:

over half the wilderness diffused,
A bed of glittering light. . . .

(128–129)

And this is perhaps the most remarkable thing about the whole dream: that, instinctively or deliberately, Wordsworth makes it a daemonic reduction of his most powerful symbol of imaginative life. I am suggesting, to be precise, that the sea in the dream represents the destructive power of the phenomenal world—and that power apprehended *under the aspect of the visual*. The inter-

14. Ibid., p. 230.
15. R. A. Foakes, *The Romantic Assertion* (London, 1958), p. 72.

pretation of the sea as imagination involves a contradiction, since the book of apocalyptic poetry is also certainly an imagination symbol, and neither dream- nor poetic-logic seems to countenance the kind of doubling such an interpretation suggests. The proper relationship between the dream book and the dream sea, however, is an important one. For, in perfect conformity with the logic of dreams, the prophetic ode uttered by the shell not only foretells but actually generates the destructive deluge: the apocalyptic impulse (here as elsewhere under the sign of the book, the visual, and the sublime) generates the sort of radical and daemonic split between the imagination and the phenomenal world which insures an "end of the world" situation and the consequent annihilation of all the products of human imagination. The dream is a parable of the poet's confrontation with the world-destructive power of the imagination. And this confrontation is dramatized through techniques of visuality-as-daemonic and of self-reductive allegory. For the imagination Wordsworth here fears to confront is exactly the visual, sublime imagination implied by the dream book itself—and the unifying act of the dream is not the rising of the waters but the reading of the book, which, in the speaker's waking context, contains the stuff of the dream, which generates the climactic moment of the dream itself, and which finally is brought back into manageable dimensions in the conclusion to the episode.

Wordsworth says, finally, that the quixotic Arab became a figure of great poignance for him:

> A gentle dweller in the desert, crazed
> By love and feeling, and internal thought
> Protracted among endless solitudes;
> Have shaped him wandering upon this quest!
> Nor have I pitied him; but rather felt
> Reverence was due to a being thus employed;
> And thought that, in the blind and awful lair
> Of such a madness, reason did lie couched.

(5. 145–152)

In fact, looking for the most general plot of the dream, we might see it as the curve of Wordsworth's attempt to identify with the Arab and his inevitable separation from that exotic self-projection. The Arab obviously represents the visual-daemonic element we have been discussing for two chapters now: indeed, he is the most obsessive character of Wordsworth's mature poetry (I except here the characters from "The White Doe of Rylstone"). And it is an essential part of the dream's meaning that Wordsworth cannot fully become his projection. Finally the apocalyptic waters are seen as being in pursuit of him, the Arab, but Wordsworth the dreamer shows surprisingly little concern for his own position vis-à-vis the deluge—an emblem of health that prepares for the final vision of the dreamer awakened and staring at the real waters before him.

Attempting now to reintegrate the dream passage into our putative series of transformations of the eye, we can see it pretty clearly as an increase of the power of the tyrant eye over the imagination's freedom and as an indication of Wordsworth's own growing awareness of the losses involved in the life of vision. The young poet is more and more torn between an orthodox eighteenth-century urge to participate in the poetry of the eye and a sense of betrayal of his own powers, of guilt at the terms involved in such poetry.

The passage represents an even more fascinating stage in Wordsworth's history, however, if one applies to it certain findings of twentieth-century psychoanalysis. Theodor Reik, in *The Compulsion to Confess*, discusses the dream mechanism in terms which significantly qualify Freud's pronouncements upon that subject. For Reik, while the content of the dream may represent uncensored wish fulfillment, the narrative form of the dream—what he calls the "dream-work"—may be taken to represent a confession of those wishes, that is, a self-generated acknowledgment of guilt at the heart of the dream itself.[16] In this way, the dream of the Arab, which certainly represents Wordsworth's growing enslavement to the visual and the daemonic, is nevertheless presented in the form of an allegory—that very form which he elsewhere eschews so vigorously and which is the most blatant manifestation of the visual and the daemonic as literary resources. So that one may say of the dream of the Arab that, while manifesting the deteriorating power of the young Wordsworth's imagination, it manifests itself in such a self-criticizing form as to hold out a subtle hope for

16. Theodor Reik, *The Compulsion to Confess* (New York, 1966), p. 227.

release from psychic bondage. It is a hope which the conclusion of the episode, the waking to the natural sea and to continuity, certainly substantiates.

The third passage in our series is from book 9, "Residence in France." The France books of *The Prelude* are a curious anomaly, for in any study of *The Prelude* as confession or poetic autobiography, they are bound to loom large in consideration of what was, for Wordsworth, the major conscious crisis of his life. But the books themselves—9, 10, and 11—have a singular air of exhaustion about them, as if written at a much lower state of agitation than anything else in the poem. It is a striking example of dichotomy between explicit and inner form in narrative; like Falstaff's Mistress Quickly, one does not know where to have them.

The split, of course, is symptomatic of English Romantic poetry. For most of the English Romantics, as for Wordsworth, England's intervention in the course of the French Revolution at the urging of Pitt and the Revolution's degeneration into the Terror represented a national and personal trauma. And the creations directly traceable to this trauma—Blake's Orc cycle, Coleridge's "Fears in Solitude," and Shelley's *Prometheus Unbound*—are among the archetypes of the Romantic experience. But explicit poetic confrontations with the historical fact itself are both scarce and, when found, nearly always imaginative failures.

In terms of our history of the eye, perhaps the most important passage from the France section is the famous incident that occurred during one of Wordsworth's ambulatory conversations with the revolutionary Beaupuis:

> Hatred of absolute rule, where will of one
> Is law for all, and of that barren pride
> In them who, by immunities unjust,
> Between the sovereign and the people stand,
> His helper and not theirs, laid stronger hold
> Daily upon me, mixed with pity too
> And love; for where hope is, there love will be
> For the abject multitude. And when we chanced
> One day to meet a hunger-bitten girl,
> Who crept along fitting her languid gait
> Unto a heifer's motion, by a cord
> Tied to her arm, and picking thus from the lane

Its sustenance, while the girl with pallid hands
Was busy knitting in a heartless mood
Of solitude, and at the sight my friend
In agitation said, "Tis against *that*
That we are fighting," I with him believed
That a benignant spirit was abroad
Which might not be withstood, that poverty
Abject as this would in a little time
Be found no more, that we should see the earth
Unthwarted in her wish to recompense
The meek, the lowly, patient child of toil.

(9. 502–524)

It is a brilliant passage, since the excitement and nobility of the visionary politics with which it concludes—more than a little reminiscent of the tone of the Fourth Vergilian Eclogue—are firmly qualified by the vision which inspires them. The peasant girl is another of those rural solitaries who people Wordsworth's major poetry and are such an important part of the fabric of his vision. But in this case the final word on the image is given by Beaupuis— " 'Tis against *that* / That we are fighting"—and the italicized *that* perfectly conveys the mixture of scorn and humanitarianism implicit in the revolutionary's attitude. To fight against *that* is to fight not only against the social cause of the girl's misery but in some degree against the vision itself—to transform it into an allegorical, i.e., hortatory, image which can be solved or alleviated only by being banished. It is an attitude which, besides being revolutionary, is also very close to the myth of conventional pastoral; and as we shall see in the next chapter, Wordsworth's final attitude toward traditional pastoral is one of rejection.[17]

In this passage, then, Wordsworth's subjection to the power of the untransfigured eye has reached a condition much like that of the humanitarian revolutionary Marmaduke with whom we began this chapter: a dead-level confusion which inevitably thwarts itself, since it cannot transcend the world of the eye for any broader form, and which effectively eliminates the oppressed with the oppression and stifles imagination with its own materials. Words-

17. It is interesting in this connection that Marxism itself contains a strong pastoral sensibility in its vision of proletarian revolution.

worth later writes of his disillusionment with the course of the Revolution and subsequent abandonment of humanitarian goals:

> I speak in recollection of a time
> When the bodily eye, in every stage of life
> The most despotic of our senses, gained
> Such strength in *me* as often held my mind
> In absolute dominion.
>
> . . . .
> I roamed from hill to hill, from rock to rock,
> Still craving combinations of new forms,
> New pleasure, wider empire for the sight,
> Proud of her own endowments, and rejoiced
> To lay the inner faculties asleep.
>
> (12. 127–131, 143–147)

But it would be a mistake to see this crisis simply as a revulsion against his revolutionary fervor: for his espousal and rejection of the Revolution are part of one movement and share the common ground of a *hyper*visual imaginative despair.

This brings us to the point of Wordsworth's recovery, around 1798, through the spiritual ministrations of Dorothy and Coleridge, and brings us equally to the last books and the first book of *The Prelude*, since the end of the poem is a return to the poetic present of the opening lines and a vindication of their exuberant optimism. It also brings us to the second series of eye passages we set ourselves to describe, those which refer not to the history of Wordsworth's developing vision but to the characteristic process of that vision in its reformed state. Here we may move somewhat more quickly than before, since the general morphology of that process has already been described from a great number of perspectives. In its starkest form, as seen in the Blind Beggar passage from book 7, it is a three-part progress:

Fixation of the eye on the object in its surface or daemonic aspects, leading to a

Darkening of the eye, and consequent nonvisual (primarily aural) admonishment by the inner powers of imagination, issuing in a

Transformed vision of the object, not as image, but as integral part, of the imaginative salvation of the personality.

We can readily identify three passages in *The Prelude* which appear, in the extended narrative time of the whole poem, to correspond to these stages. The first, of course, is the celebrated "false dawn" of *Prelude* 1, roughly the first half of the book, describing Wordsworth's failure to celebrate the present joy of his release from the city into the country. A great deal has been written about the opening of *The Prelude*; it probably remains, no matter how many readings we give the whole poem, the single most fascinating section of the work. In one of the most influential essays on book 1, M. H. Abrams identifies the "correspondent breeze" of 1. 35, as a major symbol not only of Wordsworth's career but of the entire Romantic movement.[18] Abrams's essay is the best one we have on the relations between Romanticism and radical Protestant traditions of thought—especially under the aspect of the Augustinian influence. But however important the correspondent breeze is in the history of the period, in *Prelude* 1 it is inevitably linked to an imaginative failure by the poet, his inability to sustain the powerful lyric confidence with which he begins. Richard Stang, in a valuable essay on the same passage, indicates why the breeze is an image of defeat:

> There is a very real reason why the breeze, which seems like a heavenly visitant, does not act as the quickening wind, the breath of the spirit. Such an impulse cannot come from without. The whole logic of the poem and the position Wordsworth is developing at this point in his career demands that it be an inner movement of his own spirit, *i.e.*, the stream which is his total past, and that it be unconscious.[19]

"Unconscious" is perhaps an inappropriate word to describe the state of mind Wordsworth is evolving in *The Prelude* for his imaginative health. It is nevertheless true that the failure of the opening of *The Prelude* is profoundly involved with an act of overweening, conscious will on the part of the poet, a desire to

18. M. H. Abrams, "The Correspondent Breeze: A Romantic Metaphor," in M. H. Abrams, ed., *English Romantic Poets: Modern Essays in Criticism.*
19. Richard Stang, "The False Dawn: A Study of the Opening of Wordsworth's *Prelude*," *ELH* 33 (1966): 61.

convert the present prospect into immediate lyrical energy and, thus, a fixation of the eye. As Wordsworth describes his rambling in the countryside:

> Content and not unwilling now to give
> A respite to this passion, I paced on
> With brisk and eager steps; and came, at length,
> To a green shady place, where down I sate
> Beneath a tree, slackening my thoughts by choice,
> And settling into gentler happiness.
> 'Twas autumn, and a clear and placid day,
> With warmth, as much as needed, from a sun
> Two hours declined towards the west; a day
> With silver clouds, and sunshine on the grass,
> And in the sheltered and the sheltering grove
> A perfect stillness. Many were the thoughts
> Encouraged and dismissed, till choice was made
> Of a known Vale, whither my feet should turn,
> Nor rest till they had reached the very door
> Of the one cottage methought I saw.
> No picture of mere memory ever looked
> So fair. . . .
>
> (1. 59–76)

The last lines, with their implied abandonment of the power of memory and consequent reliance on present sight for inspiration, are unmistakably bad auspices for what is to follow. This is a Wordsworth attempting to turn nature into sacrament—visible outward sign of grace. We can see the first hundred lines of *Prelude* 1 as an inversion of the sort of nature poetry which finds its finest expression in Marvell's "The Garden" or *Upon Appleton House*. The reason it is doomed to failure in terms of Wordsworth's characteristic vision, furthermore, is an index of the distance between the conservative Puritanism which informs Marvell's vision and the radical Protestantism which informs Wordsworth's. The sacramental stance which leads Wordsworth to declare,

> Poetic numbers came
> Spontaneously to clothe in priestly robe
> A renovated spirit singled out,
> Such hope was mine, for holy services.
>
> (1. 51–54)

is, as we have pointed out before, a kind of daemonism. And the extent of its daemonic force is made clearer later in book 1 when Wordsworth, under the spell of his present joy, projects a series of subjects for his epic, all of whom are famous and bloody conquerors, prime avatars of the daemonic, fixated will to domination.

So much, then, for the stage of the fixating of the eye. The middle stage of the process occurs in a brilliant passage beginning book 7—the center of the 1850 poem. Wordsworth is noting the fact that for too long the promised work has lain unattended:

> Through the whole summer have I been at rest,
> Partly from voluntary holiday,
> And part through outward hindrance. But I heard,
> After the hour of sunset yester-even,
> Sitting within doors between light and dark,
> A choir of redbreasts gathered somewhere near
> My threshold,—minstrels from the distant woods
> Sent in on Winter's service, to announce,
> With preparation artful and benign,
> That the rough lord had left the surly North
> On his accustomed journey. The delight,
> Due to this timely notice, unawares
> Smote me, and, listening, I in whispers said,
> "Ye heartsome Choristers, ye and I will be
> Associates, and, unscared by blustering winds,
> Will chant together." Thereafter, as the shades
> Of twilight deepened, going forth, I spied
> A glow-worm underneath a dusky plume
> Or canopy of yet unwithered fern,
> Clear-shining, like a hermit's taper seen
> Through a thick forest. Silence touched me here
> No less than sound had done before; the child
> Of summer, lingering, shining, by herself,
> The voiceless worm on the unfrequented hills,
> Seemed sent on the same errand with the choir
> Of Winter that had warbled at my door,
> And the whole year breathed tenderness and love.

(7. 16–42)

This, a deliberate reprise of the "false dawn" of *The Prelude*'s opening, is a magnificent version of the darkening of the eye—not only the personal eye of the poet but the eye also of day and indeed of the whole year, since winter is setting in. It startlingly converts the images of book 1 into sounds: birdsong and the primal sound, silence itself. The effect is a purification and "outering" of the correspondent breeze; for while in book 1 it is the interior breeze which turns into a tempest vexing its own creation, here it is the external gust of winter which brings turbulence and which leads to the poet's renewed dedication to his task:

> The last night's genial feeling overflowed
> Upon this morning, and my favourite grove,
> Tossing in sunshine its dark boughs aloft,
> As if to make the strong wind visible,
> Makes in me agitations like its own,
> A spirit friendly to the Poet's task,
> Which we will now resume with lively hope,
> Nor checked by aught of tamer argument
> That lies before us, needful to be told.
>
> (7. 43-51)

The breeze comes in a state of suspension of the will rather than an access of willed energy—in fact, as a gift of grace.

But the darkening of the eye is not the whole Wordsworthian process of vision. There is also a final stage at which the sense of sight is transformed by the darkening and becomes a "true" poetic fact. The effect is that described by a confessant such as the eighteenth-century Quaker Elizabeth Webb, the conversion of a previously daemonic nature into something very different through the act of confession:

> And I remember after I had made public confession to the goodness of God, my soul was as if it had been in another world: it was so enlightened and enlivened by the divine love, that I was in love with the whole creation of God. . . . So everything began to preach to me; the very fragrant herbs, and beautiful, innocent flowers had a speaking voice in them to my soul, and things seemed to have another relish with them than before.[20]

20. In Thomas Chalk, ed., *Autobiographical Narratives of the Convincement and Other Religious Experience of Samuel Crisp, Elizabeth Webb, Evan Bevan, Margaret Lucas, and Frederick Smith* (London, 1848), pp. 68–69.

Wordsworth is a considerably more tough-minded observer of
the phenomenal world than Mistress Webb or most Quaker and
Methodist religionists, but we can see the same basic shape of
experience in a passage like the first spot of time of book 12.

The spots of time, of course, raise perhaps the single most vexed
question in *Prelude* criticism, and their rich and elusive suggestive-
ness may never—and never need—be satisfactorily explicated. Their
first appearance, in book 12, is one of Wordsworth's most characteristic articulations of interaction between mind and world:

> There are in our existence spots of time,
> That with distinct pre-eminence retain
> A renovating virtue, whence depressed
> By false opinion and contentious thought,
> Or aught of heavier or more deadly weight,
> In trivial occupations, and the round
> Of ordinary intercourse, our minds
> Are nourished and invisibly repaired;
> A virtue, by which pleasure is enhanced,
> That penetrates, enables us to mount,
> When high, more high, and lifts us up when fallen.
> This efficacious spirit chiefly lurks
> Among those passages of life that give
> Profoundest knowledge to what point, and how,
> The mind is lord and master—outward sense
> The obedient servant of her will.
>
> (12. 208–223)

The 1805 version (book 11) has for the last three lines:

> We have had deepest feeling that the mind
> Is lord and master, and that outward sense
> Is but the obedient servant of her will.

And however much the more ambiguous construction of 1850 may
be a result of Wordsworth's imaginative decline, I think it is also
undeniably more appropriate to what follows. For the spots of time
represent, in the series we have been describing, the return of the
soul from the darkening of the eye to a new and fruitful relationship with the world of sight. The spots of time are a recovery,
not only in the narrat*ed* sequence of Wordsworth's enslavement

to the tyrant eye, but also in the narrative sequence (of fixation-darkening-reillumination) we have been tracing. The phrase "spot of time" is in fact a deliberate version of the kind of verbal mis-understanding of problems of time that Ludwig Wittgenstein liked to call a "muddle," imposing a spatial, visual, scenic definition on a dimension of experience which is fundamentally devoid of all three elements. But, to exploit for the moment the possibilities of typography, it is important for us to understand that these are not *spots* of time as much as they are spots of *time*. That is, their renovating virtue proceeds from the fact that they are visual mani-festations seen precisely under the sign of the temporal, as units of continuity, rather than under the sign of the visual. They reproduce the difference we noted in Wordsworth's two words for the blind beggar in London: not fixed (i.e., daemonic, precarious surface disruptions) but steadfast (the "fixed" as viewed primarily in a time continuum). In the first spot of time, for example, Wordsworth tells how as a boy he became lost, and in his attempts to get home:

Came to a bottom, where in former times
A murderer had been hung in iron chains.
The gibbet-mast had mouldered down, the bones
And iron case were gone; but on the turf,
Hard by, soon after that fell deed was wrought,
Some unknown hand had carved the murderer's name.
The monumental letters were inscribed
In times long past; but still, from year to year,
By superstitition of the neighborhood,
The grass is cleared away, and to this hour
The characters are fresh and visible:
A casual glance had shown them, and I fled,
Faltering and faint, and ignorant of the road:
Then, reascending the bare common, saw
A naked pool that lay beneath the hills,
The beacon on the summit, and, more near,
A girl, who bore a pitcher on her head,
And seemed with difficult steps to force her way
Against the blowing wind. It was, in truth,
An ordinary sight; but I should need
Colours and words that are unknown to man,
To paint the visionary dreariness
Which, while I looked all round for my lost guide,

Invested moorland waste, and naked pool,
The beacon drowning the lone eminence,
The female and her garments vexed and tossed
By the strong wind. When, in the blessed hours
Of early love, the loved one at my side,
I roamed, in daily presence of this scene,
Upon the naked pool and dreary crags,
And on the melancholy beacon fell
A spirit of pleasure and youth's golden gleam;
And think ye not with radiance more sublime
For these remembrances, and for the power
They had left behind? So feeling comes in aid
Of feeling, and diversity of strength
Attends us, if but once we have been strong.

(12. 235–271)

It is necessary to quote this very great passage at length, in order to observe all the strains of imagery and thought which find release and renewal in it. The monumental letters, kept fresh through time by the strong power of local superstition, represent a reprise and transformation of the minimum visibility of the beggar's label and of writing itself. And the peasant girl, struggling against the wind, is almost certainly a visionary, antidaemonic reprise of the French peasant Wordsworth had encountered with Beaupuis. Both are resolutely antiallegorical and carefully placed in a context of permanence which works subtly against the linear movement implicit in the passage.

Janet Spens has written a highly valuable commentary on this spot of time in her study of *The Faerie Queene*, noting that a possible source for the image of the girl with the pitcher is Spenser's figure of Corceca, or Superstitution, encountered by Una in *FQ* 1. 3. 3–12, but that Wordsworth's treatment of the figure is a nearly complete inversion of the allegorical method.[21] And when Wordsworth notes that later, in a completely different mood (being "found" in love rather than lost from his father), he revisited the same scene and drew a special imaginative strength from it, he is asserting finally that the scene, and implicitly all the visual world, is benign when encountered as an avatar of time and of the con-

21. Janet Spens, *Spenser's Faerie Queene* (London, 1934), pp. 57–59.

tinuity of the integrated self. In other words, the world of evidences is safe for the regenerated man precisely because he has no need of them as evidences. It is notable that he repeats all the elements of the scene twice, as if insisting on their visual permanence within his reintegrated consciousness—except, of course, for the perishable and central figure of the solitary peasant girl. But the girl's very omission in the second rehearsal of the scene is an assertion of her continued presence as a spot of *time*: much as the song of the Solitary Reaper continues, though finished, in the song of the retrospective narrator.

These, then, are the two series in the history of the eye which we set out to trace. The seventh passage is the point of transcendence, of the merging of the two series in a single unitary vision, the moment at which the poem redeems its beginning and takes full possession of its implicit form. It is the passage describing the ascent of Mount Snowdon in book 14. But to discuss it is also to discuss the second phrase of the formula I have drawn for *The Prelude* as confession: remembered vision, disciplined and unified by narrative speech. And to touch on this matter is also to confront, finally, the inmost confessional form of the work, its transfiguration of language into mythology, of memorial narrative into agency of salvation.

CHAPTER FOUR

EDENIC WORDS

Hence in a season of calm weather
Though inland far we be,
Our Souls have sight of that immortal sea
Which brought us hither,
Can in a moment travel thither,
And see the Children sport upon the shore,
And hear the mighty waters rolling evermore.

Wordsworth, *Ode: Intimations of Immortality from Recollections of Early Childhood*

We hear the name, and we all confess that we desire the things; for we are not delighted with the mere sound. For when a Greek hears it in Latin, he is not delighted, not knowing what is spoken; but we Latins are delighted, as would he too, if he heard it in Greek; because the thing itself is neither Greek nor Latin, which Greeks and Latins, and men of all other tongues, long for so earnestly. . . . And this could not be, unless the thing itself whereof it is the name were retained in their memory.

Augustine, *Confessions*

We have been tracing the history of Wordsworth's imagination as he reconstitutes that history in *The Prelude*. In the last chapter we discussed the basic plot of the poet's growth as his progressive enslavement to, and liberation from, an obsessively visual, allegorical, daemonic relationship to Nature—and therefore, of course, to his own experiences. This plot of liberation, furthermore, provided the liberated Wordsworth, the teller of his own tale, with a central, generative structure (fixation—blank desertion—release into vision) for confronting the worlds without and within him. Any confession tends to become a literal re-creation both of the confessant's self and of the world he inhabits. And Wordsworth's confession, with profound intuition of its own basic form, becomes a re-creation very like that of Genesis 1, where the temporal order of God's constitution of the universe is also the rational order of the hierarchy of created things.

As we have seen, the point of transcendence in *The Prelude* is the Mount Snowdon episode in book 14. It is at this point that the two processes of liberation we have been tracing—historical and structural—unite in a final moment of exemplary vision, a final attainment of the language of poetic maturity. Wordsworth himself, very clearly, intends the episode to have just such summarizing power. Introducing it, in the conclusion to book 13, he reflects upon Coleridge's praise of his first poetic efforts (a passage we have discussed in the first chapter):

> Call we this
> A partial judgment—and yet why? for *then*
> We were as strangers; and I may not speak
> Thus wrongfully of verse, however rude,
> Which on thy young imagination, trained
> In the great City, broke like light from far.
> Moreover, each man's Mind is to herself
> Witness and judge; and I remember well
> That in life's every-day appearances
> I seemed about this time to gain clear sight
> Of a new world—a world, too, that was fit
> To be transmitted, and to other eyes

Made visible; as ruled by those fixed laws
Whence spiritual dignity originates,
Which do both give it being and maintain
A balance, an ennobling interchange
Of action from without and from within;
The excellence, pure function, and best power
Both of the objects seen, and eye that sees.

(13. 360–378)

All of the elements of mediation and unification we have been discussing are present in this passage and present in a climactic articulation and interrelationship which is surely intended to set the stage for the great proof which is Snowdon. The mediating presence of Coleridge as auditor, at the beginning of the passage, prevents Wordsworth from false humility about the first fruits of his imagination. And this mediated confrontation with his own power leads him to the sense of his Mind as "witness and judge" (confessant) of his relationship to the new world of his imaginatively transfigured sight. That world is described as the source of "spiritual dignity"—what we have called imaginative maturity—and as a world whose "balance" and "ennobling interchange" of inner and outer being is a dismissal of the fragmentary and daemonic for the continuous and unitary. This new world, furthermore, is still regarded by the poet under its aspect of confessional speech to Coleridge: the prime value of the world is not its private radiance to Wordsworth but the fact that it is "fit to be transmitted, and to other eyes made visible."

And most importantly, the vision of the mature Wordsworth is articulated specifically in terms of the disciplining and liberation of the eye:

The excellence, pure function, and best power
Both of the objects seen, and eye that sees.

But here Wordsworth is not simply describing his clear sight of a new world, as he is midway through the passage, but in fact realizing that world in the language of the poem itself. For the last line, devoid of imagery and hardly distinguishable in its rhythm from prose, nevertheless imitates in its syntax precisely the ennobling interchange of inner and outer upon which Wordsworth's faith is based. For "objects" and "eye"—not symbols but the substance of "nature" and "consciousness"—are made equivalent as genitives appertaining to the unifying word "power"; and even more subtly, they are forced into grammatical interchange with each other in their common modification by a form of the word "see." For, as the passage has been talking about unification at some length, "seen" and "sees" become a concrete, syntactic example of that unity of object and subject: what might be called an ideological rhyme, unifying under the infinitive act "to see" both the passive and active voice-markers -*n* and -*s*.

This passage, I am suggesting, is an almost symphonic reprise of the great themes of *The Prelude*, preparing for the final movement which is the vision of Snowdon. The vision itself, however, begins almost anecdotally, with a deliberate reduction of the prophetic energy of its overture:

> In one of these excursions (may they ne'er
> Fade from remembrance!) through the Northern tracts
> Of Cambria ranging with a youthful friend,
> I left Bethgelert's huts at couching-time
> And westward took my way, to see the sun
> Rise, from the top of Snowdon. To the door
> Of a rude cottage at the mountain's base
> We came, and roused the shepherd who attends
> The adventurous stranger's steps, a trusty guide;
> Then, cheered by short refreshment, sallied forth.
>
> (14. 1–10)

"To see the sun rise, from the top of Snowdon"—the phrase might come from a collection of travel memoirs, as indeed might the whole paragraph. We have seen frequently before how Wordsworth channels the sublime into the quotidian and, correspondingly, how the central drive of confession is to articulate, through the most circumstantial narrative, the indwelling spark of the divine. Here, before the climactic spot of time of *The Prelude*, the poet very carefully prepares the ground of his vision with the most circumstantial of introductions.

Circumstantial, that is, in its detail. In its placement within *The Prelude*, however, the episode has already begun to function like the spots of time we discussed at the conclusion of the last chapter: as an incident, that is, whose shape remains constant and sempiternal throughout history, while its meaning varies and grows according to what, at a specific time, the narrator needs to receive from it. The episode has been introduced, at the end of book 13, as belonging to the time of Wordsworth's recovery from despair, his "clear sight of a new world." In point of fact, the poet and his friend Robert Jones had made their visit to the top of Snowdon in the summer of 1791, nearer the height than the end of his disillusionment. And, of course, as the episode develops, it becomes not simply a memory of discovery but the triumphant and present-tense, earned vision of the whole poem ("may they ne'er / Fade from remembrance!"), a message of hope to Coleridge and a presage of Wordsworth's own greater work to come. The vision of Snowdon, in other words, exists—through the confessant's language—at all times of the confessant's life, attending him with visionary power since he has once, albeit unwittingly, been strong.

For the young Wordsworth of 1791, though, the ascent of Mount Snowdon was another of those failures of the will or of the appetitive intellect which—like crossing the Alps or stealing the boat—yields up its meaning only after the search for meaning has been abandoned. Wordsworth and his friend seek a vision of the natural sublime from the mountaintop. And the force of will which leads them to set out at night also separates them—daemonically, I insist—from the event of rebirth and renewal, of continuity, which they are attempting to fixate as aesthetic experience. As Wordsworth describes their ascent, the travelers themselves soon become possessed by a correspondingly daemonic separation from each other, an imprisonment within private reflections which, ironically, blocks out the view of the very mountain they are ascending:

> The mist soon girt us round,
> And, after ordinary travellers' talk
> With our conductor, pensively we sank
> Each into commerce with his private thoughts:
> Thus did we breast the ascent, and by myself
> Was nothing either seen or heard that checked
> Those musings or diverted, save that once
> The shepherd's lurcher, who, among the crags,
> Had to his joy unearthed a hedgehog, teased

His coiled-up prey with barkings turbulent.
This small adventure, for even such it seemed
In that wild place and at the dead of night,
Being over and forgotten, on we wound
In silence as before. . . .

(14. 15–28)

The incident of the shepherd's dog, like the encounter of the travelers with the peasant in the Simplon section or like George Fox's turning aside to the spring on his descent from Pendle Hill— like any of the confrontations of the sublime and the quotidian we have seen—emphasizes the vacuity and abstraction of a will which admits only the drive toward the sublime, only the daemonic, Promethean urge to grasp immediately the divine or nature.

So far, in the preparation for the episode, we have seen the poet move from an introductory rhapsody—an overture—on the unitary imagination (13. 360–378), into a matter-of-fact recounting of the circumstances of the ascent (14. 1–10), into this narration of the ascent itself, in which the fragmenting, isolating will to fix the sight and daemon-ize the imagination takes on increasingly grim overtones. It is a development of tone and mood as careful, as architectonic, as any in Wordsworth's poetry. And the next lines, in which the vision begins to be made manifest, are surely among the poet's most breathtaking narrative performances:

With forehead bent
Earthward, as if in opposition set
Against an enemy, I panted up
With eager pace, and no less eager thoughts.
Thus might we wear a midnight hour away,
Ascending at loose distance each from each,
And I, as chanced, the foremost of the band;
When at my feet the ground appeared to brighten,
And with a step or two seemed brighter still;
Nor was time given to ask or learn the cause,
For instantly a light upon the turf
Fell like a flash. . . .

(14. 28–39)

No exegesis can hope to do justice to this magnificent passage; but the confessional terms for *The Prelude* which we have been developing help, at any rate, to catch the sources of its power. The first lines, in the manner of the Stolen Boat episode, identify the experiences of daemonic will and intense muscular effort: Wordsworth is literally spurning the earth as he pantingly ascends the mountain. Most brilliantly, however, the image which describes his willful separation from quotidian nature—"in opposition set against an enemy"—is qualified by the phrase "as if," which denies the willfulness of the experience in the very act of affirming it. For the image itself of man set in opposition against the earth is daemonic in the extreme; and yet its presentation under the reflective, ruminative marker "as if" affirms the daemonic as part of the language of continuity. The actual experience of opposition to the Earth is, of course, that of the Wordsworth of 1791; but the silent, intense thoughts of that Wordsworth as he climbs Snowdon do not allow for words this self-conscious or self-critical. The words themselves are those of the present poet, narrating his last great anecdote of continuity and community; and they are words whose daemonic imagery, superimposed upon a past daemonic experience, dramatize the unity of the present narrator and his 1791 self. With the phrase "as if," Wordsworth conveys his belief in his past warfare with the Earth only as a delusion he has overcome and can now command with words. The "as if" clause, in fact, belongs to what I have called "confessional time": neither wholly to the past nor wholly to the memorial present but to that mysterious, narrative field where present and past are related, not sequentially or causally, but by mutual penetration and fructification.

As the climbers continue their ascent, they become—although there are only three of them—a "band": a word suggesting purposive and usually illegal action. And Wordsworth is "foremost" among them, both in muscular advance up the mountain and in daemonic single-mindedness. And although Wordsworth most probably did not have *The Borderers* in mind while writing the passage, it is difficult not to see a continuity and a triumph in this image of the leader of a daemonic band, advancing toward a vision which resolves the problems of will, causality, and action of the earlier drama.

The last five lines describe the beginning of the vision itself. Wordsworth had ascended the mountain to seek the light of the rising sun; what he is given—by nature and through memory—is a light which cannot be localized, dispersed as it is throughout all things, and a light which cannot be sought purposively or causally, since it is itself a moment of process rather than, like sunrise, an artificial fixation of process. Two lines describe the brightening of the ground before the poet. But the brightening is at first so subtle, so gradual, that he remembers it as imperceptible intimation rather than "fact": "appeared to brighten" and "seemed brighter still." The brightening is, of course, due to a chance collocation of the moon, mist, and clouds. And the full revelation of the moon occurs, as Wordsworth says, without "time given to ask or learn the cause" —a line which brilliantly indicates that, while the rational, disjunctive cause is there, the time of the revelation makes such questioning irrelevant.

What it is Wordsworth saw is impossible of paraphrase. It is a vision of things at their vanishing point, returning to the primal state of indeterminacy in which all shapes and transformations are possible—yet at the same time, things revealing, in their very malleability, their eternal presence and the everlasting mystery of their substance:

> For instantly a light upon the turf
> Fell like a flash, and lo! as I looked up,
> The Moon hung naked in a firmament
> Of azure without cloud, and at my feet
> Rested a silent sea of hoary mist.
> A hundred hills their dusky backs upheaved
> All over this still ocean; and beyond,
> Far, far beyond, the solid vapours stretched,
> In headlands, tongues, and promontory shapes,
> Into the main Atlantic, that appeared
> To dwindle, and give up his majesty,
> Usurped upon far as the sight could reach.
> Not so the ethereal vault; encroachment none
> Was there, nor loss; only the inferior stars
> Had disappeared, or shed a fainter light
> In the clear presence of the full-orbed Moon,
> Who, from her sovereign elevation, gazed
> Upon the billowy ocean, as it lay
> All meek and silent, save that through a rift—
> Not distant from the shore whereon we stood,
> A fixed, abysmal, gloomy, breathing-place—
> Mounted the roar of waters, torrents, streams

Innumerable, roaring with one voice!
Heard over earth and sea, and, in that hour,
For so it seemed, felt by the starry heavens.

(14. 38–62)

Rereading this passage, one is continually surprised at how little, actually, is given to the eye. Even the Moon, the bright center of the vision, exists in a clarity which is austere rather than dazzling; the firmament of azure in which she hangs naked bears more than a nominal resemblance to *l'azur*, denuded and inhuman, which was later so to obsess Mallarmé. The roar of waters which concludes the passage is of course the apocalyptic might of a new deluge which we have already seen operating in Wordsworth's deepest perceptions. And it, too, like the pure and unprismatic light of the moon, is an image of primal sensation, almost without what Lockean epistemology would call "secondary qualities," specific modulations determining its identity as this sound or this light. The remarkable— and characteristically Wordsworthian—thing about the passage, though, is that it does retain the pressure of reality, in spite of its minimal differentiation. Wordsworth's reflections on the scene are among the most powerful of his passages and are carefully kept disjunctive from the scene itself, so as not to impinge upon that scene's own mute authority.

When into air had partially dissolved
That vision, given to spirits of the night
And three chance human wanderers, in calm thought
Reflected, it appeared to me the type
Of a majestic intellect, its acts
And its possessions, what it has and craves,
What in itself it is, and would become.
There I beheld the emblem of a mind
That feeds upon infinity, that broods
Over the dark abyss, intent to hear
Its voices issuing forth to silent light
In one continuous stream. . . .

(14. 63–74)

That the vision should partially dissolve into air, as Wordsworth says, is a further touch of realization, since the vision itself

had been of the most airy, the most transient and fortuitous collocation of mist and landscape. Its further dissolution into air, its
final passage across the borderline between the minimal and the
insubstantial is a retrospective affirmation of the reality of the vision
itself.

But a more important aspect of this passage is the ambiguous
and seemingly clumsy phrase "in calm thought / Reflected," which
appears to have no real referent in the sentence. In 1805 the construction had been avoided by a straightforward meditative transition, much in the manner of a seventeenth-century metaphysical
evidence:

> A meditation rose in me that night
> Upon the lonely Mountain when the scene
> Had pass'd away, and it appear'd to me
> The perfect image of a mighty Mind,
> Of one that feeds upon infinity. . . .

(1805, 13. 67–71)

But in fact the 1850 construction is both more accurate in its
implications and closer to the sort of perception Wordsworth is
concerned with in *The Prelude*. Its very vagueness and the impre-
cision of its time sense (not "that night" but at, or in, some time
between "then" and the narrative "now") suggest again the confessional merging of event and afterthought: what has been called
the "suspension of the will to relational knowledge."[1] Furthermore,
while 1805 calls the vision explicitly an "image" of the mind feeding
upon infinity, 1850 refers to it as a "type" or an "emblem." And
whether or not Wordsworth was wholly aware of, or wished to use,
the traditional implications of those words,[2] they certainly imply
a more complex and tenuous inherence of meaning in object than
does the straightforward "image."

The key word in the whole passage is "Reflected," for while
its most obvious meaning is "reflection" in the sense of meditation
or ratiocination, it is impossible to construe the phrase grammatically
with this meaning. If we wish to read the sentence grammatically,

---

1. Geoffrey Hartman, *The Unmediated Vision* (New York, 1966), p. 5.
2. See James A. W. Heffernan, "Wordsworth on Imagination: The
Emblemising Power," *PMLA* 81 (1966):389–99.

with "Reflected" referring to "it," the meaning toward which "Reflected" tends is reflection in its purely optical, non-intellectual sense, like reflections in a pool of water. Such an implicit meaning for the word gives the whole construction "in calm thought / Reflected" a complexity which is almost a direct reversal of 1805's more simple-minded "A meditation rose in me that night."

This sort of reflection, a paradox in the psychology of Words-worth's own day, is the source of much of the imaginative power of *The Prelude* and the key to Wordsworth's radically original imagery. Its sense is elaborated, furthermore, in an earlier passage from *The Prelude*, one of Wordsworth's most famous images for the introspective, confessional technique of his great poem. In book 4, the book which originally was to have been the last of *The Prelude*, he is speaking to Coleridge of the progress of his poem up to the point of his first self-dedication to the powers of poetry during a summer vacation from Cambridge:

> As one who hangs down-bending from the side
> Of a slow-moving boat, upon the breast
> Of a still water, solacing himself
> With such discoveries as his eye can make
> Beneath him in the bottom of the deep,
> Sees many beauteous sights—weeds, fishes, flowers,
> Grots, pebbles, roots of trees, and fancies more,
> Yet often is perplexed and cannot part
> The shadow from the substance, rocks and sky,
> Mountains and clouds, reflected in the depth
> Of the clear flood, from things which there abide
> In their true dwelling; now is crossed by gleam
> Of his own image, by a sun-beam now,
> And wavering motions sent he knows not whence,
> Impediments that make his task more sweet;
> Such pleasant office have we long pursued
> Incumbent o'er the surface of past time
> With like success. . . .

(4. 256–273)

On the simplest level, of course, this is a gracious conceit for the rambling, ruminative nature of *The Prelude* as autobiography. But examined more closely, from the viewpoint of the narrator—

the man in the boat—as confessional narrator, it is an inversion of usual ideas about the nature of the "real" and the operation of the intellect. For the "real" things in this image are not the trees, sky, and clouds of the boatman's world—the present world of the confessor—but rather the submerged flowers and roots of time past. And the narrator's present understanding of those images, "the gleam of his own image," occurs not as a result of any directed act of the will but rather as an unwilled gift to the introspective intellect, literally "in calm thought / Reflected" through the medium of time past. Here again, as in the Snowdon passage, Wordsworth has intuitively touched very near the nerve of much contemporary psychology. It is the problem Wordsworth eleswhere describes as that of the retrospective duality of consciousness:

> . . . often do I seem
> Two consciousnesses, conscious of myself
> And of some other Being.
>
> (2. 31–33)

This duality, as is implied by the word "seem" in the passage, is primarily an illusion of the voluntary intellect; and the two passages of reflection indicate the terms of its imaginative, if not discursive, resolution. In terms of Wordsworth's own image for the problem from book 4, the situation is the same as that of looking out a window at a landscape; anyone who has ever ridden a bus through a nighttime countryside will have a strong impression of what the image means. Looking out the window of the bus, the passenger sees alternatively both the passing countryside and the reflected interior of the bus—including his own image—independently of any willed concentration of his eyes. In fact, it takes a concerted effort to see only one or the other. One of the discoveries of modern psychology, furthermore, has been the extent to which our natural, relaxed perception of such a visual field is a function not of analytic powers but rather of the general, gestalt organization of our whole sensory environment. Maurice Merleau-Ponty discusses this problem in a passage which suggests but in no way surpasses in insight or imaginative power the Wordsworthian locution:

> Movement and repose distribute themselves for us in our sur-
> roundings, not according to the hypotheses our intellect happens

to construct, but according to the manner in which we fix ourselves within the world and according to the situation our body assumes therein.[3]

We can now see more clearly what importance it has for *The Prelude* that the vision of Snowdon takes its meaning "in calm thought / Reflected." The passage is a precise parallel to the situation of the observer and the window. Wordsworth, the present-tense confessor, regards his past experience on Snowdon. Does the meaning of that experience, the "type" and "emblem" of a mighty cosmic mind, arise from the experience in the past or from the present-time meditations of the narrator? Exactly; it arises from either and neither. The crucial phrase, "in calm thought / Reflected," with its implication of the past phenomenon superimposed upon the present and involuntary intellect of the narrator, is a deliberate way of placing the experience within neither time but rather above and around their confluence. What Merleau-Ponty calls "the manner in which we fix ourselves within the world" is, for Wordsworth here, the manner of fixation of the confessor, which allows the reflective confluence of past and present time into not two distinct consciousnesses but one temporal and yet liberated consciousness. This consciousness can draw meaning from the visible world without either the daemonic fixation of the visual into allegory or its evaporation in intellectualized evidences.

And that is the point of the rupture of time which the whole Snowdon passage represents. For not only is the experience of 1791 transported as an imaginative coda into the last book of *The Prelude*; but the substitution of the deliberately vague time sense of "Reflected" for the line "A meditation rose in me that night" has the effect of widening the distance between vision and meditation, translating the time of meditation into the universal confessional time of the redeemed narrator.

The meditation part of the vision is one of Wordsworth's most explicit and most triumphant statements of human power and human unity. But before proceeding to a discussion of that meditation, I shall discuss further some of the confessional problems in

---

3. Maurice Merleau-Ponty, *Sens et non-sens* (Paris, 1948), p. 92 (my translation).

the history of thought and in Wordsworth's own career which find their definitive articulation in the Snowdon episode. The ambiguity of the word "reflected" and its centrality to the process of Wordsworth's narration raise particularly the problems of "double vision" and "duality of consciousness" which are so crucial to the history of the form.

In discussing duality of consciousness in confession, we come close to the central linguistic energies of the form. For, quite simply, confession for the confessant *is* language: consciousness is the syntax of that language, and salvation is its semantics. The confessant is in the business of saying "I"—the oddest word in language, since its meaning demands to be filled by the total experience of its speaker, to the extent that it even, normally, loses its identity as a word.[4] For the confessant, however, the word "I" tends to become recognizably a word again, and this is the chief source of disruption and unease in confession. For if I, filled with the consciousness of my renovation and blessing, try to tell the steps of my life leading up to my conversion and rebirth, it is inevitable that I should be overwhelmingly aware of the gap between the I who previously lived life on a lower plane of experience and the new I telling the story. Conversion, while it bases itself upon the providentially insured continuity of the self, nevertheless, in its very violence and psychic depth, tends to break down that continuity.

The most conventional method of overcoming this duality is to assert that the spirit of God, in some way, was present even in one's earliest youth and most abysmal excesses. But this assertion itself, in the subtlest of the confessants, carries a stronger assertion about language—the perennial power of the Word—as the agency of that presence of God. It is speech which one remembers: the speech of a preacher, or the silent speech of God himself, but speech which allows the present narrator to see into the grace

4. Cf. Roland Barthes, *Elements of Semiology* (New York, 1970).

which was at work even in his daemonic past. As the early Quaker Elizabeth Webb writes in her letter to Anthony William Boehme:

> I was convinced that the Quakers held the principles of truth, and that their ministry was the true ministry: but I dwelt then far from any of them, only thus it had happened:—When I was about twelve years old, I was at a meeting or two of theirs, and the doctrine of one man that preached there, proved to me . . . like bread cast upon the waters, for it was found after many days: the sound of his voice seemed to be in my mind when I was alone, and some of his words came fresh into my remembrance; and the voice and the words suited with the exercise of the mind.[5]

The type and emblem of a mighty mind which Wordsworth finds not at the time of Snowdon but "in calm thought / Reflected," has unmistakable linguistic and structural similarities to this sort of experience.

The connection of language, memory, and continuity is even more explicit, of course, in Augustine's use of "The Preacher" Ambrose, as we have already seen in the opening of the *Confessions*. As a Manichaean, Augustine delighted in the rhetorical skill of the Christian Ambrose. But looking back on his former aesthetic taste for the Preacher's words, he finds that they were even then elements of the truth living within him: "Together with the words which I would choose, came also into my mind the things which I would refuse; for I could not separate them" (5. 24).

The situation may be described almost graphically. For conversion, in its soul-shattering excitement, tends to sunder the present I of redeemed experience and the past I of benighted, daemonic experiences. And confession, whose aim is to render permanent and unassailable the experience of conversion, heals that daemonic split of I's by asserting past language to have been the unfolding manifestation of the divine Word one is now prepared to recognize and speak. The narrative is a mirror reflection of the life, and as such it completes and eternalizes the unity toward which the life strives. In this connection, I shall examine a number of confessional

---

5. Thomas Chalk, ed., *Autobiographical Narratives of the Convincement and Other Religious Experience of Samuel Crisp, Elizabeth Webb, Evan Bevan, Margaret Lucas, and Frederick Smith* (London, 1848), p. 58.

passages which deal with the relationship of language and unitary memory, including two of Wordsworth's most profound and characteristic memorial passages.

The first passage predates the development of confession as a form; and, though describing a conversion-experience, it fails to resolve the pronominal ambiguity of past and present I we have been discussing. It is from Paul's Second Letter to the Corinthians:

> I have to boast. There is nothing to be gained by it, but I will go on to visions and revelations given me by the Lord. I know of a man fourteen years ago—whether in the body or out of it, I do not know, God knows—being actually caught up to the third heaven. And I know that this man—I do not know whether it was in the body or out of it, God knows—was caught up into Paradise, and heard things that must not be told, which no human being can repeat. On this man's account I am ready to boast, but about myself I will boast only of my weaknesses.
>
> (2 Corinthians 12:1–5)

The "man," of course, is Paul. But the disjunction between his conversion experience and his conscious life after that experience is so strong that he finds it impossible to make the narrative act of connecting them by a single I. He will boast of his weaknesses in the first person, since that is the I dependent upon the grace of God, which is his present self; but by a fine grammatical construction, he can only identify his past ecstatic self with the present I in the form of a first person accusative—not the conscious, narrative "I" but the passive and acted-upon "me" whose life was absolutely transformed by a gift of supernal vision.

Augustine describes a far subtler experience of pronominal ambiguity when, in the *Confessions*, he narrates his divided consciousness at the moment of his conversion:

> Myself when I was deliberating upon serving the Lord my God now, as I had long purposed, it was I who willed, I who nilled, I, I myself. I neither willed entirely, nor nilled entirely. Therefore was I at strife with myself, and rent asunder by myself. And this rent befell me against my will, and yet indicated, not the presence of another mind, but the punishment of my own.
>
> (8. 21)

It is obvious that in this displacement of self-awareness into two conflicting I's not only the ideal of narrative continuity but implicitly the operation of the rule of memory itself is at stake. And equally, the very gravitation of I into opposed forces indicates the strength and continued presence of the confessor's memory. It is a potential breach which in its violent possibilities testifies to the strength of the memorial fabric. For it is the memory of election, of choice by a higher power, which makes it possible to avoid confrontation with the Doppelgänger of one's past self.

Theodor Reik, in *The Compulsion to Confess*, narrates a remarkable conversation with his eight-year-old son Arthur which illumines the problem of memory and the twin self. Arthur is questioning his father about the inner voice of conscience which causes his problems with washing his hands before dinner, masturbating, and crossing the street without looking both ways:

[Reik, Sr.] "Is that really a voice?"

"No, there isn't anybody there. It is memory that tells me that."

"Why memory?"

Arthur pointed vividly to his head, "Well, cleverness, the brain. When, for instance, you say on the day before, 'If the child runs and falls,' and I run the next day, then the thought tells me, 'Don't run!' . . . But now I know what the inner voice is! *It is a feeling of one's self and the language of somebody else!*"[6]

"The feeling of one's self and the language of somebody else," regardless of its applications to Reik's theory of superego and id antagonism, is a nearly perfect description of the difficulty of the religious confessor in using the same I to describe his present and past selves. The other I, either the accusing voice of a bad conscience or the unawakened self of the preconversion past, is a full-fledged double, and the confessional confrontation with this double is fraught with all the psychic perils associated with such an experience—perils avoided only by the same forces that generate them, language and memory. Augustine describes such a powerful self-confrontation in the story of his listening to the tale of the convert Pontitianus:

Such was the story of Pontitianus; but Thou, O Lord, while he was speaking, didst turn me round toward myself, taking me from

6. Theodor Reik, *The Compulsion to Confess* (New York, 1966), p. 316.

behind my back where I had placed me, unwilling to observe myself; and setting me before my face, that I might see how foul I was, how crooked and defiled, bespotted and ulcerous. And I beheld and stood aghast; and whither to flee from myself I found not.

(8. 15)

Here, literally, as in John Nelson's experience with the preacher discussed in chapter 1, the "language of somebody else" effects a radical transformation in the "feeling of one's self"; and we may read if we wish the whole immense verbal web of the *Confessions* as a memorial attempt to find the appropriate language for both halves, pre- and post-conversion, of the Saint's self.

Georges Gusdorf, in a fine article, "Conditions et limites de l'autobiographie," provides what will be for the moment our final word on the general dimensions of this problem. Writing of formal autobiography and its tendency toward an artificial superimposition of present conditions on the past, he says:

The original sin of autobiography is. . . . that of logical coherence and rationalization. The telling is a conscious act, and as the consciousness of the narrator organizes the telling, so it inevitably appears to him that he has organized his life. Put another way, the constitutive reflection of self-consciousness is transformed, by a kind of inevitable optical illusion, to the level of the event itself. . . . Autobiography is condemned to substitute perpetually the perfected [*le tout fait*] for the durational [*au se faisant*].[7]

Confession, on the other hand, which we have continually distinguished from conventional autobiography, is concerned precisely because of its reverence for the radical, crucially overturning moment of conversion with maintaining a narrative transaction between the present *tout fait* and the past *se faisant*. Thence its strong linguistic awareness of pronominal ambiguity and all that it implies and its particularly "Wordsworthian" character. Both the religious confessions and *The Prelude* demonstrate the same grammar of memory.

7. In Günter Reichenkron and Erich Haase, eds., *Formen der selbstdarstellung: Analekten zu einer Geschichte des literarischen Selbstportraits* (Berlin, 1956), p. 117 (my translation).

The most famous instance of pronomial displacement in *The Prelude*, of course, is the Boy of Winander passage from book 5. It is one of the earliest fragments to find its way into *The Prelude*, and it has the honor of standing first among the poet's grouping of his "Poems of Imagination." And it is a transferral, with Pauline violence, of the past self into another I:

> There was a Boy: ye knew him well, ye cliffs
> And islands of Winander!—many a time
> At evening, when the earliest stars began
> To move along the edges of the hills,
> Rising or setting, would he stand alone
> Beneath the trees or by the glimmering lake,
> And there, with fingers interwoven, both hands
> Pressed closely palm to palm, and to his mouth
> Uplifted, he, as through an instrument,
> Blew mimic hootings to the silent owls,
> That they might answer him; and they would shout
> Across the watery vale, and shout again,
> Responsive to his call, with quivering peals,
> And long halloos and screams, and echoes loud,
> Redoubled and redoubled, concourse wild
> Of jocund din; and, when a lengthened pause
> Of silence came and baffled his best skill,
> Then sometimes, in that silence while he hung
> Listening, a gentle shock of mild surprise
> Has carried far into his heart the voice
> Of mountain torrents; or the visible scene
> Would enter unawares into his mind,
> With all its solemn imagery, its rocks,
> Its woods, and that uncertain heaven, received
> Into the bosom of the steady lake.
>   This Boy was taken from his mates, and died
> In childhood, ere he was full twelve years old.
> Fair is the spot, most beautiful the vale
> Where he was born; the grassy churchyard hangs
> Upon a slope above the village school,
> And through that churchyard when my way has led
> On summer evenings, I believe that there
> A long half hour together I have stood
> Mute, looking at the grave in which he lies!

(5. 364–397)

This superb passage has undergone a weight of critical analysis which must seem to approach the point of textual exhaustion, and it is not my intention to retrace the brilliance of its images of confrontation. A fascinating aspect of the passage, however, is its very curious texture of verb tenses—a texture we can easily understand as a further mutation of pronomial ambiguity, if we wish to see Wordsworth as the Boy. "There was a Boy"—the section begins in what is obviously intended as a perfect tense (*le tout fait*). But of course it is one of the inherent ambiguities of English that the verb *to be* can serve as perfect or imperfect. So that the "perfect" of "There was a Boy," implying his present nonexistence, easily glides into the "imperfect" durational tense implied in "would he stand alone" and "Blew mimic hootings" (*le se faisant*). Neither one of these implied tenses, of course, necessarily hints at the boy's continued existence as another I, the I of the narrator. But the next permutation of tense definitely does. The phrase "a gentle shock of mild surprise / Has carried far into his heart . . ." cannot be read in normal English as meaning anything else than that the boy still exists at the time of the writing. One could not now say, for example, that Milton *has* opposed the restoration of the Stuart line, in spite of the fact that generations of schoolboys *have* been taught to translate the Latin perfect tense by a "have . . ." construction. It would be a mistake, though, to read the verb "Has carried" as a slip from an earlier manuscript version or as a simple syntactical error. For it is precisely, again, the confessional narrative tense, which asserts a connection between past and present selves and which subsumes and transforms conventional narrative in a memorial resurrection of the Doppelgänger which one's youth always is.

The most problematic example of pronomial ambiguity in Wordsworth's poetry, however, is not to be found in *The Prelude* itself but rather in "Home at Grasmere," the monumental wreckage which is as far as Wordsworth ever got with *The Recluse*. Written in 1800, "Home at Grasmere" is later than the Boy of Winander passage of *The Prelude* but predates the great bulk of it in composition. And the transition between the two poems is itself a measure of Wordsworth's increased understanding of the essentially confessional nature of his genius. "Home at Grasmere" begins with a reminiscent vision resembling the opening of "Tintern Abbey":

Once to the verge of yon steep barrier came
A roving school-boy; what the adventurer's age
Hath now escaped his memory—but the hour,
One of a golden summer holiday,
He well remembers, though the year be gone—
Alone and devious from afar he came;
And, with a sudden influx overpowered
At sight of this seclusion, he forgot
His haste. . . .

(1–9)

The first three lines are a triumphantly simple projection, in dia-
grammatic form, of the celebrated two consciousnesses of *Prelude*
2. 25ff. The past experience and the present repenetration of it are
tenuously related—memorially as well as gramatically—to the "steep
barrier" which is ambivalently both the most striking fact of the
present-tense observer and the least important aspect of his observa-
tion. The steep barrier itself avoids being emblematic by a richness
of suggestion too strong for a simple emblem to support. It is the
barrier against the apocalyptic sense, the obsessive spot which, like
a true *omphalos*, is a concentration of antinatural powers and therefore a herald of the death of the purely natural imagination. The
power of the passage—and it is a power almost impossible to grasp
through any sort of rhetorical analysis, though the rhetoric is
compelling—is that it transforms the apocalyptic associations of the
spot into an antiapocalyptic binding of the imagination to nature.
But the most remarkable thing is the way in which that binding
is actually achieved. For here, at the outset of Wordsworth's most
confident and joyous poem, it is articulated in explicitly confessional
terms:

Since that day forth the Place to him—*to me*
(For I who live to register the truth
Was that same young and happy Being) became
As beautiful to thought, as it had been
When present, to the bodily sense; a haunt of pure affections. . . .

(46–50)

The italicized *to me* is, in spite of its emphasis, a perfectly smooth
and inevitable rounding-off of what should be recognizable by

now as a unique version of experience. The identification of the poet and the schoolboy unifies the past, other time of the boy's story with the unfolding present of the narration and transvalues the verb *became* into the confessional tense, which can regard natural experience as a continuum and redeem the spot's apocalyptic intimations. The second and third lines of the passage—"For I who live to register the truth / Was that same young and happy Being"— is a parenthesis as brilliant and profound in its implied weight of narrative power as any single passage from *The Prelude*.

Having achieved and articulated, in his vision from the top of Snowdon, the unification of the dual consciousness, Wordsworth proceeds to describe the gift this unity brings:

> There I beheld the emblem of a mind
> That feeds upon infinity, that broods
> Over the dark abyss, intent to hear
> Its voices issuing forth to silent light
> In one continuous stream; a mind sustained
> By recognition of transcendent power,
> In sense conducting to ideal form,
> In soul of more than mortal privilege.
> One function, above all, of such a mind
> Had Nature shadowed there, by putting forth,
> 'Mid circumstances awful and sublime,
> That mutual domination which she loves
> To exert upon the face of outward things,
> So moulded, joined, abstracted, so endowed
> With interchangeable supremacy,
> That men, least sensitive, see, hear, perceive,
> And cannot choose but feel. The power, which all
> Acknowledge when thus moved, which Nature thus
> To bodily sense exhibits, is the express
> Resemblance of that glorious faculty
> That higher minds bear with them as their own.

(14. 70–90)

The gift is language—a language whose rolling periodic rhythms both mask and reveal the daring simplicity at the heart of its complications. For here present and past, self and other, unitary and daemonic, are not simply asserted to be one continuum but are acted out in the resplendence of their continuity. "There I beheld" is neither the time of the 1791 ascent nor the time of the present writing of the words. It is "in calm thought / Reflected," precisely the confluence of those two times mirrored in a mind that feeds upon infinity. For the emblem which the poet beholds in confessional time is at once an image of a power and a mind beyond nature and man, generating both; and at the same time it is an image of his own mind exercising its fullest and most visionary power of unification. The whole magnificent passage, in fact, is an extended confrontation with the other I of transcendent vision in terms which make that transcendence immanent within the syntax itself. The line ". . . intent to hear / Its voices . . ." may refer either to the mind or to the poet beholding the emblem of that mind. But this double reference is not "ambiguity," as the new critics have established that term. It is, rather, the entirely unambiguous assertion that both referents are substantially one, differentiated only in their mode of manifestation. For while the reflections of the narrator are kept carefully in the past-confessional tense, the operations of the mind are described in a perennial present—"feeds" and "broods." But even as this apparent disjunction of times is affirmed, the first half of the passage abounds with present and past participles— "issuing," "sustained," "conducting"—which enforce a sense of common and indeterminately continuous duration between the reflecting mind of the narrator and the universal mind that he perceives.

Midway through the passage, as the perceiving and perceived minds continue to approach each other, the primal experience itself—historical, daemonic fact—recedes even further back. For the pluperfect "*Had* Nature shadowed there" is immediately overwhelmed by the complex, heavily participial sentence, which describes the mutual domination—of nature and nature, nature and man, the poet's timeless vision and the poet's mortal consciousness. And in the last sentence of the passage, the poet yokes the eternal and the time-bound with a verb. The power he has been reflecting upon, he now says,

> . . . is the express
> Resemblance of that glorious faculty
> That higher minds bear with them as their own.

All the verbs are present-tense indicative: the activity of the universal mind and that of the reflecting narrator have become one, and the confessional past has developed inevitably into the prophetic present tense. And the "higher minds" which now displace the universal mind, in remaining human, substantial, and plural, incarnate the poet's vision in an ideal of community and history.

The total effect of the passage, in fact, is to evolve a language in which the visionary power of the imagination is indistinguishable from the syntax in which that imagination manifests itself: a language "In sense conducting to ideal form," until ideal form and sense become absolutely appropriate signs of each other. Jung, among other moderns, has written of the peculiar nature of this sort of language, as a permanent possibility of the psyche:

> The deeper "layers" of the psyche lose their individual uniqueness as they retreat further and further into darkness. . . . Hence "at bottom" the psyche is simply "world." In this sense . . . in the symbol the *world itself* is speaking.[8]

Word and world, in such a language, are at their minimum point of divergence, if divergent at all. But for Wordsworth, the language is not gained by going deeper and deeper into the psyche as much as it is earned by confronting and refurbishing one of the most permanent myths of language, that of Eden.

The sort of language I am talking about here is what I call in the title of this chapter "Edenic words," that is, language which attempts to attain to a prelapsarian condition of naming. Adam's only recorded act in the Garden of Eden is, of course, his naming of the beasts, plants, stones, etc., in a language which fits perfectly together the structures of word and thing. This is the Edenic situation of language, and in fact this act of quasi-divine naming is the only possible or appropriate act of Edenic man. For the perfect balance of appetites, objects, and understanding which is Eden

---

8. C. G. Jung, *Psyche and Symbol* (New York, 1958), p. 138.

cannot issue in any action less symmetrical than the spontaneous generation of the word which absolutely reflects an absolute condition. And the fall of man from this situation necessarily entails the parallel fall of language: the myth of the Serpent is doubled in the myth of the Tower of Babel. Such, in fact, was the tacit assumption of European linguistics until the late seventeenth century. The greatest efforts of such philologists as Athanasius Kircher, J. C. Becanus, and John Webb were directed toward locating the Edenic language by a process of extrapolation from its known "dialects."[9]

The breakdown of this language myth has been recounted often enough. Beginning most explicitly with Bacon's *Novum Organum*, the idea has grown throughout the last three centuries that an Edenic correlation of word and thing is not simply a lost power of speech but one which never could have been, and never could be, possible. The consequent severing of word from reality, thought from the objects of thought, is the most crucial linguistic event of the modern age, and it is nowhere more tellingly articulated than in Hobbes's epigram: "For *true* and *false* are attributes of speech, not of things."[10] The general effects of this split in Romantic poetry have been traced by Paul de Man, who speaks of the nostalgia of Romantic language for the object which it seeks to become, and which it never can become, precisely because it is language.[11] And in our own age, a thinker as seminal as Ludwig Wittgenstein, who was engaged in his own private and lifelong agony over the chances of a meaningful language, invoked the Edenic myth with mingled disdain and—in a Romantic sense—nostalgia:

> For we are most strongly tempted to imagine that giving a name consists in correlating in a peculiar and rather mysterious way a sound (or other sign) with something. How we make use of this peculiar correlation then seems to be almost a secondary matter. (One could almost imagine that naming was done by a peculiar sacramental act, and that this produced some magic relation between the name and the thing.)[12]

9. See Don Cameron Allen, "Some Theories of the Growth and Origin of Language in Milton's Age," *Philological Quarterly* 28 (1949): 5-16.

10. Thomas Hobbes, *Leviathan* (New York, 1962), p. 36.

11. See, again, Paul de Man, "Intentional Structure of the Romantic Image," in *Romanticism and Consciousness*, ed. Harold Bloom (New York, 1970).

12. Ludwig Wittgenstein, *The Brown Book* (New York, 1965), p. 172.

A magic relation between word and thing—this is what language, particularly visionary language, must seek in spite of itself, even if it is only the broken magic of Man exiled from the Garden. And the Wordsworth who, as we have seen, becomes the emblem of power he beholds and becomes it through the agency of his own words—this poet occupies a central place in the history of the word. Not, indeed, for his solution to the problem, as much as for the desperate precision with which he sees the terms and the need for a solution. He writes in his most exuberant passage on language, the "Prospectus" to *The Excursion*:

> Paradise, and groves
> Elysian, Fortunate Fields—like those of old
> Sought in the Atlantic Main—why should they be
> A history only of departed things,
> Or a mere fiction of what never was?
> For the discerning intellect of Man,
> When wedded to this goodly universe
> In love and holy passion, shall find these
> A simple produce of the common day.
> —I, long before the blissful hour arrives,
> Would chant, in lonely peace, the spousal verse
> Of this great consummation:—and, *by words
> Which speak of nothing more than what we are,*
> Would I arouse the sensual from their sleep
> Of Death. . . .
>
> (47–61, italics mine)

These lines, written before the bulk of *The Prelude*, are a brilliant commentary on the imaginative activity we have been witnessing in the Snowdon passage. Another Wordsworth text, however, postdating the 1805 *Prelude*, casts an even clearer light on the poet's complex attitude toward language. I am speaking of his series of essays upon epitaphs. These essays may be taken partially as a critical commentary on the linguistic insight the poet gained in writing the original *Prelude*. And they indicate the visionary power with which Wordsworth, during his great decade, expanded the criterion of "language ordinarily used by men" of the *Preface* to *Lyrical Ballads*—that most famous and, probably, most misunderstood Wordsworthian pronouncement.

The essays upon epitaphs should, I think, come to be recognized
as essential to the study of Wordsworth. Only the first and com-
paratively least interesting one was published (in *The Friend*,
February 22, 1810), as "Upon Epitaphs"; the other two, "The
Country Church-Yard" and "Critical Epitaphs Considered," were
edited by Grosart from manuscripts. Together they form an extended examination of what Wordsworth considers the appropriate
language of the deepest sort of human truth.

The first essay, from *The Friend*, eloquently develops the
relationship between the true language of poetry and the common
speech of rural epitaphs. In what may be his closest approach to an
expression of the Quaker inner light, Wordsworth writes of the
charity necessary in reading an epitaph.

> We are not anxious unerringly to understand the constitution of
> the minds of those who have soothed, who have cheered, who have
> supported us: with whom we have been long and daily pleased or
> delighted. The affections are their own justification. The light of
> love in our hearts is a satisfactory evidence that there is a body
> of worth in the minds of our friends or kindred, whence that light
> has proceeded.[13]

Much like the "conversational sublime" we have described in the
first chapter, the epitaph, as a unit of continuity between the
generations, assumes an extraliterary, human mediatorship—"it is
truth hallowed by love—the joint offspring of the worth of the dead
and the affections of the living."[14] This mediatorship, furthermore,
is linked explicitly to memory: it functions as a point of contact
with the earlier imaginative power of the individual's youth. The
overtones of the great theme of the Immortality Ode are unmistakable:

> If we look back upon the days of childhood, we shall find that the
> time is not in remembrance when, with respect to our own individual
> Being, the mind was without this assurance [of immortality]; whereas,
> the wish to be remembered by our friends or kindred after death,

13. *The Prose Works of William Wordsworth*, 3 vols., ed. A. B. Grosart
(London, 1876) 2:35.
14. Ibid., p. 36.

or even in absence, is, as we shall discover, a sensation that does not form itself till the *social* feelings have been developed, and the Reason has connected itself with a wide range of objects.[15]

The sense of immortality, of autonomous imaginative power, ages naturally into the social compulsion to communicate, to convert, to be remembered, and thus it necessitates the mediatorship we have seen operating in Wordsworth's own confessional language in *The Prelude*.

It is in the second and third essays upon epitaphs, however, that the full implications of these sentiments find expression. The second essay is largely concerned with what Wordsworth's generation would have regarded as the criterion of sincerity; Wordsworth insists, as he had done in *The Friend*, that a primary condition for approaching epitaph verse is an act of critical charity and good faith:

> Literature is here [i.e., in epitaph verse] so far identified with morals, the quality of the act so far determined by our notion of the aim and purpose of the agent, that nothing can please us, however well executed in its kind, if we are persuaded that the primary virtues of sincerity, earnestness and a moral interest in the main object are wanting.[16]

It seems obvious that what Wordsworth is doing here is denying the tension between language and referent, between word and significance—in modern terms, between "tenor" and "vehicle"—which is so basic to earlier versions of metaphor.

The criterion of absolute appropriateness is a rich vein in Wordsworth's poetry and implies a number of things. "Words which speak of nothing more than what we are," words which in their absolute purity of reference both recover the past and avoid its allegorical transformation into an ideational, dehumanizing schematism, are, as it were, the verbal incarnation of memory. And therefore, like memory itself, they become an element of the poetry beyond rational analysis: they are not agents of mediation; they are mediation.

15. Ibid., p. 28.
16. Ibid., p. 54.

This is a crucial point. Hartman's *The Unmediated Vision,*
although certainly taking a good deal of its theoretical impetus
from the energies of Wordsworth's poetry, tends to understate this
aspect:

> Whereas the older poet, even when as extreme as Meister Eckhart,
> knew and acknowledged mediation, the modern either does not
> acknowledge or does not know a mediator for his orphic journey.
> He passes through experience by means of the unmediated vision.
> Nature, the body, the human consciousness—that is the only text.[17]

But it is not, of course, the only text. There is also the book itself,
what we normally call the text, and Hartman damages his argument
by attempting to expand the substantive meaning of text to human
experience, while at the same time ignoring the substantiality of
text in its conventional connotation. Most such phenomenological
approaches, indeed, fail to take into account the physical existence
of the book. For the apocalyptic vision which Wordsworth tries
so to avoid and which later poets, in their various ways, embrace—
vision beyond mediating nature—is still necessarily vision within
text. And thus the poet's attitude toward that text becomes immensely important, since it determines whether or not he chooses
to use language itself as the necessary mediation between apocalypse
and the world or whether language itself becomes for him a self-
annihilating moment of prophecy:

> I warn everyone who hears the message of prophecy in this book
> read, that if anyone adds anything to it, God will inflict upon him
> the plagues that are described in this book; and if anyone removes
> from this book any of the prophetic messages it contains, God will
> remove from him his share in the tree of life and the holy city
> which are described in this book.
>
> (Revelation 22:18–19)

John's obsessive repetition of "this book" is a strong indication of
the importance of the verbal text in apocalyptic poetry, both as
amelioration and reinforcement of the apocalyptic message.

We have already discussed, in this connection, the nature of

17. Hartman, *The Unmediated Vision,* p. 155.

Wordsworth's answer to the central exegetical question, "where is the text?" With Luther, and with the great confessors of radical Protestantism, Wordsworth's answer is one which emphasizes the social, humanizing, and mediatory function of the potentially world-annihilating Word.

Returning to the essays on epitaphs, we see how this verbal criterion works itself out in Wordsworth's attitude toward the poetry of the Augustans. Examining Pope's epitaph on Mrs. Corbet, a highly antithetical and structured verse, he remarks:

> The Author forgets that it is a living creature that must interest us and not an intellectual existence, which a mere character is. Insensible to this distinction the brain of the Writer is set at work to report as flatteringly as he may of the mind of his subjects; the good qualities are separately abstracted (can it be otherwise than coldly and unfeelingly?) and put together again as coldly and unfeelingly.[18]

Pope's verses on Mrs. Corbet (who died of breast cancer) are not his finest but are a fairly polished and witty example of the verbal energies Wordsworth is repudiating:

> Here rests a Woman, good without pretence,
> Blest with plain Reason and with sober Sense;
> No Conquests she, but o'er herself desir'd,
> No Arts essay'd, but not to be admir'd.
> Passion and pride were to her soul unknown,
> Convinc'd, that Virtue only is our own.
> So unaffected, so compos'd a mind,
> So firm yet soft, so strong yet so refin'd,
> Heav'n, as its purest Gold, by Tortues try'd;
> The Saint sustain'd it, but the Woman dy'd.

The slight sense of bathos a modern reader may experience in reading this is probably due not so much to the poem's intrinsic nature as to the unfortunate resemblance of lines like the eighth—"so firm yet soft, so strong yet so refin'd"—to the advertising slogan of a brand of cigarette. But it is a remarkable substantiation of

---

18. *The Prose Works of William Wordsworth*, 2:56.

Wordsworth's point about language. The words are daemonic here: they become the autonomous organizing terms of Mrs. Corbet's personality and, finally, the terms of her dehumanization. The final line, "The Saint sustain'd it, but the Woman dy'd," from the standpoint of what we have already seen of Wordsworth's concern for the wholeness and continuity of the human experience, is bound to call forth a shuddering denial, for it exhibits a daemonism (albeit a eudaemonic one) of the most severe order and, furthermore, one which Pope's use of language in this little epitaph makes inevitable.

Wordsworth was not blind to the greatness of Pope. But he did realize the antithetical nature of the Augustan poetic to his own deepest concerns. The third essay on epitaphs, while acknowledging the power of couplet rhetoric, makes a brilliant point about its opposition to the Wordsworthian ideal—and incidentally comes as close as any of Wordsworth's prose to an explicit repudiation of the daemonic:

> If a man has once said . . . "Evil, be thou my good!" and has acted accordingly, however strenuous may have been his adherence to this principle, it will be well known by those who have had an opportunity of observing him narrowly that there have been perpetual obliquities in his course; evil passions thwarting each other in various ways. . . . It is reasonable then that . . . Dryden and Pope, when they are describing characters like Buckingham, Shaftesbury, and the Duchess of Marlborough, should represent qualities and actions at war with each other and with themselves; and that the page should be suitably crowded with antithetical expressions.[19]

We need only remind ourselves of the really unforgettable passages in the poetry of Pope, with their frighteningly concentrated and barely restrained hatred—such as the "Sporus" portrait in the *Epistle to Dr. Arbuthnot*, which was apparently a favorite of Byron's—to realize the daemonic quality of his language. Whether that daemonism, of course, is simply a result of the satirist's mask, or whether it is a necessary corollary of the assumptions of eighteenth-century poetic diction, is open to much question; but for Wordsworth, all these considerations are inextricably interrelated, and they are all deadly for his own imagination. It is

19. Ibid., p. 60.

especially significant in this connection that Wordsworth's most Popean use of words in *The Prelude* occurs at the end of book 1, as he is remembering the winter evening card games of his boyhood:

> . . . some, plebeian cards
> Which Fate, beyond the promise of their birth,
> Had dignified, and called to represent
> The persons of departed potentates,
> Oh, with what echoes on the board they fell!
> Ironic diamonds—clubs, hearts, diamonds, spades,
> A congregation piteously akin!
> Cheap matter offered they to boyish wit,
> Those sooty knaves, precipitated down
> With scoffs and taunts, like Vulcan out of heaven. . . .
>
> (1. 522–531)

This is undoubtedly a reprise of the game of Ombre in *The Rape of the Lock*, canto 3; but it is also a remarkable inversion and dismissal of Popean wit and language. For if *The Rape of the Lock* is the language's most glorious use of the daemonic and the diminutive for satire, the card game in *The Prelude* represents an intentional diminution of those verbal resources themselves. We remember the giant forms of daemonic heroism which had haunted Wordsworth's epic hopes at the beginning of this book and his gradual memorial triumph, in incidents like the Skating and Stolen Boat episodes, over a daemonic ideal of nature in favor of a rhetoric of human continuity. Now, at his great moment of renewal and rededication at the end of book 1, he again examines the daemonic and, in a curiously involuted compliment to one of the masterpieces of the language, finds that view of human existence and experience "cheap matter offered . . . to boyish wit." It is to be the characteristic Wordsworthian attitude throughout *The Prelude* and all the major poetry toward any myth or metaphor which distorts the language of "the produce of the common day."

Before proceeding in this discussion of Wordsworth's language in *The Prelude*, then, it is advisable to examine one of his few exercises in the kind of verbalization he disliked in Pope. It is not from *The Prelude* but was composed in 1804 during the intense period of writing which produced the larger poem. I quote it in full:

She was a Phantom of delight
When first she gleamed upon my sight;
A lovely Apparition, sent
To be a moment's ornament;
Her eyes as stars of Twilight fair;
Like Twilight's, too, her dusky hair;
But all things else about her drawn
From May-time and the cheerful Dawn;
A dancing Shape, an Image gay,
To haunt, to startle, and way-lay.

I saw her upon nearer view,
A Spirit, yet a Woman too!
Her household motions light and free,
And steps of virgin-liberty;
A countenance in which did meet
Sweet records, promises as sweet;
A Creature not too bright or good
For human nature's daily food;
For transient sorrows, simple wiles,
Praise, blame, love, kisses, tears, and smiles.

And now I see with eye serene
The very pulse of the machine;
A Being breathing thoughtful breath,
A Traveller between life and death;
The reason firm, the temperate will,
Endurance, foresight, strength, and skill;
A perfect Woman, nobly planned,
To warn, to comfort, and command;
And yet a Spirit still, and bright
With something of angelic light.

The poem is about marriage and, more importantly, about the problem of knowing another person in and through the body. And the subtlety with which it approaches the problem is at least as great as any of the contemporary existential or phenomenological treatments of this crucial and intricate theme. Like Pope's epitaph on Mrs. Corbet, it is a description of a woman; like the epitaph, it is written in heavily end-stopped couplets; and like the epitaph, it abounds in general terms—"Endurance, foresight, strength, and skill." But as a way of knowing, as a verbal structure, it is polar to the Pope verse.

Each of the three ten-line stanzas of the poem can be described as a recognition of the subject and can be analyzed into the three characteristic forms through which, in fact, we may be said to recognize any person. To the internal question "Who is this?" we usually say to ourselves either "This is William Wordsworth" (or more generally, "This is a man") or "This is the person with these recognizable characteristics" (this longish nose, weak chin, thoughtful expression, etc.) or "This is the author of *The Prelude*" (or "This is a poet," "This is the Distributor of Stamps," etc). Each stanza, that is, is a movement of perception from name to appearance to function.

Now, observing the permutations of these three terms for forms of knowing within the poem, we can see that each stanza generates a set of prime coordinates:

1. *Name:* "She was a Phantom of delight."
    Appearance: "a moment's ornament."
    Function: "A dancing Shape."
2. *Name:* "A Spirit, yet a Woman too!"
    Appearance: "A countenance."
    Function: "human nature's daily food."
3. *Name:* "The very pulse of the machine."
    Appearance: "A Being breathing thoughtful breath."
    Function: "A perfect Woman . . . yet a Spirit still."

This breakdown is itself, of course, daemonic in the extreme and tends to obscure the single, unified movement of the poem through all three sets of coordinates. But it is useful in trying to see how that movement develops. The first stanza, which by itself could almost be confused with a courtly compliment by a chaste Lovelace or a leisurely Pope, is by far the most conventional in its description; it is also the most daemonic in its use of words. Not only do the key phrases "Phantom," "Apparition," "Shape," and "Image" carry an implication of a disembodied, sublimated sensuality, but the terms of visualization are explicitly ornamental, disjunctive, and obsessive. The lady's eyes and hair are visualized in conventional imagistic terms, but more importantly, they are visualized singly, that is, not in terms of an integrated, human perception. The language perfectly reflects the overcoming of the eye by the very power of the visual; and the dance which is the function-term of this stanza is not the dance of Yeats's cosmic figure in "Among School Children" but a momentary, faery dance which precisely startles and waylays the observer.

In stanza 2 the perception becomes humanized. Familiarity reveals the Woman within the apparition, the human body which articulates the spirit. And this revelation is in terms of a perception which is primarily unitary. The ornamental features of the woman's face are organized into "a countenance, in which did meet / Sweet records, promises as sweet." And an important part of that countenance-recognition is the transformation of movement as function into movement as appearance: the startling dance of the first stanza, which had been the ornamental apparition's definitive activity, is now refined into "Her household motions light and free," which is the woman's characteristically human feature. But if stanza 1 represented the overcoming of subject by the brilliance of its object, this stanza in its incipient humanization represents the inversion of that relationship. First she had gleamed upon the poet's sight; now he sees her with a more active eye, and this is to some extent an intellectual dominance of the object; her function, then, is as food for experience, as a relatively passive performer of the transient and surface human activities.

The love which is assigned to the woman as function in the second stanza, though, literally grows to transform the language and perception of the third. The poet now sees "with eye serene"—or as he had said in the great passage from "Tintern Abbey":

> . . . with an eye made quiet by the power
> Of harmony, and the deep power of joy,
> We see into the life of things.
>
> (47–49)

And it is important to understand that it is into the life of things that the poet does see. The name term here, "The very pulse of the machine," has struck a number of intelligent readers as a rather uncomplimentary one for the lady. Actually, it is by far the most intensely intimate name in the poem. For it is the final name perception, the perception that is neither beyond nor of the humanity of the body but which is a vision of humanity through and within the body. Nor should the phrase "pulse of the machine" suggest any deference to a Cartesian or Pauline soul-body dichotomy, such as that implied in Gilbert Ryle's phrase "the ghost in the machine." For "pulse" is itself a powerfully embodied articulation of life force; and "machine," in fact, must refer not only to the woman's body but to the whole complex process of the poet's perception of that body. Perception itself becomes here literally *con*ception, as the woman's appearance is transformed beyond even the humanity of "countenance" into the powerful and inexplicably rich phrase, "A Being breathing thoughtful breath." Remarkably, this stanza, while incarnating the height of humanized perception, contains the greatest percentage of generalized terms. Unlike the example of the Pope epitaph, however, the general terms here are not categories for the delimiting of the woman's character but are rather qualities spontaneously generated from the contemplation of her physical and psychic individuality. They are, in fact, not generalizations in the normal sense at all but terms which in their very bareness and nearly prosaic quality bring home the "creaturality" of the perception. And the woman's function terms in this last stanza, "To warn, to comfort, and command," are appropriately terms implying in the fullest sense a community with the poet, a mutuality in which each creature is reciprocally subject and object to the other, in which each is most definitively a person. The last two lines, in their graceful rounding back to the spirit images of the first two stanzas, are one of those characteristic Wordsworthian assertions of grace which convince because they seem earned. There are few poems which describe so well the way in which one human being comes to know another and perhaps none which articulate that process in such a complex yet basically unitary language.

For it would be an error to assume that any of the perception terms we have been tracing is lost in the last stanza. Each of the coordinates retains its organic importance in the development of the final intuition, as each of the stages in the history of the eye we described in the last chapter retains its memorial autonomy, and each phase of Wordsworth's confessional relationship with his auditor is essential for every other phase in *The Prelude*. "She was a Phantom" has its very great usefulness for a study of *The Prelude* because it demonstrates, writ small, the complex balance between the past and present selves as both continuous and discontinuous, which is our theme here. And that very discontinuity-within-continuity, as "She was a Phantom" makes almost graphically clear, is a function of the operation of the rule of memory in the language game which is the poem.

In the first two sections of the Snowdon episode, we have seen the poet move from a confessional unification of past and present into a new, Edenic language which acts out as well as asserts the power and blessedness he has earned through memory. Continuing our examination of the passage as a moment of transcendence, we now observe the third and final movement. Much has been said in this study about Wordsworth's avoidance of the metaphoric and allegorical; that urge has been described as similar to the Protestant confessant's horror of the sacramental and liturgical. But in the final movement of the Snowdon episode, one should not be surprised to see Wordsworth employing his most self-consciously religious, hieratic language. Having introduced the higher minds who represent a human incarnation of the universal mind of the middle section, he now proceeds to describe these minds' activity:

> They from their native selves can send abroad
> Kindred mutations; for themselves create
> A like existence; and, whene'er it dawns
> Created for them, catch it, or are caught
> By its inevitable mastery,
> Like angels stopped upon the wing by sound
> Of harmony from Heaven's remotest spheres.
> Them the enduring and the transient both
> Serve to exalt; they build up greatest things
> From least suggestions; ever on the watch;
> Willing to work and to be wrought upon,
> They need not extraordinary calls
> To rouse them; in a world of life they live
> By sensible impressions not enthralled,
> But by their quickening impulse made more prompt
> To hold fit converse with the spiritual world,
> And with generations of mankind
> Spread over time, past, present, and to come,
> Age after age, till Time shall be no more.

Such minds are truly from the Deity,
For they are Powers; and hence the highest bliss
That flesh can know is theirs—the consciousness
Of Whom they are, habitually infused
Through every image and through every thought,
And all affections by communion raised
From earth to heaven, from human to divine. . . .

                                                    (14. 93–118)

Almost every line of this great passage contains a phrase or image
from the vocabulary of religious conversion. It begins with the
doubling of active and passive responses to Nature which we have
seen operating throughout the vision. But here, the dual relationship which was "seen" / "sees" at the opening becomes the doubling
of "create" / "created," that is, no longer a matter simply of perception but of an activity like that of God himself. The godlike
minds of the visionary are compared to those of angels and are
shown in their characteristic activity of building up "greatest things
from least suggestions"—definitively the activity of *The Prelude*'s
narrator and most strikingly what happens in the Snowdon incident
itself. And from the vantage of this newly asserted power and
divinity, Wordsworth can expand the sense of his own mediating
and edified audience from the person of Coleridge and the "happy
few" like himself to include the generations of men even down to
the moment of final apocalypse. And as if even the simile of angels
were to be taken literally, Wordsworth in the conclusion to the
passage puns on the higher visionary minds as

            . . . truly from the Deity,
    For they are Powers. . . .

Powers, that is, as one of the traditional choirs of angels. And
Powers, also, as real incarnations of the supernal power "which all
acknowledge when thus moved" and which has been the subject
of his confessional reflection.

    The reader who has followed *The Prelude* to this point cannot
himself but acknowledge, thus moved, the mastery and sweep of
Wordsworth's language here. For, true to his own fundamental
linguistic principles, the poet is not using metaphor or allusion in
this passage, for all its liturgical and hieratic vocabulary. He is,
rather, celebrating the abolition of the Fall of man. For if, as we
have said, the modern fissure of word and meaning involves, in its

origin, a denial of the Fall and of the original, "Edenic" state of consciousness, then Wordsworth's way of healing that fissure is to assert not simply the original and lost power of Edenic words but their real possibility in the here-and-now. His treatment of the image of angels is an index of his seriousness; for, refusing to allow the image to stand as image, he translates it into the word "Powers," whose meaning and range have been guaranteed through the language of the passage itself. As point of transcendence, in fact, the Snowdon episode here transcends even the terms of this study. For at this moment, the growth of poetic imagination is not simply like Protestant versions of the indwelling of God in the soul; that growth has, rather, become the indwelling of the only God Wordsworth—or the modern era—can imagine, allowing him to use the language of Christian theology not as image or allusion but as absolutely appropriate to his own sense of his poetic gift.

This negation of the Fall is, of course, a constant theme in the Protestant confessions themselves; we have already alluded to it as the theme of "Paradise Regained." The confessions of self-proclaimed "great sinners," such as John Newton or Silas Told,[20] assert that, for the converted and redeemed, original sin and the effects of the Fall have been obliterated through the sacrifice of Christ, and the converted man has become innocent, like a preternatural child. The image of the child, in fact, in his pristine closeness to God, plays at least as important a role in these confessions as it does in Wordsworth's own poetry. And specifically as a mode of liberation from the Fall—of man and of his language—the image of the child displays profound connections with the Snowdon episode and the theme of Edenic words.

Who is the child? What are his links with the world, and why does he remain a lifelong agent of salvation in spite of the fact that man's own relationship to the world and the self changes radically during his career?

> Emphatically such a Being lives,
> Frail creature as he is, helpless as frail,
> An inmate of this active universe.
> For feeling had to him imparted power
> That through the growing faculties of sense
> Doth like an agent of the one great Mind

20. See appendix 3.

Create, creator and receiver both,
Working but in alliance with the works
Which it beholds.—Such, verily, is the first
Poetic spirit of our human life,
By uniform control of after years,
In most, abated or suppressed; in some,
Through every change of growth and of decay,
Pre-eminent till death.

(2. 252–265)

The relationship of this very early passage from *The Prelude* to the climactic vision on Mount Snowdon is inescapable. And always, in Wordsworth's awareness of the primordial energy of the child, is the sober awareness that the child must change. The child, that is, is *an* ornament against the voluntarist intellect, an archetype against the will. The child is what must grow, as in the primal linguistics of the soul "child" necessarily implies a later "man." The child of the confessors is not, then, a myth of absolute primal innocence but rather a symbol, "smaller than small, bigger than big,"[21] of all that the man will become, innocence and guilt, but yet in a uniquely blessed balance, a balance that in its very physical inevitability of growth and change insures the ultimate wholeness-in-time of the later man.

Augustine's is the least rhapsodic intellect imaginable about the child's absolute goodness, and yet book 1 of the *Confessions* concludes with a powerful memorial salutation of that infantile, other I:

Yet, Lord, to Thee, the Creator and Governor of the universe, most excellent and most good, thanks were due to Thee our God, even hadst Thou destined for me boyhood only. For even then I was, I lived, and felt; and had an implanted providence over my well-being—a trace of that mysterious Unity whence I was derived; I guarded by the inward sense the entireness of my senses, and in my thoughts on things minute, I learnt to delight in truth, I hated to be deceived, had a vigorous memory, was gifted with speech, was soothed by friendship, avoided pain, baseness, ignorance. In so small a creature, what was not wonderful, not admirable?

(1. 31)

21. The phrase is Jung's, in *Psyche and Symbol* and other works, for the libido.

In the Latin, the "mysterious Unity whence I was derived" of this majestic passage is equally interpretable as referring either to prenatal unity in the godhead or to the unity of father and mother in the sexual act, wellspring of the individual's physicality and hence of his psychic uniqueness. The passage, read with the latter bias, is a use of language and primal symbology matched in later confessional literature only by *The Prelude* itself:

> Blest the infant Babe,
> (For with my best conjecture I would trace
> Our Being's earthly progress,) blest the Babe,
> Nursed in his Mother's arms, who sinks to sleep
> Rocked on his Mother's breast; who with his soul
> Drinks in the feelings of his Mother's eye!
> For him, in one dear Presence, there exists
> A virtue which irradiates and exalts
> Objects through widest intercourse of sense.
> No outcast he, bewildered and depressed:
> Along his infant veins are interfused
> The gravitation and the filial bond
> Of nature that connect him with the world.
>
> (2. 232–244)

For the child is not only the central symbol of the confessional recovery of Edenic speech; it is also the prime form of confessional narration. From the standpoint of the present narrator, any past stage of the self is always archetypally the "child," that which was to grow; and this attitude assures not only an avoidance of the daemonic, willful separation of temporal selves but also the truth to spiritual fact of confessional language and the transformation of past guilt into the necessary evidence of one's glorification. Paul's First Letter to the Corinthians, which has already been cited, is involved with, among other things, the purity of evangelical speech (the Corinthians had taken to prophesying in ecstatic tongues) and the symbology of the child:

> For our knowledge is imperfect and our preaching is imperfect. But when perfection comes, what is imperfect will pass away. When I was a child, I talked like a child, I thought like a child, I reasoned like a child. When I became a man, I put aside my childish ways.

For now we are looking at a dim reflection in a mirror, but then
we shall see face to face.

(1 Corinthians 13:9-12)

The "child" here is the earlier Paul (Saul) who had persecuted the
Christians; and although he is put aside by the Apostle, the implication is strong that his imperfection is a necessary prelude to the later
man's perfection. We cannot pass without remarking again the
presence here of the ancient theme of mirror-reflection in the confrontation of present and past selves.

Wordsworth, in regarding the child of his past self at twenty-
two, provides yet another example of this imaginative form:

> . . . until not less
> Then two-and-twenty summers had been told—
> Was Man in my affections and regards
> Subordinate to her [Nature], her visible forms
> And viewless agencies: a passion, she,
> A rapture often, and immediate love
> Ever at hand; he, only a delight
> Occasional, an accidental grace,
> His hour being not yet come.

(8. 348-356)

The last line is of course deliberately christological, not in a theological but rather in a linguistic, imaginative context, implying as
it does the inevitable growth-to-be of human sympathy in the
twenty-two-year-old "child" and the hour to come, not only of
Man as a wider ground of natural and imaginative sympathy, but
also of the particular man narrating this process.

I have attempted to discuss the Snowdon passage, without
scanting its own intrinsic brilliance, as a kind of visionary com-
pendium both of *The Prelude* and of Wordsworth's imaginative
life during the period of *The Prelude*'s composition. In this way, I
believe, it is possible to see this last vision of the poem as an access
of power and confidence which, in fact, radiates over the entire
web of the poem. From the vantage point of this passage, which has
been the central vantage point of the present chapter, it is possible

to observe the distinctively confessional elements of *The Prelude* in their deepest relationships with one another and with the fabric of Wordsworth's vision.

The sense of the human community as mediatory is manifested in the poem's confessional address to Coleridge, a mode of address which implies the carefully humanized and antidaemonic sense of human growth in both the physical and psychic world. Both this mediation and this humanization, furthermore, necessitate Wordsworth's delicate reapportionment and balance of the senses—particularly the sense of sight—in a narrative structure which can at the same time give equal weight to the experiences of the past and to the present state of enlightenment which those experiences have created. And, finally, as the confluence and triumph of these confessional elements, the poem articulates the ideal of Edenic words— an ideal epitomized in the myth of the *child* who will, necessarily, grow to be a *man*. It is, for Wordsworth as for so many mythmakers in the history of thought, the fullest vision of recovery in this our only world of that oneness with the past which is the paradise of historical man.

It is an intuitive balance of subject, narration, and imagination which is astounding both in its achievement and in its felt influence on the history of Western thought and verbalization. It was not, of course, an achievement which Wordsworth was to keep faith with. The story of his first failings of power and then of his long decline into a poetic life-in-death are not our concern here. But it would not be possible to conclude without mentioning that a man has only one life, and therefore only one confession to write, and that Wordsworth's continued testimony to the imaginative election he found within himself, for some reason, never filled the great form projected by *The Prelude*, whose tragically ironic title we note here for the last time.

The Excursion is perhaps a great poem—whatever that sanction implies—but it demonstrates a falling-off of the power to speak Edenic words. This is quite explicit in the dialogue of the Wanderer and the Solitary, which throughout books 3, 4, and 5 centers in the meaning of our words for happiness and our myths of a pastoral Eden. The Wanderer's defense of daemonic superstition as at least marginally conducing to reverence for the world and his comparative insouciance toward the phenomenal reference of language in a headlong rush toward a quasi-Platonic doctrine of Forms are betrayals of the poem's own "Prospectus" and a new and ominous departure in the poet's career. Likewise, in what is perhaps Wordsworth's last major poem, *The White Doe of Rylstone*, human history has been transformed into something very different from *The Prelude*. Emily's final attainment of exaltation above her melancholy history may represent, as many have said, a new mysticism in Wordsworth, of a more spiritual nature than the rule of memory in *The Prelude*. But it also represents a deep cleavage in what had been his central symbolic resource, what we have called the primal symbol. The Doe and the Banner that Emily weaves, the living creature and the artifact, carry on a subtle emblematic warfare throughout the poem. And the final immortal triumph of Emily's spirit in the former after having been betrayed by the latter is an implicit defeat of the imagistic and symbolic power which had once belonged to the miraculous child of the major years.

But in spite of Wordsworth's later failures and in spite even of the remarkable but minor successes of these poems of the decline, *The Prelude* stands not only as the single great work of the poet's career but also as one of the very great revolutions in the human spirit. Few poems can claim to have made radically new avenues of experience available to the secular imagination, but *The Prelude* is certainly one of these few, generating a sense of the self in time, whose wonders and terrors we are still exploring at the moment these words are written. This sense takes its dim origin from the saints and madmen of English Christianity of the seventeenth and eighteenth centuries, but it is Wordsworth's indelible honor to have transformed it into a "prelude," not only to his own century and poetic era, but to our own most deeply human triumphs and perils. The last line of Augustine's *Confessions* is "it shall be opened," heralding the opening on *this* earth of an epoch to which the first great confessor stands as patriarch. And the poetic confession we have been exploring here, heralding an epoch more resolutely secular and fiercely aspiring than any which had gone before, ends with another opening, characteristically the linguistically compact and complex opening of the comparative adverb, in the assurance that the unaided human spirit is, within the physical universe which is its home and its heritage,

> In beauty exalted, as it is itself
> Of quality and fabric more divine.

APPENDIX
ONE

❧

JAMES NAYLER

James Nayler raises the problem of enthusiasm as daemonic to perhaps its highest pitch of violence and tragedy—in English religious history, at least. He was to the early Quaker movement more or less what George Whitefield was later to be to the Methodist, or what Paul had been to the Petrine, church: an intensely energetic and charismatic early convert who bid fair to take the leadership of the sect away from its original founder not so much through guile as through simple magnetism. Nayler's acceptance of the inner light was fully as unshakable as Fox's. Unlike Fox, however, Nayler was not assiduously careful to avoid the full incarnational, christological implications of the doctrine. Nayler's trust in—and imprisonment by—language is in fact at the heart of his tragedy. For if the inner light is the indwelling of Christ, and if "indwelling" means what it says, then one cannot really, fully distinguish one's own converted self from the converting and saving self of Christ. And, in fact, to do so can even be a kind of blasphemy against the light. This is the classic problem of the divine becoming the daemonic, and Nayler is only more self-conscious—and more intelligent—than most in his dramatization of it.

As his popularity increased, so did the conviction of his followers that he actually was the Messiah come again. And in Nayler's courageously literalistic interpretation of Quaker doctrine, it was impossible for him to refute his own idolaters. The climax of the situation came when in October 1656 a group of his cultists led him

191

into Bristol seated on a horse, throwing their cloaks in the mud before him and chanting continually "Holy, Holy, Holy." Nayler, who had just been released from an imprisonment for his religious views, was brought to trial immediately, found guilty of blasphemy, and punished barbarously. What makes his trial significant for our concerns is the insistence with which Nayler, before his accusers, holds to the strict letter of the inner light doctrine: he is literally a man held captive by language, by precisely what we have already spoken of as the daemonic power of names. Asked, for example, whether that worship is due him which is due Christ, he replies: "If they did it to the visible, they were to blame, but if to the invisible, that worship is due to me, according to my measure, as was due to Christ."[1] What is equally remarkable about Nayler—something Knox neglects to mention—is that after his terrible punishment and more terrible humiliation he makes a full spiritual recovery, writes some of his most moving tracts, and becomes the only one of the early Society of Friends to admit and come to terms with the possibility of a second fall from the light.[2] In his later tract *Milk for Babes* (1661), referring to his own messianic possession and to the possibility of it in others, he writes in explicitly daemonic terms of the danger of the "strong man" within:

> There is the strong man to be bound, before the Babe can reign. . . .
> The strong man having got a possession within, is not easily
> bound . . . give yourselves no rest until the strong man bow.[3]

1. Quoted in Ronald A. Knox, *Enthusiasm* (New York, 1961), p. 165.
2. Geoffrey F. Nuttall, *James Nayler: A Fresh Approach*, Suppl. 26 to *Journal of the Friends' Historical Society* (London, 1954), p. 162.
3. Ibid., p. 165.

APPENDIX TWO

❧

WILLIAM COWPER

The fixation of the eye, the sacramental betrayal of the living spirit of God, the warfare between Book as "text" and Book as "Word," all of these elements have their most self-conscious and most carefully literary manifestation in a confession which Wordsworth could not have known at the time of writing *The Prelude*. William Cowper's *Memoir* (1816), though, can be read almost as a critical commentary on that poem's central method—so much so that Cowper seems closer to Wordsworth as a confessor than he does as a poet of the pre-Romantic sublime. It is a confession in which concerns of spiritual salvation and imaginative health mingle and are equated under Cowper's major and tragic flaw, his predisposition toward melancholy and insanity. Early in the short narrative, Cowper tells of his despair at having to stand a public examination for the position of Keeper of the Journals of the House of Commons, a position that was originally to have been a comfortable and retired sinecure for him. One day, trying to escape from his panic at the prospect, he went with some friends into the country around Southampton and was immensely refreshed at the natural view he witnessed there:

> Here it was that on a sudden, as if another sun had been kindled that instant in the heavens on purpose to dispel sorrow and vexation of spirit, I felt the weight of all my misery taken off; my heart became light and joyful in a moment; I could have wept with transport had I been alone. I must needs believe that nothing less

than the Almighty fiat could have filled me with such inexpressible delight, not by a gradual dawning of peace, but, as it were, with a flash of his life-giving countenance. . . . But Satan and my own wicked heart quickly persuaded me that I was indebted for my deliverance to nothing but a change of scene and the amusing varieties of the place. By this means he turned the blessing into a poison. . . .[1]

We recognize in this passage a distinctly Wesleyan flavor in the concern with instantaneous conversion and in the comparative flatness of the language; the Wesleyan narratives tend to be written in less excited, and therefore to some modern ears more compelling, prose than those of the Quakers. But what is really exciting and has almost the air of an original aesthetic discovery here is Cowper's instinctive merging of a central problem of earlier religious confessors with a central, if submerged, problem of pre-Romantic poetry: what might be described in general terms by the phrase "the one life within us and abroad." Cowper came to regard this episode in his life as the "unpardonable sin," his one disastrous failure to trust to the divinity within nature—or as we would put it in more Wordsworthian terms, to transcend sight for vision:

No favourable construction of my conduct in that instance, no argument of my brother's who was now with me, nothing he could suggest in extenuation of my offences could gain a moment's admission. Satan furnished me so readily with weapons against myself that neither scripture nor reason could undeceive me.[2]

This despair, coupled with its secular analogue, Cowper's fear of his public examination, eventually led him on the morning of the proposed examination to attempt suicide no less than three separate times, to withdraw from the candidacy for the post, and to enter the asylum (how appropriate that word is for this pathologically shy man!) of Dr. Nathaniel Cotton at St. Alban's, whence he dates the beginning of his full conversion to Christ and Calvinist evangelicalism. The story of this and Cowper's later fits of melancholy is,

1. William Cowper, *Memoir*, ed. Maurice J. Quinlan, *Proceedings of the American Philosophical Society* 97 (1953):368.
2. Ibid., p. 376.

of course, well known from such biographical studies as Lord David
Cecil's *The Stricken Deer*; but the Cowper of the *Memoir* finally
establishes himself as a much more perspicuous, tough-minded individual than the "outer" Cowper of Cecil's overdone book.[3] One
tends to forget too readily that a man writing about his insanity,
far from being a study in psychic aberrancy, can often be the most
viable exemplar of the sane available to us.

In Cowper's case, his precise narrative control of the confession is, besides a heartening picture of a man making peace
(however temporary) with his private desert places, a valuable
commentary on the structuring powers of Protestantism as an
imaginative fact. The central symbol of Cowper's confession, the
madhouse from which he was to come forth in a new birth of faith,
is rather like a final exaggeration or aggravation of elements at work
in a whole line of earlier religious confessions, and it helps us bring
into focus the problems of the visual world and the daemonic. His
penetration to the roots of the experience is extraordinary. Here is
Cowper, for example, discussing his difficulties in actually studying
for his examination (he was given about a year to peruse the journals
and acquaint himself with the duties of the post):

> I expected no assistance from anybody there, all the inferior clerks
> being under the influence of my opponent, and accordingly I
> received none. The journal books were indeed thrown open to
> me—a thing which could not be refused, and from which perhaps
> a man in health and with a head turned to business might have
> gained all the information he wanted—but it was not so with me.[4]

The inner split in Cowper's personality readily projects an analogous
division into the world around him, and he sees the offices of the
journals transformed by the same daemonic fears that have begun to
possess him. It is a cruel but appropriate irony that the cynosure of
his despair should be, again, the journal—books rather like a malign
reduction of his visual field corresponding to his earlier "unpardonable sin" in being unable to transcend the visual field at the
other end of the scale, the natural prospect at Southampton.

---

3. David Cecil, *The Stricken Deer* (Indianapolis, 1930). For a fine discussion
of the *Memoir*, see John N. Morris, *Versions of the Self* (New York, 1966).
    4. Cowper, *Memoir*, p 370.

We see, in fact, the daemonic-visual syndrome of Cowper's madness beginning to transform the world of "experience" into a negative sacrament, a downward viaticum into a universe of absolutely hostile things. And it is here, at the level of sacramental theology, that the connections between Wordsworthian Romanticism and the radical tradition in Protestantism appear in their most inevitable aspects. For the mistrust of sacrament, absolute in the Quakers and a constant, if restrained, element in Wesleyan Methodism, is the most obvious element not only of radical ritual but of radical confessional narrative.

APPENDIX
THREE

❧

SILAS TOLD

Told's narrative, besides being one of the most readable and novelistic of confessions, is an intensely interesting example of the power of the Edenic ideal of language and of the complex problem of the two consciousnesses from which this idea is generated. It is a double narrative, in which Told relates his life history once from a realistic, autobiographical viewpoint (in which he frequently attains a tone combining elements of Defoe and Smollett) and once again from the viewpoint of the numinous, literally reshaping the first narrative into a history of his approach to God. The meeting point of the two narratives is his encounter with an evangelical bricklayer in 1736:

> Here my readers will permit me to enter upon my religious life, and therefore I think it prudent to revert back to my earliest days; and as I have already in the beginning set forth the manner and mystery of God's working upon my soul, to the time of my admission into Edward Colson's Hospital, so I shall occasionally intersperse my changes of station in this life, as well as those of a spiritual nature.[1]

Here the two consciousnesses and the confessional speech which is their unification are literally and simultaneously present in the book.

---

1. *An Account of the Life and Dealings of God with Silas Told* (London, 1806), p. 60.

Since Told was a very atypical Methodist (personally an amusing but outrageous snob and religiously a violent visionary), his confession betrays more than is usual the effort involved in attaining the right language of conversion. He cannot quite bring himself to the truly Edenic, christological narration of his past before he has given that other I a full projection on its own disjunctive, rowdy, and swashbuckling terms. And Told's narrative proper concludes with a truly brilliant passage in which he finally achieves the full Edenic language of confession in an experience with strangely Wordsworthian overtones. After his conversion, he experiences one final series of temptations to disbelieve his own election, and in agony he walks alone into a field, wishing himself a dog, a cow, a murdered man, anything insensate and unconscious. It is not difficult to see that he is in fact experiencing the perpetual disease involved in consciousness, the disease attendant upon trying to be one's whole self, past as well as present. Then he finds a secluded spot in the field:

> When I had secluded myself therein, being alone, on a sudden, in the twinkling of an eye, "a hand struck me a weighty blow on the top of my head," which in some measure affected my senses; but I instantly found myself crying with a loud voice, "Praise God, praise God," and, looking up, I beheld the ethereal universe, replete with the Glory of God. . . .[2]

The temporary deprivation of sense and sudden access of phenomenal vision are, of course, by now recognizable and profound Wordsworthian locutions—here some twenty years before Wordsworth's major poetry. But the incalculably brilliant insight in this passage, by a man of anything but a reflective temperament, is involved in the phrase in quotation marks, "a hand struck me a weighty blow on the top of my head." It is a quotation—from the other I of Told's own past self, referring to his earliest religious experience at twelve years of age:

> Sitting one day in my order, and reading Sherlock on Death. I suddenly laid down the book, leaned my right elbow on my right knee, and with my hand supporting my head, and I meditated in the most solemn thought, upon the awfulness of eternity: Suddenly

2. Ibid., p. 85.

I was struck with a hand on the top of my head, followed by a voice with these words, "Dark! dark! dark!" and although it alarmed me prodigiously, yet, upon the recovery from so sudden a motion, I found myself broad awake in a world of sin.[3]

The later passage, in which, memorially and verbally, Told is able to align his present state with the experience of the twelve-year-old Silas, represents a triumph of language and refinement of psychic power which transforms the long intervening period of guilt and transgression into a testimony to the redemptive power of God and the individual religious memory of the confessor. And it leads immediately afterward to a nearly apocalyptic vision of the one man which is the Christian communal self as the redeemer not only of the soul but of time past:

And immediately some articulate voice asked me the following question: "How did you find yourself an hour ago?" I then recollected that I was in a wretched and lost state. The voice again suggested, "All the world is but as one man, and one man as all the world."[4]

3. Ibid., p. 62.
4. Ibid., p. 87.

BIBLIOGRAPHY

Abrams, M. H. *The Mirror and the Lamp: Romantic Theory and the Critical Tradition.* New York: W. W. Norton, 1958.

———. "The Correspondent Breeze: A Romantic Metaphor." In *English Romantic Poets: Modern Essays in Criticism.* Edited by M. H. Abrams. New York: Oxford University Press, 1960.

Allen, Don Cameron. "Some Theories of the Growth and Origin of Language in Milton's Age." *Philological Quarterly* 28(1949):5–16.

Augustine, Saint. *The Confessions.* Translated by Edward B. Pusey. New York: Pocket Books, 1958.

Bateson, F. W. *Wordsworth: A Reinterpretation.* London: Longmans Green, 1963.

Beatty, Arthur. *William Wordsworth: His Doctrine and Art in Their Historical Relations.* Madison: University of Wisconsin Press, 1962.

Beer, J. B. *Coleridge the Visionary.* New York: P. F. Collier, 1962.

Berkeley, George. *Philosophical Writings.* Edited by David M. Armstrong. New York: P. F. Collier, 1965.

Blake, William. *Poetry and Prose.* Edited by David V. Erdman. New York: Doubleday, 1965.

Bloom, Harold. *The Anxiety of Influence: A Theory of Poetry.* New York: Oxford University Press, 1973.

———. *Blake's Apocalypse: A Study in Poetic Argument.* New York: Doubleday, 1965.

———. *Shelley's Mythmaking.* New Haven: Yale University Press, 1959.

———. *The Visionary Company: A Reading of English Romantic Poetry.* New York: Doubleday, 1963.

———, ed. *Romanticism and Consciousness: Essays in Criticism.* New York: W. W. Norton, 1970.

Bostetter, Edward E. *The Romantic Ventriloquists.* Seattle: University of Washington Press, 1963.

Boulger, James D. *Coleridge as Religious Thinker.* New Haven: Yale University Press, 1961.

Bunyan, John. *Grace Abounding to the Chief of Sinners.* Edited by G. B. Harrison. London: J. M. Dent & Sons, 1963.

————. *The Life and Death of Mr. Badman.* Oxford: Oxford University Press, n.d.

Burke, Kenneth. *A Grammar of Motives.* New York: Meridian Books, 1962.

————. *The Philosophy of Literary Form.* New York: Vintage Books, 1961.

————. *The Rhetoric of Religion: Studies in Logology.* Boston: Beacon Press, 1961.

Byron, George Noel Gordon, Lord. *The Selected Letters of Lord Byron.* Edited by Jacques Barzun. New York: Grosset & Dunlap, 1953.

Campbell, Joseph, ed. *Pagan and Christian Mysteries: Papers from the Eranos Yearbooks.* New York: Harper & Row, 1963.

Chalk, Thomas, ed. *Autobiographical Narratives of the Convincement and Other Religious Experience of Samuel Crisp, Elizabeth Webb, Evan Bevan, Margaret Lucas, and Frederick Smith.* London, 1848.

Christensen, Francis. "Intellectual Love: The Second Theme of *The Prelude.*" *PMLA* 80(1965–66):69–75.

Chomsky, Noam. *Language and Mind.* New York: Harcourt, Brace & World, 1968.

Coleridge, Samuel T. *The Complete Poetical Works.* Edited by E. H. Coleridge. Oxford: Oxford University Press, 1960.

Cowper, William. *Letters of William Cowper.* 2 vols. Edited by J. G. Frazer. London, 1912.

————. "Memoir of William Cowper: An Autobiography." Edited by Maurice J. Quinlan. *Proceedings of the American Philosophical Society,* 97(1953):359–382.

Crisp, Stephen. *A Memorable Account of the Christian Experiences, Gospel Labours, Travels and Sufferings of that Ancient Servant of Christ Stephen Crisp.* London, 1694.

Curtius, Ernst Robert. *European Literature in the Latin Middle Ages.* New York: Harper & Row, 1963.

Danby, John F. *The Simple Wordsworth: Studies in the Poems, 1797–1807.* New York: Barnes & Noble, 1961.

Davie, Donald. *Articulate Energy: An Inquiry into the Syntax of English Poetry.* London, Routledge & Kegan Paul, 1955.

Davis, Walter R. *Idea and Act in Elizabethan Fiction*. Princeton: Princeton University Press, 1970.

De Quincey, Thomas. *Confessions of an English Opium Eater and Other Writings*. Edited by Aileen Ward. New York: New American Library, 1966.

Dodds, E. R. *The Greeks and the Irrational*. Berkeley: University of California Press, 1951.

Eliot, T. S. *On Poetry and Poets*. New York: Noonday Press, 1961.

Fergusson, Francis. *The Idea of a Theater: The Art of Drama in Changing Perspective*. New York: Doubleday, 1953.

Ferry, David. *The Limits of Mortality: An Essay on Wordsworth's Major Poems*. Middletown: Wesleyan University Press, 1959.

Fletcher, Angus. *Allegory: The Theory of a Symbolic Mode*. Ithaca: Cornell University Press, 1964.

Foakes, R. A. *The Romantic Assertion: A Study in the Language of Nineteenth Century Poetry*. London: Methuen, 1958.

Fox, George. *The Journal of George Fox*. Edited by Rufus M. Jones. New York: Capricorn Books, 1963.

Frye, Northrop. *Fables of Identity*. New York: Harcourt, Brace & World, 1963.

Gill, Frederick C. *The Romantic Movement and Methodism*. London: Epworth Press, 1937.

Gottfried, Leon. *Matthew Arnold and the Romantics*. Lincoln: University of Nebraska Press, 1963.

Gray, Thomas. *Poems of Thomas Gray*. Edited by Austin Lane Poole. London: Oxford University Press, 1961.

Guardini, Romano. *The Conversion of St. Augustine*. New York: Henry Regnery, 1960.

Hardy, John Edward. *The Curious Frame: Seven Poems in Text and Context*. South Bend, Ind.: University of Notre Dame Press, 1962.

Harper, George McLean. "Coleridge's Conversation Poems." In *English Romantic Poets: Modern Essays in Criticism*. Edited by M. H. Abrams. New York: Oxford University Press, 1960.

Hartman, Geoffrey. "The Poet without Golden Daffodils." *Book Week*, March 6, 1966, p. 4.

———. *The Unmediated Vision*. New York: Harcourt, Brace & World, 1966.

———. *Wordsworth's Poetry, 1797–1814*. New Haven: Yale University Press, 1964.

Heffernan, James A. W. "Wordsworth on Imagination: The Emblemising Power." *PMLA* 81(1966):389–99.

Hirsch, E. D. *Wordsworth and Schelling*. New Haven: Yale University Press, 1960.

Hobbes, Thomas. *Leviathan*. New York: Capricorn Books, 1962.

Hobhouse, Stephen. *William Law and Eighteenth Century Quakerism*. New York: Macmillan, 1928.

Hollander, John. *The Untuning of the Sky*. Princeton: Princeton University Press, 1961.

James, D. G. *The Romantic Comedy*. London: Oxford University Press, 1954.

Jung, C. G. *Psyche and Symbol*. New York: Doubleday, 1958.

———. *Symbols of Transformation: An Analysis of the Prelude to a Case of Schizophrenia*. 2 vols. New York: Harper & Row, 1962.

———, and Kerenyi, C. *Essays on a Science of Mythology*. New York: Harper & Row, 1963.

Kaske, R. E. "*Sapientia et Fortitudo* as the Controlling Theme of *Beowulf*." In *An Anthology of Beowulf Criticism*. Edited by Lewis E. Nicholson. South Bend, Ind.: University of Notre Dame Press, 1963.

Knox, Ronald A. *Enthusiasm: A Chapter in the History of Religion*. New York: Oxford University Press, 1961.

Köhler, Wolfgang. *Gestalt Psychology*. New York: New American Library, n.d.

Kroeber, Karl. *Romantic Narrative Art*. Madison: University of Wisconsin Press, 1966.

Langbaum, Robert. "Magnifying Wordsworth." ELH 33 (1966): 271–78.

———. *The Poetry of Experience: The Dramatic Monologue in Modern Literary Tradition*. New York: W. W. Norton, 1963.

———. *The Modern Spirit: Essays on the Continuity of Nineteenth and Twentieth Century Literature*. New York: Oxford University Press, 1970.

Leavis, F. R. *Revaluation*. New York: W. W. Norton, 1963.

Lévi-Strauss, Claude. *Totemism*. Boston: Beacon Press, 1963.

Lewis, C. S. *The Allegory of Love*. New York: Oxford University Press, 1961.

Lindenberger, Herbert. *On Wordsworth's Prelude*. Princeton: Princeton University Press, 1963.

Luther, Martin. *Martin Luther: Selections*. Edited by John Dillenberger. New York: Doubleday, 1961.

McCaffrey, Isabel Gamble. *Paradise Lost as "Myth."* Cambridge: Harvard University Press, 1959.

McLuhan, Marshall. *The Gutenberg Galaxy*. Toronto: University of Toronto Press, 1964.

Madsen, William G. "The Idea of Nature in Milton's Poetry." In *Three Studies in the Renaissance*. New Haven: Yale University Press, 1958.

Malinowski, Bronislaw. *Magic, Science, and Religion*. New York: Doubleday, 1954.

Martz, Louis L. *The Paradise Within*. New Haven: Yale University Press, 1964.

———. *The Poetry of Meditation*. New Haven: Yale University Press, 1962.

———., ed. *The Meditative Poem*. New York: Doubleday, 1963.

Merleau-Ponty, Maurice. *Sens et non-sens*. Paris: Nagel, 1948.

Miller, Perry, ed. *The American Puritans*. New York: Doubleday, 1956.

Milton, John. *Complete Poems and Selected Prose*. Edited by Merritt Y. Hughes. New York: Odyssey Press, 1957.

———. *Poetical Works*. Edited by Charles Grosvenor Osgood. New York: Oxford University Press, 1935.

Monk, Samuel Holt. *The Sublime*. Ann Arbor: University of Michigan Press, 1960.

Nelson, John. *Extract from the Journal of John Nelson*. New York, 1831.

Newton, John. *The Works of the Reverend John Newton*. 2 vols. Philadelphia, 1834.

Nuttall, Geoffrey F. "James Nayler: A Fresh Approach." *Journal of the Friends' Historical Society*, London, 1954, supp. 26.

Overton, J. H. *John Wesley*. London, 1891.

Pascal, Roy. *Design and Truth in Autobiography*. Cambridge: Harvard University Press, 1960.

Perkins, David. *The Quest for Permanence: The Symbolism of Wordsworth, Shelley, and Keats*. Cambridge: Harvard University Press, 1959.

Pope, Alexander. *The Poems of Alexander Pope*. Edited by John Butt. New Haven, Yale University Press, 1963.

Pottle, Frederick A. "The Eye and the Object in the Poetry of Wordsworth." In *Centenary Studies Presented at Cornell and Princeton Universities*. Princeton: Princeton University Press, 1951.

Price, Martin. *To the Palace of Wisdom*. New York: Doubleday, 1965.

Reichenkron, Günter, and Haase, Erich, eds. *Formen der Selbstdarstellung: Analekten zu einer Geschichte des literarischen Selbstportraits*. Berlin: Duncker & Humblot, 1956.

Reik, Theodor. *The Compulsion to Confess: On the Psychoanalysis of Crime and Punishment*. New York: John Wiley & Sons, 1966.

Rogers, Hester Ann. *A Short Account of the Experience of Mrs. Hester Ann Rogers.* New York, 1811.

Roppen, Georg, and Sommer, Richard. *Strangers and Pilgrims: An Essay on the Metaphor of Journey.* Oslo: Universitetsforlaget, 1964.

Rousseau, Jean-Jacques. *Les Confessions.* Edited by François Mauriac. Paris: Livre de Poche, 1963.

Salvesen, Christopher. *The Landscape of Memory.* Lincoln: University of Nebraska Press, 1965.

Sharrock, Roger. "Spiritual Autobiography in *The Pilgrim's Progress.*" *Review of English Studies* 24(1948):102–20.

Shelley, Percy Bysshe. *Poetical Works.* Edited by Thomas Hutchinson. Oxford: Oxford University Press, 1961.

Shepherd, T. B. *Methodism and the Literature of the Eighteenth Century.* London: Epworth Press, 1940.

Shklovsky, Victor. "Sterne's *Tristram Shandy*: Stylistic Commentary." In *Russian Formalist Criticism: Four Essays.* Translated by Lee T. Lemon and Marion J. Reis. Lincoln: University of Nebraska Press, 1965.

Shumaker, Wayne. *Literature and the Irrational.* New York: Washington Square Press, 1966.

Spens, Janet. *Spenser's Faerie Queene.* London: Edward Arnold, 1934.

Spenser, Edmund. *Poetical Works.* Edited by J. C. Smith and E. de Selincourt. London: Oxford University Press, 1960.

Stang, Richard. "The False Dawn: A Study of the Opening of Wordsworth's *Prelude.*" *ELH* 33(1966):53–65.

Stauffer, Donald. *The Art of Biography in Eighteenth Century England.* Princeton: Princeton University Press, 1941.

Steiner, George. *Language and Silence.* New York: Atheneum, 1967.

Sterne, Laurence. *Tristram Shandy.* Edited by James A. Work. New York: Odyssey Press, 1940.

Sypher, Wylie. *Four Stages of Renaissance Style.* New York: Doubleday, 1955.

Thomas a Kempis. *Of the Imitation of Christ.* Translated by Abbot Justin McCann. New York: New American Library, 1962.

Thompson, Bard, ed. *Liturgies of the Western Church.* New York: Meridian Books, 1964.

Told, Silas. *An Account of the Life and Dealings of God with Silas Told, Late Preacher of the Gospel.* London, 1806.

Traherne, Thomas. *Centuries, Poems, and Thanksgivings.* Edited by H. M. Margoliouth. Oxford: Oxford University Press, 1958.

van den Berg, J. H. *The Changing Nature of Man.* New York: Dell, 1964.

Waldock, A. J. A. *Paradise Lost and Its Critics.* Cambridge: Cambridge University Press, 1964.

Warren, Austin. *Richard Crashaw.* Ann Arbor: University of Michigan Press, 1957.

Weil, Simone. *The Iliad, or the Poem of Force.* Wallingford: Pendle Hill Press, 1962.

Wellek, René, and Warren, Austin. *Theory of Literature.* New York: Harcourt, Brace, 1956.

Wesley, John. *The Journal of John Wesley.* 4 vols. London: J. M. Dent & Sons, 1930.

Wimsatt, William K., Jr. *The Verbal Icon: Studies in the Meaning of Poetry.* New York: Noonday Press, 1960.

Wittgenstein, Ludwig. *The Blue and Brown Books.* New York: Harper & Row, 1965.

————. *Philosophische Bemerkungen.* Oxford: Oxford University Press, 1964.

Wordsworth, William. *The Poetical Works of William Wordsworth.* 5 vols. Edited by Ernest de Selincourt and Helen Darbishire. Oxford: Oxford University Press, 1949.

————. *The Prelude.* Edited by Ernest de Selincourt and Helen Darbishire. Oxford: Oxford University Press, 1959.

————. *The Prose Works of William Wordsworth.* 3 vols. Edited by A. B. Grosart. London, 1876.

————., and Wordsworth, Dorothy. *The Early Letters of William and Dorothy Wordsworth, 1787–1805.* Edited by Ernest de Selincourt. Oxford: Oxford University Press, 1935.

Wright, Luella M. *The Literary Life of the Early Friends.* New York: Columbia University Press, 1932.

INDEX

Abrams, M. H., 3, 39, 138
Aeschylus, 12
Ambrose, Saint, 37
Areopagitica. See Milton, John, *Areopagitica*
Arnold, Matthew, 25, 60
Augustine, Saint, 3, 4, 13, 29. *See also* Confessions (Saint Augustine)

Barthes, Roland, 160
Bateson, F. W., 25
Beatty, Arthur, 75
Becanus, J. C., 171
Beer, J. B., 76
Berkeley, George, 2, 4, 109
Berryman, John, 2
Blake, William, 103, 127
Bloom, Harold, 1, 81 n, 96
Böhler, Peter, 114
Boehme, Anthony William, 161
The Borderers. See Wordsworth, Willam, *The Borderers*
Bostetter, Edward E., 91
Boulger, James D., 76
Bunyan, John, 33, 111–12
Burke, Kenneth, 16, 38 n, 69 n

Cecil, David, 195
Chatterton, Thomas, 40
Christensen, Francis, 22–23
The Christian Doctrine. See Milton, John, *The Christian Doctrine*

Cicero, 21
Coleridge, Samuel Taylor, 1, 7, 16–27, 149
  The Prelude: Coleridge as auditor of, 16–27; Conversation Poems and, 44–50
  Religious Musings, 75–81
Confession: antisacramentalism of, 110–14; the daemonic in, 11–14, 74–75; described, 3–5; edification and mediation in, 28–34; internalization of politics in, 38–39; pronomial ambiguity in, 160–68
Confessions (Saint Augustine), 190; auditor in, 36–39; figure of the child in, 186–87; language of self-consciousness in, 161, 163–64; pear tree episode in, 7–9; tyranny of the visual in, 109–10
Conversation Poems. *See* Coleridge, Samuel Taylor, Conversation Poems
Cowper, William, 193–96
Crane, Hart, 2
Crisp, Stephen, 39, 113–14
Curran, Stuart, 13
Curtius, E. R., 17

Davie, Donald, 81
Defoe, Daniel, 187
De Man, Paul, 34, 75 n, 171

De Quincey, Thomas, 25, 59
Dodds, E. R., 12–14
Donne, John, 5

Eliot, T. S., 60
Epistle to Dr. Arbuthnot. See Pope,
    Alexander, *Epistle to Dr. Ar-
    buthnot*
Erasmus, 118
Essays on epitaphs. *See* Words-
    worth, William, Essays on epi-
    taphs
The Excursion. See Wordsworth,
    William, *The Excursion*

Fergusson, Francis, 16
Ferry, David, 25
Fletcher, Angus, 13
Foakes, R. A., 87, 132
Fox, George, 5, 33, 83–86, 110–11,
    114
Freud, Sigmund, 12
The Friend. See Wordsworth,
    William, Essays on epitaphs

Gibbon, Edward, 4, 83
Godwin, William, 70–71
Gray, Thomas, 53
Grosart, A. B., 173
Guilt and Sorrow. See Words-
    worth, William, *Guilt and Sor-
    row*
Gusdorf, Georges, 164

Hardy, John Edward, 47
Hartley, David, 2, 12
Hartman, Geoffrey, 7 n, 21, 34, 61,
    107, 115, 129, 132, 156 n, 175
Hazlitt, William, 25
Heidegger, Martin, 2, 110
Herbert, George, 32
Hirsch, E. D., 83
"Home at Grasmere." *See* Words-
    worth, William, "Home at
    Grasmere"
Hume, David, 2, 4, 83

Jackson, Thomas, 27
James, William, 110
John, Saint, 175
Jung, C. G., 170, 186 n

Keats, John, 2
Kircher, Athanasius, 171
Knox, Ronald, 192
Köhler, Wolfgang, 89

Langbaum, Robert, 25 n, 88–89, 90–
    91
Lévi-Strauss, Claude, 70
Lindenberger, Herbert, 21, 22–23
Locke, John, 4, 108–10
Lowell, Robert, 14
Luther, Martin, 4, 15, 29, 112–13,
    118–20

Mallarmé, Stéphane, 155
Manichaeanism, 13
Mark, Saint, 99
Martz, Louis L., 32, 63, 65, 69
Marvell, Andrew, 139
Merleau-Ponty, Maurice, 158–59
Methodism, 4, 27, 113
Mill, John Stuart, 25
Milton, John, 205
    Areopagitica, 66
    The Christian Doctrine, 67
    Paradise Lost, 43–44, 46–47
    Paradise Regained, 13, 63–70, 77

Nayler, James, 82, 84, 191–92
Nelson, John, 5, 17 n, 29–31, 164
Newton, John, 5, 26–29, 185
"Nutting." *See* Wordsworth, Wil-
    liam, "Nutting"

"Ode: Intimations of Immortality
    from Recollections of Early
    Childhood." *See* Wordsworth,
    William, "Ode: Intimations of
    Immortality from Recollec-
    tions of Early Childhood"
The Old Cumberland Beggar. See
    Wordsworth, William, *The
    Old Cumberland Beggar*

Paradise Lost. See Milton, John,
    Paradise Lost
Paradise Regained. See Milton,
    John, *Paradise Regained*
Paul, Saint, 61, 162, 187–88
Paxton, Frances, 114
Pope, Alexander, 205
    Epistle to Dr. Arbuthnot, 176–78

The Rape of the Lock, 178, 180–81
Pottle, Frederick A., 89
The Prelude. See Wordsworth, William, *The Prelude*

Ransom, John Crowe, 63
The Rape of the Lock. See Pope, Alexander, *The Rape of the Lock*
The Recluse. See Wordsworth, Wlliam, *The Recluse*
Reik, Theodor, 134, 163
Religious Musings. See Coleridge, Samuel Taylor, *Religious Musings*
Resolution and Independence. See Wordsworth, William, *Resolution and Independence*
Rilke, Ranier Maria, 99
Rogers, Hester Ann, 32–33
Rousseau, Jean-Jacques, 4
Ryle, Gilbert, 182

Sartre, Jean-Paul, 2, 110
Shelley, Percy Bysshe, 2
"She was a Phantom of delight." *See* Wordsworth, William, "She was a Phantom of delight"
Smollet, Tobias, 197
The Society of Friends, 4, 27, 33, 113–14
Socrates, 12
"The Solitary Reaper." *See* Wordsworth, William, "The Solitary Reaper"
Spens, Janet, 18, 144
Spenser, Edmund, 17, 144–45
Stang, Richard, 138
Sterne, Laurence, 52–53, 57

Thomas a Kempis, 59
"Tintern Abbey." *See* Wordsworth, William, "Tintern Abbey"
Told, Silas, 5, 185, 197–99

van den Berg, J. H., 112–13
Vaughan, Henry, 5, 115–16

Webb, Elizabeth, 141, 161
Webb, John, 171
Weil, Simone, 17
Wellek, René, 119
Wesley, John, 27, 114
The White Doe of Rylstone. See Wordsworth, William, *The White Doe of Rylstone*
Whitman, Walt, 2
Wilde, Oscar, 25
Willey, Basil, 108–9
Wittgenstein, Ludwig 2, 9, 10, 171
Woodring, Carl, 80
Wordsworth, Dorothy, 6–7, 79, 98, 137
Wordsworth, William
   The Borderers, 71–75, 100–104, 124
   Essays on epitaphs, 173–74, 176–77
   The Excursion, 10, 172, 189
   Guilt and Sorrow, 45, 124
   "Home at Grasmere," 166–68
   "Nutting," 5–7
   "Ode: Intimations of Immortality from Recollections of Early Childhood," 147
   The Old Cumberland Beggar, 102–5
   Preface to *Lyrical Ballads*, 15
   The Prelude: book 1, 89–98, 121–22, 138–40; book 3, 128–29; book 5, 129–35, 165–66; book 7, 105–8, 140–41; book 8, 122–27; book 9, 135–37; book 12, 142–45; book 14, 148–60, 168–75, 183–88; Coleridge as auditor of, 52–57; title of, 16–19, 42–44, 81, 86–88
   The Recluse, 34
   Resolution and Independence, 40–42
   "She was a Phantom of delight," 179–83
   "The Solitary Reaper," 115–18
   "Tintern Abbey," 8, 78–80, 181
   The White Doe of Rylstone, 190
Wright, Luella M., 27, 39

Yeats, William Butler, 13, 181

THE JOHNS HOPKINS UNIVERSITY PRESS

This book was composed in Janson text and Weiss Initials I display by
Maryland Linotype Composition Company from a design by Beverly
Baum. It was printed on 60 lb. Warren paper and bound in Columbia
Bayside Linen by The Maple Press Company.

Library of Congress Cataloging in Publication Data

McConnell, Frank D   1942-
    The confessional imagination.

    Bibliography: p.
    1. Wordsworth, William, 1770-1850. The prelude.
2. Confession in literature. I. Title.
PR5864.M25   821'7   73-19333
ISBN 0-8018-1574-6